ALIVE IN CHRIST

GRADE 7

Jesus Christ and the New Testament

aliveinchrist.osv.com

The Subcommittee on the Catechism, United States Conference of Catholic Bishops, has found this catechetical series, copyright 2014, to be in conformity with the *Catechism of the Catholic Church*.

Nihil Obstat
Rev. Fr. Jeremiah L. Payne, S.Th.L.
Censor Librorum, Diocese of Orlando

Imprimatur
✠ Most Rev. John Noonan
Bishop of Orlando
January 20, 2014

Alive in Christ Grade 7 Student Book
ISBN: 978-1-61278-018-4
Item Number: CU5108

5 6 7 8 9 10 11 12 015016 23 22 21 20 19
Webcrafters, Inc., Madison, WI, USA; October 2019; Job# WC1910031

© Our Sunday Visitor

Opening Lesson 1
Welcome to Alive in Christ, Grade 7. This chapter introduces you to the different parts of your book and invites you to learn, love, and celebrate your Catholic faith.

UNIT 5 Morality

A New Year

♡ Let Us Pray

Leader: O, Lord, you have given us so much, in the gifts of creation; the stars, the planets, and life on Earth. Help us understand what it means to be alive in you and for you.

"O LORD, our Lord,
how awesome is your name through all the earth!
I will sing of your majesty above the heavens."
Psalms 8:2

All: Help us be alive in you, Lord. Amen.

📖 Scripture

"But God, who is rich in mercy, because of the great love he had for us, even when we were dead in our trangressions, brought us to life with Christ ... raised us up with him, and seated us with him in the heavens in Christ Jesus, that in the ages to come he might show the immeasurable riches of his grace in his kindness to us in Christ Jesus. For by grace you have been saved through faith, and this is not from you; it is the gift of God; it is not from works, so no one may boast. For we are his handiwork, created in Christ Jesus for the good works that God has prepared in advance, that we should live in them."
Ephesians 2:4–10

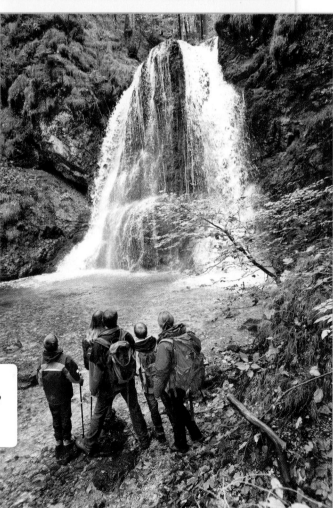

Have you ever thought...

- What does your Catholic faith mean to you?
- How do you stay connected to Christ?

Getting Started

Every chapter in your book begins with a Getting Started section that introduces you to the topics that will be covered in the chapter. You'll discover important points about Jesus, Sacred Scripture, Sacred Tradition, and Church history. In this section you will also complete charts, webs, tables, and other graphic organizers with information you have already learned about chapter topics. Sometimes you will return to these pages to complete the charts as you work through the chapters.

> *****
> In this box you will find direction for completing the graphic organizers and charts.
>
> Fill in the chart with some things you know about the Catholic Church. One example has been provided for you.

The Church celebrates Seven Sacraments.

What I've Learned

The Church and My Life Today As a member of the Catholic Church and a disciple of Christ, your relationship with Jesus and the Church is a part of your life every day. Our faith is connected to who we are and therefore to everything we do. Place a check mark next to the statements that most apply to you. Draw a star next to things you have questions about.

○ I take time to pray and read the Bible.

○ I think about the teachings of Jesus and the Church when I'm making decisions.

○ I've stood up for what I believe, even when it's been hard.

○ My relationship with Jesus influences my life.

○ I participate in Mass every week.

○ I've told someone outside of my Church about my faith.

○ I trust that God has a plan for my life.

○ I think it's part of my responsibility as a Catholic to serve others.

What is one thing from the list above that you want to work on this year?

_____

_____

_____

_____

_____

_____

Who or what do you think will help you do this?

_____

_____

_____

_____

_____

_____

_____

Seventh Grade

Where will this year take you?

A new year is ahead of you. Your book will guide you on your journey in life and faith this year as you discover more about your connection with Jesus Christ and learn how to make it stronger.

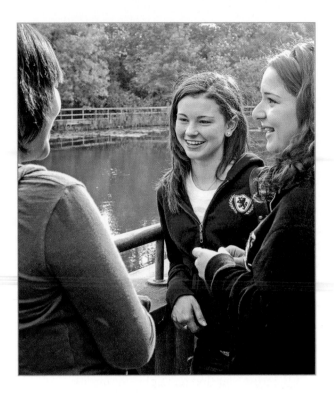

This symbol lets you know that the reading that follows is from **Sacred Scripture**. In every chapter you will spend time with God's Word, meeting Jesus in a different and exciting way. You'll get to know him through his closest friends and followers. You'll find out what was important to him and why those things are still important to us today.

Scripture

Thus faith comes from what is heard, and what is heard comes through the word of Christ.   **Romans 10:17**

Go to the Source

Read *Romans 10:14–17* to learn what Saint Paul says about the importance of spreading the Good News.

You'll ask questions about topics that matter to you, and discover what Jesus and the Church have to say about them. You'll also have opportunities to Go to the Source— to read more about certain passages of Scripture and their background and apply it to what you have learned, and to your life today.

Each chapter in your book begins and ends with prayer. Every time you start class, you will have the chance to thank God, ask for his help, pray for others, and praise God just for being who he is. You'll learn about different prayer forms—prayers of praise and adoration, blessing, intercession, petition, and thanksgiving—and how to practice these forms in personal prayer and devotional practices.

Every chapter also includes tools to help you interact with chapter content and better understand what you're learning. You may be underlining, highlighting, completing thoughts, or more.

Each chapter also contains Catholic Faith Words, like Sacred Scripture referenced above, important vocabulary terms that help you better understand core Catholic teachings—the "what" and "why" of your faith. These terms are highlighted and defined throughout your book.

Your book also contains features such as Where It Happened, which explains the location and context of events in biblical or Church history. You'll see photographs from historical sites as they appear today, often as special places of pilgrimage for people of all Christian communities.

The Catholics Today feature connects you to that Church history and how your faith is still in action right now. You'll learn about how Catholics all over the world live their faith by the ways we pray and worship, how we serve others, and the choices we make.

At the end of each chapter you will find a Catholics Believe section, which summarizes what you have learned about Church teachings, and how Catholics put the core doctrines of our faith into practice.

The Our Catholic Tradition section in the back of your book provides valuable information on Sacred Scripture, Sacred Tradition, prayer, devotions, and other reference material. There is also a Church History timeline to help you visualize the growth of the Catholic Church from her very beginning.

In the back of your book you will also find the Catholic Social Teaching: Live Your Faith section. This reference material explains the core principles that connect Catholics to all people through how we care about and for others because of our common human dignity, given by God. You'll learn about how the Catholic Church and her members respond to the needs of people—especially through the Corporal and Spiritual Works of Mercy—and what the Church has to say and share about the issues facing everyone around the world today.

Catholic Faith Words

Sacred Scripture the Word of God written by humans acting under the Holy Spirit's inspiration and guidance; another name for the Bible

LIST AND DISCUSS

List three things you want to find out about who Jesus is and what it means to follow him.

_____

_____

_____

Compare your thoughts with a classmate you haven't met before. Then work in small groups to find out what your class is wondering about.

_____

_____

_____

Detail from a Desis mosaic image of Jesus in the Hagia Sophia (Holy Wisdom) church in Istanbul, Turkey. The Hagia Sophia was a central church of Christianity for over nine hundred years.

Jesus in Sacred Scripture

You have already learned that the Bible is made up of two parts: the Old Testament and the New Testament. Together, they make up what we call Sacred Scripture, and their unity comes from the unity of God's plan of salvation for all people. That plan and God's truth are recorded in both Testaments as our salvation history.

The Catholic **canon of Scripture**, or the Church's complete list of inspired books included in Sacred Scripture, contains seventy-three books. Forty-six books make up the Old Testament, and twenty-seven books can be found in the New Testament. We cannot read and understand the New Testament without the background of the Old Testament, or the other way around!

The Old Testament tells about God the Father's relationship with the Hebrew people before the birth of Jesus, his presence in their lives, and the covenant, or sacred agreement, he made with them. The Old Testament includes the laws, history, and stories of God's Chosen People.

The New Testament is about the birth, life, ministry, teachings, suffering, Death, and Resurrection of Jesus Christ. Jesus was a Jew who preached about the Kingdom of God to his fellow Jews at the time. Jesus fulfilled the promise of the Old Testament prophets

Catholic Faith Words

canon of Scripture the Church's complete list of inspired books included in Sacred Scripture of a Messiah. He also fulfilled the Law of Moses as explained in the Old Testament, by giving the people a new law of love. He taught that God's covenant of love is for everyone, not just the Chosen People.

In the New Testament we discover accounts, stories, and parables that tell of God's love through Jesus and the Holy Spirit. The Gospels according to Matthew, Mark, Luke, and John proclaim the Good News of Jesus today, just as they did to the early followers of Christ. The Gospels were formed in three stages; first, in the life and teaching of Jesus, then through the oral tradition of storytelling and preaching, and then in the written Gospels themselves. You can discover more about the formation of the Gospels in the New Testament on page 364 in the Our Catholic Tradition section of your book.

When we study the Scriptures—in the Old Testament and the New Testament—we learn not only about God's past saving actions, but also about how he is still saving us today. Jesus in present in the Seven Sacraments, and in the Church's liturgy and worship.

You will come to better know Jesus and his teachings through studying the New Testament and seeing how he accomplished his mission during his time on Earth. You will come to realize in a deeper way how Christ's actions and the Word of God in Scripture and Tradition continue to guide and strengthen Catholics in the present time. You are connected to the early Christian followers, and God is calling you to be part of your parish and school community and part of the greater Catholic community.

> **What is one thing you would like to know about Jesus in the New Testament?**

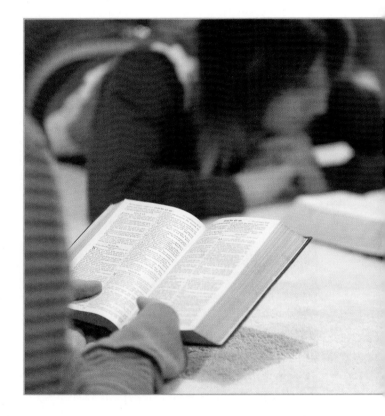

IDENTIFY

Identify three times when you have connected with the Word of God through Sacred Scripture, in Church, in school, or in your own reading.

1. _____

2. _____

3. _____

Jesus Christ, the Catholic Church, and You

Have you ever looked back at pictures of yourself as a young child and wondered how you could ever have been that small? Have you ever read something you wrote last year in class or in a journal and wondered what you were thinking at the time?

Sometimes it can feel like we grow into entirely new people in just one year. This time in your life is like that. You have learned a lot about yourself over the last few years, but the person you see in the mirror might feel like a stranger to you sometimes.

So many things in your life are changing. But there is one thing you can count on to remain the same: the love of God, who never changes. His wisdom, his Church, and his love will always be there for you. Your family and school and parish are also there to help you as you continue your faith journey.

We live in a world where everything changes all the time, and not always for the better. There are few things we can depend on to help us no matter what. That's why our Catholic faith is so important. Things are different, and better, when you let the **Holy Trinity**—God the Father, his Son, Jesus, and the Holy Spirit—into your life. Learning about the Trinity will help you through the ups and downs in your life, and give you the strength to become who God wants you to be: someone who is Alive in Christ.

Catholic Faith Words

Holy Trinity the mystery of one God in three Divine Persons: Father, Son, and Holy Spirit

Are You Ready?

Jesus loves you for who you are right now. He calls you to begin this next part of your life with hope, trusting in the Father's plan for you. As you move through this book and study Christ's words and life in the New Testament, he speaks to you and asks you to live as his disciple. He wants to get to know you, to spend time with you, to strengthen you, and to challenge you to be the person God made you to be.

Fill in the chart with your thoughts about the next year. As you work through your book over the next few months, come back and update your chart with your progress or how your thoughts have changed.

The Next Year	
What I know about Jesus:	_____
What I know about the Bible:	_____
My goals for the coming year:	_____
My faith helps my goals by:	_____
How is Christ alive in me now?	_____
How can I be alive in Christ?	_____

Our Catholic Life

Each chapter in your book has an Our Catholic Life section. It builds on what you have read in the chapter and focuses in a special way on what it means to be Catholic. Text, images, and an activity will help you better understand how to grow closer to **God, Jesus, and the Church.** Topics covered will include learning more about the Catholic faith, background on the meaning and celebration of the Seven Sacraments, discovering how to live as Christ calls us to, understanding different forms of prayer, advice on how to be an active member of your Church, and ways to help others come to know Jesus Christ through our own words and actions.

> What are you looking forward to learning most this year?

People of Faith

Holy Men and Women

You will also be introduced to People of Faith, men and women of all ages who loved God and did his work to help build the Kingdom on Earth. Some were figures of Church history such as the Apostles, some were men and women religious— priest, monks, religious sisters—and some served as part of the laity, without taking vows or being ordained. They are officially recognized by the Catholic Church as Venerables, Blesseds, and Saints. You will learn about their lives and some of the people they met, influenced, or were influenced by, and discover how their lives changed as they accepted God's grace and made a commitment to live a Christian life.

For more, go to
aliveinchrist.osv.com

IDENTIFY

Think of someone you know who has been a role model of Catholic faith for you. This person could be a priest, a teacher, or someone in your community, even a good friend. Explain how they share their faith and are an example to you on the lines below.

_____

_____

_____

_____

_____

_____

_____

_____

♥ Celebration of the Word

Leader: Let us take time, here and now, to gather for prayer, in the name of the One who calls us to "come and follow."

Jesus said, "I am the light of the world. Whoever follows me will not walk in darkness, but will have the light of life" **John 8:12.**

Reader 1: Lord Jesus, I want to be alive in you and your Word.

Help me to trust you and know you will show me how to love.

Let your light shine in me for friends who are searching,

and for all who are lost and can't find the way.

All: Let us be alive in you, Jesus Christ.

Leader: Jesus called to Peter and Andrew as they sat in their boats, "Come after me, and I will make you fishers of men" **Mark 1:17.**

Reader 2: Lord Jesus, I want to be alive in you and your Word.

Let me be ready when you cast your net.

Send me in search of the others you call to.

Help me to lead all the lost ones to you.

All: Let us be alive in you, Jesus Christ.

Leader: Jesus said, "Whoever serves me must follow me" **John 12:26.**

Reader 3: Lord Jesus, I want to follow.

Help me to stand by the things that I say.

Remind me that actions speak louder than words.

Give me a mission to go out and serve all that I can.

Send me as witness to all your Good News.

All: Let us be alive in you, Jesus Christ.

About the Pre-Test

As you begin the year, you may be asked to complete the Pre-Test that starts on the next page. The Pre-Test corresponds with major concepts you will learn this year, and your teacher will use the results to determine individual and class knowledge related to the topics. This Pre-Test and the Post-Test at the end of the year will help your teacher assess your knowledge and understanding of Catholic teachings, beliefs, and practices.

Circle the letter of the response that correctly completes the statement.

1. God is ____, which means he always was, is now, and always will be.
   a. faithful
   b. eternal
   c. holy
   d. love

2. The Church's complete list of inspired books included in Sacred Scripture is called ____.
   a. the canon of Scripture
   b. Sacred Tradition
   c. Church doctrine
   d. natural law

3. Through ____, God promised to remain in a relationship with his People.
   a. his law
   b. his grace
   c. the covenant
   d. the spiritualities

4. ____ is the free, loving gift of God's life and help.
   a. Solidarity
   b. Inspiration
   c. Grace
   d. Conscience

5. The ____ is the term for the mystery surrounding the Son of God taking on human nature.
   a. Annunciation
   b. Nativity
   c. Miracle
   d. Incarnation

6. A prayer that acclaims God for his nature is a prayer of ____.
   a. intercession
   b. thanksgiving
   c. blessing
   d. praise

7. Jesus' ____ teach us about the meaning and path to true happiness and the ways to live in the Kingdom of God.
   a. Ten Commandments
   b. miracles
   c. Beatitudes
   d. first books of the Bible

8. The Paschal Mystery refers to ____.
   a. Jesus' Incarnation and birth
   b. Jesus' Passion, Death, Resurrection, and Ascension
   c. Jesus' teachings to the Apostles
   d. both a and b

9. Jesus instructed the Apostles to travel in such a way that they ____.
   a. would meet with important people
   b. could gather monetary treasures for the Church
   c. would trust in God to provide for them
   d. could leave a place quickly if they were persecuted

10. The Church is organized into ____ that has different levels of leadership and membership.
    a. a hierarchy
    b. the Magisterium
    c. a canon
    d. an encyclical

11. Contemplative prayer is ___.
   a. based on songs
   b. group prayer
   c. part of the Mass
   d. wordless prayer

12. You are obliged to form your ___ well, so that it will lead you to what is truthful and just.
   a. education
   b. free will
   c. conscience
   d. soul

13. The deliberate ending of a pregnancy by killing the unborn child is known as ___.
   a. suicide
   b. scandal
   c. abortion
   d. euthanasia

14. The Cardinal Virtues include all of the following except ___.
   a. prudence
   b. justice
   c. charity
   d. fortitude

15. Much of Catholic liturgy has its roots in the ___ traditions that Jesus took part in as he grew up.
   a. Jewish
   b. Roman
   c. Apostolic
   d. Gentile

16. The process by which, through the power of the Holy Spirit and the words and actions of the priest, the bread and wine are transformed into the Body and Blood of Christ is known as ___.
   a. discernment
   b. conversion
   c. transubstantiation
   d. transfiguration

17. We show our ___ when we are sorry for our sins and pledge to try to not sin again.
   a. contrition
   b. forgiveness
   c. suffering
   d. confession

18. A ___ is the purpose for which God made us and the particular way to answer and live out his call.
   a. spirituality
   b. vocation
   c. reparation
   d. covenant

19. When we act with ___, we give God and our neighbor what is due to them.
   a. prudence
   b. hope
   c. justice
   d. temperance

20. A soul that is in Purgatory is in the process of being ___.
   a. judged
   b. punished
   c. rewarded
   d. cleansed

21. ___ is the God-given ability that helps individuals judge whether actions are right or wrong.
    a. Free will
    b. Conscience
    c. Reason
    d. Judgment

22. The ___ Commandment instructs us not to kill another person.
    a. First
    b. Tenth
    c. Third
    d. Fifth

23. When we attempt to indirectly correct the damage caused by sin, we are making ___.
    a. reparation
    b. contrition
    c. conscience formation
    d. reconciliation

24. ___ is the courage to do what is right even if others disagree with or challenge you.
    a. Justice
    b. Temperance
    c. Fortitude
    d. Prudence

25. The ___ Commandment identifies lying as a sin that damages our character and integrity.
    a. Tenth
    b. Eighth
    c. Fourth
    d. Sixth

26. The ___ is the event of the Angel Gabriel telling Mary she would be the Mother of God.
    a. Assumption
    b. Annunciation
    c. Ascension
    d. Attribution

27. The name ___ means "God is with us."
    a. Jesus
    b. Mediator
    c. Christ
    d. Emmanuel

28. Jesus told ___, or stories that taught moral or spiritual truths.
    a. passages
    b. parables
    c. poems
    d. pastiches

29. Jesus told the Beatitudes during the ___.
    a. Last Supper
    b. Journey to Jerusalem
    c. Sermon on the Mount
    d. wedding at Cana

30. Letters from the Pope to the Church community are known as ___.
    a. spiritual treasury
    b. encyclicals
    c. evangelical counsels
    d. spiritualities

Respond to the following items.

Name the three Divine Persons of the Holy Trinity.

31. _____

32. _____

33. _____

Name the Marks of the Church that we profess in the Creed.

34. _____

35. _____

36. _____

37. _____

Think about the following images of Jesus. Describe what each means.

38. Light of the World

_____

_____

39. Bread of Life

_____

_____

40. Vine

_____

_____

41. Jesus used parables about nature and everyday life to describe the Kingdom of God. How would you describe the Kingdom of God?

_____

_____

42. What are the Sacraments?

_____

_____

43. What is the Paschal Mystery?

_____

_____

44. Name the Seven Sacraments.

_____

_____

45. What is the mission of the Catholic Church?

_____

_____

_____

46. What are some steps in making good decisions?

_____

_____

_____

47. Which four books of the New Testament are the Gospels?

_____

_____

48. Name two parables Jesus told in the Gospels.

_____

_____

_____

49. Describe how the Church is the Body of Christ.

_____

_____

_____

50. Who are the Saints and why are they important to us?

_____

_____

_____

The King Returns

♥ Let Us Pray

Leader: Jesus, our Lord,

Your throne stands firm from of old;
　　you are from everlasting.
Your decrees are firmly established;
　　holiness befits your house, LORD,
　　for all the length of days.   **Psalm 93:2, 5**

All: You are from everlasting, O Lord! Amen.

📖 Scripture

Pilate said to Jesus, "Are you the King of the Jews?" Jesus answered, "Do you say this on your own or have others told you about me?" Pilate answered, "I am not a Jew, am I? Your own nation and the chief priests handed you over to me. What have you done?" Jesus answered, "My kingdom does not belong to this world. If my kingdom did belong to this world, my attendants [would] be fighting to keep me from being handed over to the Jews. But as it is, my kingdom is not here." So Pilate said to him, "Then you are a king?" Jesus answered, "You say I am a king. For this I was born and for this I came into the world, to testify to the truth. Everyone who belongs to the truth listens to my voice."   **John 18:33b–37**

Have you ever thought...

- What happens when people do not accept the truth of Jesus?
- Why did Jesus, the King, spend so much time serving the needs of others?

Marking the End and a New Beginning

The Church celebrates the life and ministry of Jesus as the focus of the season of Oridinary Time. The Feast of Christ the King marks the end of the liturgical year. As the last Sunday in Ordinary Time, it falls on the Sunday before Advent begins.

The feast recalls that by Pilate's order Jesus was called "King of the Jews" when he was on the Cross. During his life on Earth, Jesus never pursued political power. That was not his goal. By rejecting political gains, he was the very opposite of the common image of the king who goes to war or maintains armies to gain or preserve power. His new focus was on being the king of our hearts, the Prince of Peace. He is the king of God's Kingdom, which is not of this world.

The Feast of Christ the King looks forward, too. It predicts the end time, when Jesus will come in glory to gather the faithful to himself and give them the fullness of life they longed for on Earth—a life in union with his Father in Heaven. This feast reflects the richness of the Kingdom of God, where good and faithful servants will be reunited with one another. We will join with the angels in praising God. The righteous, those who seek God sincerely and respond to his grace, will reign with God forever. The feast makes us want to change our behavior, so that we will be known as good and faithful servants.

> Why would Jesus have avoided gaining political power?

> How should longing for God's Kingdom change our behavior on Earth?

Faithfulness to Our King

The Feast of Christ the King invites us to be faithful to Church teachings. **Faithfulness** helps us to keep our promises and follow through on our commitments. Being faithful to God and others is about being loyal and trustworthy, so people can count on us to do what we say we will.

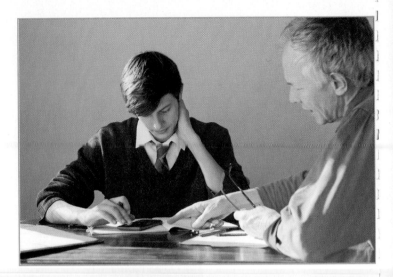

It's easy to focus on God's desire for us to be with him forever in eternal glory. What is difficult is persevering in doing what is good and turning away from sin and evil, so that through the grace of God, we can be in God's presence forever. This perseverance, or steadfastness, is faithfulness. A faithful person is dedicated to his or her task of bringing glory to God.

We cultivate faithfulness by hanging on through troubled times, by constantly maintaining that vision of our goal. We nurture this Fruit of the Holy Spirit by being faithful in small things, such as a promise to a friend, saying daily prayers, or helping with household tasks without being asked. Like every Fruit of the Holy Spirit, faithfulness will deepen with practice and as we remain responsive to God's grace in the Sacraments and our lives.

Fruits of the Holy Spirit

The twelve **Fruits of the Holy Spirit** are qualities that can be seen in us when we let the Holy Spirit work in our hearts. This season we are focusing on **faithfulness**.

EXPLAIN

Look up these Scripture verses on faithfulness. Which passage gives you the best advice or inspiration to be faithful? Explain your answer below.

Matthew 8:23–26   **Matthew 9:18–25**   **Revelation 2:9–10**

_____

_____

_____

_____

_____

_____

_____

♥ A Prayer of Praise

Pray the Sign of the Cross together.

Reader 1: Today we honor Christ the King with these words from the Book of Revelation:

From Jesus Christ, the faithful witness, the firstborn of the dead and ruler of the kings of the earth.
To him who loves us and has freed us from our sins by his blood,
who has made us into a kingdom, priests for his God and Father,
to him be glory and power forever [and ever]. Amen.

All: To him be glory and power forever and ever. Amen.

Reader 2: Behold, he is coming amid the clouds,
   and every eye will see him,
   even those who pierced him.
All the peoples of the earth will lament him.
   Yes. Amen.

All: To him be glory and power forever and ever. Amen.

Reader 3: "I am the Alpha and the Omega," says the Lord God,
"the one who is and who was and who is to come, the almighty."

All: To him be glory and power forever and ever. Amen.   **Revelation 1:5–8**

Leader: Let us now go forth to faithfully serve God.

All: God, grant us faithfulness. Amen.

▶ *Sing or play "Mighty King"*

Being Ready

♥ Let Us Pray

Leader: Lord Jesus, we want to see your face.

"O Shepherd of Israel, lend an ear …
  Seated upon the cherubim, shine forth. …
  Stir up your power, and come to save us."   **Psalm 80:2–3**

We ask this in your name, O Lord.

All: Lord, rouse your power and come to save us. Amen.

📖 Scripture

Beware that your hearts do not become drowsy from carousing and drunkenness and the anxieties of daily life, and that day catch you by surprise like a trap. For that day will assault everyone who lives on the face of the earth. Be vigilant at all times and pray that you have the strength to escape the tribulations that are imminent and to stand before the Son of Man.
Luke 21:34-36

© Our Sunday Visitor

Have you ever thought...

- What are the anxieties in your life?
- How does Advent prepare us to think about our own redemption?

Art of a Jesse Tree, which symbolizes Jesus as the root of the tree of Jesse, the father of the biblical King David.

Awaiting Jesus

We often use the word "advent" to mean "the coming of" or "the onset," as in the phrase, "the advent of the internet age." But with a capital "A," the term can only mean one thing: the time when we anticipate the coming of Jesus.

Advent is the four weeks at the beginning of the liturgical year, leading up to the Christmas season. During Advent, the priest wears purple vestments at Mass, and churches are also decorated in purple to remind us to repent and remember that Christ is our King. We begin the Church year with hope and anticipation. We renew ourselves with the age-old story of God redeeming his People.

Throughout Advent, we gather with other Christians and listen to the prophets telling us to prepare for the coming of the Lord. We recall the story of the Incarnation, Jesus becoming man, and we hear the teachings of John the Baptist. We also pray before the Advent wreath and make small acts of sacrifice and penance, and celebrate the feast days of the Solemnity of the Immaculate Conception, Our Lady of Guadalupe, Saint Nicholas, and others.

These days, we are in a second Advent. We are waiting for Jesus to come again. He came once as our Messiah, our Savior, and he will come again at the end of the world. We must prepare our hearts and minds for that time when Jesus Christ comes again. In the meantime, we must have patience and wait.

> How can we anticipate the coming of Jesus now?

> What hopes do you have for the new liturgical year?

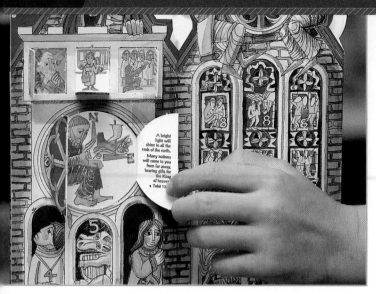

Modeling Patience

Advent can be a very trying time. Too many things wrestle for our attention: tests at school, presents to buy or make, Christmas plays and concerts to prepare for and attend, caroling parties, and tree decorating.

One Fruit of the Holy Spirit that will sustain us through this season is **patience**. Patience provides steadfastness in the face of difficulties because we trust God is with us and will somehow make things good and right. Patience helps us keep our focus on what is important rather than on distractions. The focus of Advent is preparing ourselves for Christ, making space for him in our lives.

We need to model ourselves after the Jewish people, who waited thousands of years for the Messiah. What sustained them in the storm of wandering and persecutions was trusting that the Messiah would come, that the prophecies would be fulfilled. They prepared the way for the Lord. During Advent we hear the words of the prophets calling us to be active in our anticipation, to prepare, through our words and deeds, as we wait.

Fruits of the Holy Spirit

The twelve **Fruits of the Holy Spirit** are qualities that can be seen in us when we let the Holy Spirit work in our hearts. This season we are focusing on **patience**.

CONSIDER

There's a difference between waiting for something and waiting for someone. Name one situation in each category and describe what our impatience might look like and how we might become more patient.

_____

_____

_____

_____

_____

_____

_____

_____

♥ A Waiting Prayer

Pray the Sign of the Cross together.

Leader: Make known to me your ways, Lord;
 teach me your paths.

Guide me by your fidelity and teach me,
 for you are God my savior,
 for you I wait all the day long.

All: To you, O Lord, I lift my soul.

Leader: Good and upright is the Lord;
 therefore he shows sinners the way.

He guides the humble in righteousness,
 and teaches the humble his way.

All: To you, O Lord, I lift my soul.

Leader: All the paths of the Lord are mercy and truth
 toward those who honor his covenant and his decrees.

The counsel of the Lord belongs to those who fear him;
 and his covenant instructs them.

All: To you, O Lord, I lift my soul.
Psalm 25:4–5, 8–9, 10, 14

Leader: Let us go forth with patience to celebrate Advent.

All: We ask this through Jesus Christ. Amen.

▶ *Sing or play "O Come O Come Emmanuel"*

Our Gift

♥ Let Us Pray

Leader: Lord Jesus, Let it be said of us, your people,

"Let the heavens be glad and the earth rejoice …
> before the LORD who comes,
> who comes to govern the earth.
To govern the world with justice
> and the peoples with his faithfulness." **Psalm 96.13**

All: Let us exult before the Lord. Amen.

📖 Scripture

When the angels went away from them to heaven, the shepherds said to one another, "Let us go, then, to Bethlehem to see this thing that has taken place, which the Lord has made known to us." So they went in haste and found Mary and Joseph, and the infant lying in the manger. When they saw this, they made known the message that had been told them about this child.

All who heard it were amazed by what had been told them by the shepherds. And Mary kept all these things, reflecting on them in her heart. Then the shepherds returned, glorifying and praising God for all they had heard and seen, just as it had been told to them.   **Luke 2:15–20**

Have you ever thought...

- Why did Jesus come to Earth?

- How can God the Father be so generous that he offered us his Son?

God With Us

Christmas—the word carries many images: gifts, decorations, music, and favorite foods. While these are all part of the celebration of Christmas, it is easy to lose sight of the heart of this season, which we celebrate from the Christmas Eve Vigil until the Feast of the Baptism of the Lord. Christmas is the day Christians all over the world remember and give thanks for God's greatest gift—the gift of his Son. At Christmas we celebrate the Incarnation, the sacred mystery of God becoming man, Jesus. Jesus Christ, the Second Divine Person of the Holy Trinity, chose to enter our world as a human being. "For God so loved the world," Saint John says, "that he gave his only Son" (John 3:16). Jesus, God made man, entered our human existence to save us from sin and death. That is the miracle of Christmas. That is why we celebrate with customs and traditions that remind us of this incredible gift.

It is a challenge to keep focused on the meaning of Christmas in the midst of so many distractions. You must make a choice to take the time to sift through all those distractions. You can do that by making time to pray and to read from Scripture. Allowing yourself the time and quiet to hear God's voice will help you to appreciate more deeply God's love and generosity. Jesus is the Father's gift to the world. He is the Father's gift to you. Open your heart to receive what God is offering you.

> **What can you do during the Christmas season to more clearly hear God's voice?**

> **What does it mean to you to say that while God offers us the gift of salvation, we must choose to receive it?**

True Generosity

During the Christmas season, we can't help but think of gifts. We are preoccupied with what others might want, and we are constantly quizzed about what we want. We sometimes fail to see that we have already received the greatest gift of all: God's Son.

As we celebrate Christmas, God is our model for generosity. He gave us his only Son as a tiny, dependent baby. **Generosity** is one of the Fruits of the Holy Spirit. We live generously when we share our gifts (talents), time, and possessions with others out of gratitude for God.

Mary is a model of generosity, too, in the way that she shared Jesus with others. She welcomed the shepherds and the Magi. She took Jesus to the Temple, to see Simeon and Anna.

We tend to give temporary pleasures, such as clothes and electronics, as gifts. To be truly generous, we need to give of ourselves, to find a way to share Christmas peace and joy with others. Then we will be more like God and Mary, our models of generosity.

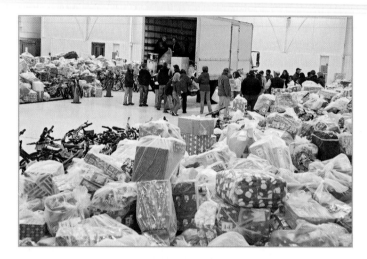

Fruits of the Holy Spirit

The twelve **Fruits of the Holy Spirit** are qualities that can be seen in us when we let the Holy Spirit work in our hearts. This season we are focusing on **generosity**.

LIST AND IDENTIFY

Name small acts of generosity that you can take in each of these situations.

For an extended family member who might be lonely: _____

_____

For a family who is homeless: _____

_____

For a classmate who seems unhappy: _____

_____

For a single parent of one of your friends: _____

_____

For a teacher who is facing his or her first holiday without a loved one: _____

_____

♥ An Adoration Prayer

Pray the Sign of the Cross together.

Leader: The people who walked in darkness
   have seen a great light;
Upon those who dwelt in the land of gloom
   a light has shone.

All: You have brought them abundant joy
   and great rejoicing;
They rejoice before you as people rejoice
at harvest, as they exult when dividing the
spoils.

Leader: For a child is born to us,
a son is given us;
   upon his shoulder dominion rests.
They name him Wonder-Counselor,
God-Hero,
   Father-Forever, Prince of Peace.

All: His dominion is vast
   and forever peaceful,
Upon David's throne, and over his kingdom,
   which he confirms and sustains
By judgment and justice,
   both now and forever.
The zeal of the Lord of hosts
will do this!   Isaiah 9:1-6

Leader: Glory to God in the highest,
and on earth peace to people of good will.

All: We praise you,
we bless you,
we adore you,
we glorify you,
we give you thanks for your great glory,
Lord God, heavenly King,
O God, almighty Father.

Lord Jesus Christ, Only Begotten Son,
Lord God, Lamb of God, Son of the Father,
you take away the sins of the world,
   have mercy on us;

you take away the sings of the world,
   receive our prayer;

you are seated at the right hand of the Father,
   have mercy on us.

For you alone are the Holy one,
you alone are the Most High,
Jesus Christ,
with the Holy Spirit,
in the glory of God the Father.
Amen.

Leader: Go forth and live generously to
honor Christ, our newborn King.

All: We thank God for this gift. Amen.

▶ *Sing or play "O Come All Ye Faithful"*

The Annunciation

♥ Let Us Pray

Leader: Lord God, Help us be like Mary. Help us say, as she did,

"I delight to do your will, my God;
your law is in my inner being!" **Psalm 40:9**

All: May we come to do your will, just as Mary did. Amen.

📖 Scripture

The angel Gabriel was sent from God to Nazareth, to a virgin named Mary. And coming to her, he said, "Hail, favored one! The Lord is with you." But she was greatly troubled at what was said and pondered what sort of greeting this might be. Then the angel said to her, "Do not be afraid, Mary, for you have found favor with God. Behold, you will conceive in your womb and bear a son, and you shall name him Jesus. He will be great and will be called Son of the Most High … and of his kingdom there will be no end." But Mary said to the angel, "How can this be, since I have no relations with a man?" And the angel said to her in reply, "The holy Spirit will come upon you, and the power of the Most High will overshadow you. Therefore the child to be born will be called holy, the Son of God." … Mary said, "Behold, I am the handmaid of the Lord. May it be done to me according to your word." **Luke 1:26–35, 38**

Have you ever thought...

- How does someone become open to doing God's will?

- Can I be like Mary?

Mary with the infant Jesus

Mary with Jesus at the Wedding at Cana

Mary with the body of Christ after the Crucifixion

Mary as Jesus' Mother

The season of Lent includes the Feast day on which the Church remembers Mary's "yes" to God's plan for her life. This day is known as the Feast of the Annunciation, and occurs on March 25. The feast is timed so that nine months elapse between it and Jesus' birth on December 25. On this feast day, and others devoted to Mary, the priest wears white vestments.

In the moment when Mary agreed to be Jesus' mother, everything changed. With her words and through the power of the Holy Spirit, Jesus became man. God became one of us, taking on human form while still maintaining his divinity. The world went from being in Old Testament times into the the time of the new covenant, the era of God with us. In a way that had never been before, God came for all people.

In this moment, Mary responded faithfully despite the many emotions that must have been going through her mind and heart. She was troubled by the Angel Gabriel's greeting, and she expressed confusion over how God's will would be done. Despite this, she didn't falter in her agreement.

The Church honors Mary above all other Saints because her "yes" set the example for all Christian believers. She was willing to serve God by bringing Jesus into the world. Her deed of goodness served all humanity.

> How did Mary's "yes" change the world?
> Why is Mary a model for us?

Mary's Goodness

Mary's willingness to participate in God's plan showed her goodness. She could have refused, because, as he did for all of us, God gave her the gift of free will. She could have chosen an easier life than that of being the Messiah's mother, with the sorrows and cares that would come with it. She chose, however, to be part of our redemption, and that shows goodness on her part.

Goodness is one of the Fruits of the Holy Spirit. It is one of the qualities that show that the Holy Spirit is working in our hearts. Because God is our creator and is good, we are good. Goodness is showing love and honor to God. It is desiring and doing what is best for another person. When Mary

agreed to be Jesus' mother, she knew that she was doing something good. She knew it would bring her troubles and sorrows, yet she still agreed.

We are invited to be models of goodness for others, just as Mary was a model of goodness. We can choose to do the right thing, even when making that choice leads to difficulties for us. Our actions can be signs that point others toward the Messiah.

Fruits of the Holy Spirit

The twelve **Fruits of the Holy Spirit** are qualities that can be seen in us when we let the Holy Spirit work in our hearts. This season we are focusing on **goodness**.

SUMMARIZE

Work with a classmate to look up these Scripture accounts of Mary and summarize each passage to each other. Then choose one account and explain how it shows Mary's goodness.

Luke 1:39–56   Luke 2:21–35   Luke 2:41–52   John 2:1–11

_____

_____

_____

_____

_____

_____

♥ A Marian Prayer

Pray the Sign of the Cross together.

Leader: A reading from the Book of Isaiah.

"The Lord himself will give you a sign:
the young woman, pregnant and about to
bear a son, shall name him Emmanuel."
Isaiah 7:14

The word of the Lord.

All: Thanks be to God.

Leader: To celebrate the Annunciation,
the feast that commemorates Mary's
agreement to be Jesus' mother,
we pray for her to show her goodness
by helping us.

All: Mary, please help us grow in goodness.

Leader: Let us end our celebration of the
Annunciation by reciting the prayer inspired
by this feast.

All: Hail, Mary, full of grace,
the Lord is with thee.
Blessed art thou among women
and blessed is the fruit of thy womb, Jesus.

Holy Mary, Mother of God,
pray for us sinners,
now and at the hour of our death.
Amen.

Leader: Go forth and show your goodness,
just as Mary did.

All: Amen.

▶ *Sing or play "O Sanctissima"*

Conquering Temptation

♥ Let Us Pray

Leader: We gather to ask for God's help in avoiding sin, for

> "Truly, I love your commandments
> more than gold, more than the finest gold.
> Thus, I follow all your precepts;
> every wrong way I hate." **Psalm 119:127–128**

All: We ask for God's guidance. Amen.

📖 Scripture

Then Jesus was led by the Spirit into the desert to be tempted by the devil. … the devil took him to the holy city, and made him stand on the parapet of the temple, and said to him, "If you are the Son of God, throw yourself down. For it is written:

"'He will command his angels concerning you' and 'with their hands they will support you, lest you dash your foot against a stone.'"

Jesus answered him, "Again it is written, 'You shall not put the Lord, your God, to the test.'"

Then the devil took him up to a very high mountain, and showed him all the kingdoms of the world in their magnificence, and he said to him, "All these I shall give to you, if you will prostrate yourself and worship me."

At this, Jesus said to him, "Get away, Satan! It is written:

'The Lord, your God, shall you worship and him alone shall you serve.'"

Then the devil left him and, behold, angels came and ministered to him. **Matthew 4:1–11**

Have you ever thought...

- What makes human beings so open to temptations?
- How do people overcome temptation?

Becoming Strong

Lent is forty days of work. For Catholics who live in the Northern hemisphere, it begins in winter, with long nights yielding a few more precious minutes of light to each successive day as spring approaches. With the added sun comes the warmth that wakens the dormant earth, stirring plants to flower and reveal God's glory as Easter arrives.

We are like the natural world: we have lots of growing to do between winter's barrenness and Easter's brightness. We have to examine ourselves to determine what keeps us from growing in God's ways. Once we recognize those things, we must find ways to help us die to sin in order that we would grow in grace. Often, the problem is temptation. This can come from within us, as envy or false pride. It can come from outside of us, from a world that holds up consumerism and selfishness as the good. Much of Lent focuses on growing the virtues that will help us fight temptation. As we grow closer to God, everything else falls into the right order.

Lenten practices such as fasting, doing works of penance, and almsgiving to people who are poor or who are in need help us remember Jesus' sacrifice and build our strength, too.

Prayer is also a vital practice during Lent. During the season we pray for faith to appreciate the gift of life, for the generosity of spirit that will help us give to others, and for hope to conquer obstacles in our lives. We also pray on behalf of others, asking Jesus to give them strength. We pray especially for those preparing for Baptism and joining the Catholic Church.

> **What kind of growth do you want to achieve this Lent?**

> **Which temptations do you find especially difficult to overcome?**

Focusing on Self-Control

Lent provides us with many opportunities to counter temptation. The readings at Mass ask God to help us, because we are all sinners. Many parishes schedule additional times for us to take part in the Sacrament of Penance and Reconciliation, the Sacrament that helps us receive God's forgiveness and grace after we have examined our consciences and become aware of sin.

On a personal level, many people give up favorite things until Easter. Others try to change a bad habit into a good one. With these simple practices, they are developing **self-control**, one of the Fruits of the Holy Spirit. Self-control is about striving to overcome temptation and do God's will. It is cooperating with God's grace to focus on what's important and resist the things that keep us from becoming the people he wants us to be.

The Gospel reading at the beginning of this lesson shows how Jesus handled temptation with self-control. His responses to the devil's tempting words focus on living out God's instructions to us. Jesus showed us how to be in the world, yet keep the things of this world in proper order and not be deceived or distracted by the power of evil.

Fruits of the Holy Spirit

The twelve **Fruits of the Holy Spirit** are qualities that can be seen in us when we let the Holy Spirit work in our hearts. This season we are focusing on **self-control**.

© Our Sunday Visitor

IDENTIFY AND PLAN

In the space below, identify areas where you feel people your age need to grow in self-control. Next to each problem area, write a way that faith can help people overcome the temptation.

Problem Area	How It Can Be Addressed

♥ A Prayer of Petition

Pray the Sign of the Cross together.

Leader: Have mercy on me, O God, in your goodness;

in the greatness of your compassion wipe out my offense.

Thoroughly wash me from my guilt and of my sin cleanse me.

All: Create a clean heart in me, O God.

Reader 1: A clean heart create for me, O God,
and a steadfast spirit renew within me.

Cast me not out from your presence,
and your Holy Spirit take not from me.

All: Create a clean heart in me, O God.

Reader 2: Give me back the joy of your salvation,
and a willing spirit sustain in me.

I will teach transgressors your ways,
and sinners shall return to you.

All: Create a clean heart in me, O God.
Based on Psalm 51:3–4, 12–13, 14–15

Leader: Let us go forth to fight temptation with self-control.

All: Our Father, who art in heaven,
hallowed be thy name;
thy kingdom come,
thy will be done
on earth as it is in heaven.
Give us this day our daily bread,
and forgive us our trespasses,
as we forgive those who trespass against us;
and lead us not into temptation,
but deliver us from evil. Amen.

 Sing or play "Create in Me"

Triduum

♥ Let Us Pray

Leader: Lord God, during Holy Week we honor the Passion and Death of your Son. The prophet Isaiah wrote,

"[He] bore the sins of many,
    and interceded for the transgressors."   Isaiah 53:12

All: May he win pardon for our sins. Amen.

Scripture

Therefore, since we have a great high priest who has passed through the heavens, Jesus, the Son of God, let us hold fast to our confession. For we do not have a high priest who is unable to sympathize with our weaknesses, but one who has similarly been tested in every way, yet without sin. So let us confidently approach the throne of grace to receive mercy and to find grace for timely help.   Hebrews 4:14–16

Have you ever thought...

- Do think there is anyone is your life who would die to save your life?

- Do you wonder what motivates fire personnel or police officers to put themselves in harm's way?

Jesus Suffers for Us

Holy Week is the most solemn week of the year. During the seven days from Passion (or Palm) Sunday to Easter, we remember Jesus' triumphant arrival in Jerusalem, the institution of the Holy Eucharist, and Jesus' Death and burial. The week ends with the Easter Vigil, when we celebrate our Savior's triumph over death. It is an intense week in the Church.

On Good Friday we recognize the depth of our Savior's sacrifice. Just hours after celebrating Passover with his companions, he is deserted by his friends. He is handed over to officials who have him scourged. His own people shout a death sentence for him. He carries his Cross up a hill, meeting his mother and other women on the way. He falls several times, to the point where Simon is pressed into service to help him.

At the top of the hill, Christ is nailed to the Cross and hoisted up between two criminals. He also says to those who have persecuted him, "Father, forgive them, they know not what they do" (Luke 23:34). He even tells a criminal being crucified by his side that he will be welcomed in Heaven. Finally, Jesus gives up his spirit, and a soldier pierces his side with a lance. The body is taken down and placed in a tomb.

The accumulated effect of these events is hard to imagine. What sort of love would sustain a person through these trials? Only a love that comes from God. Only a love that is meant to redeem others.

> **How does Jesus model God's mercy and forgiveness?**

> **What could you do to be merciful and forgiving?**

Ultimate Charity

Good Friday is the day when we witness Jesus' ultimate act of love for us, his Death upon the Cross. We are forever in his debt for this redemption. Our best way of showing that we appreciate his selfless love for us is to pass that love on to others. We do that when we follow his teachings and act with love, or **charity**, toward one another.

Fruits of the Holy Spirit

The twelve **Fruits of the Holy Spirit** are qualities that can be seen in us when we let the Holy Spirit work in our hearts. This season we are focusing on **charity**.

The Great Commandment points us toward charity. It directs us to love God above all, and to love our neighbors as we love ourselves. Charity, both a fruit of the Holy Spirit and a Theological Virtue, is the foundation of all other virtues. It is the unselfish love we return to God and share with others.

Jesus asks us to love as he did. Although we might not be asked to give our very lives, as Jesus did, this means giving of ourselves to other. We can spend time with others, observe the Corporal and Spiritual Works of Mercy, and find other ways to selflessly give of ourselves.

WRITE

Write a short meditation on the ways that Jesus showed charity throughout his life. Include a sentence or two about how you intend to follow his lead. Read the meditation often during Holy Week.

_____

_____

_____

_____

_____

_____

_____

_____

Our Reason for Joy

There is much to be joyful about at Easter. All of nature echoes the joy of the season, with greenery, blossoms, and new life. If we quietly contemplate the season, we will experience inner **joy** as well.

If we have been diligent during Lent and Triduum, we have been serving God and our fellow humans with love. We have denied ourselves pleasures in order to develop self-control. We have given alms and time to worthwhile causes to increase our charity to others. Those self-giving acts have opened us up to Christ's sacrifice and the Easter joy of his presence in our lives.

Joy is a Fruit of the Holy Spirit. It comes from the growing awareness that God and his love are with us no matter our personal circumstances or achievements.

Now that we are in the habit of serving with love, we will want to continue to share Christ's joy with others. Then it will grow even more.

Fruits of the Holy Spirit

The twelve Fruits of the Holy Spirit are qualities that can be seen in us when we let the Holy Spirit work in our hearts. This season we are focusing on joy.

WRITE

Write a short reflection on your own reasons for feeling Easter joy. Include observations on nature, your relationships, or ways you have changed for the better during Lent.

_____

_____

_____

_____

♥ A Prayer of Mercy

Pray the Sign of the Cross together.

Leader: In you, O LORD, I take refuge; let me never be put to shame. In your justice rescue me.

Into your hands I commend my spirit; you will redeem me, O LORD, O faithful God.

All: Father, into your hands I commend my spirit.

Leader: For all my foes I am an object of reproach, a laughingstock to my neighbors, and a dread to my friends; they who see me abroad flee from me.

I am forgotten like the unremembered dead; I am like a dish that is broken.

All: Father, into your hands I commend my spirit.

Leader: But my trust is in you, O LORD; I say, "You are my God.

In your hands is my destiny; rescue me from the clutches of my enemies and my persecutors."

All: Father, into your hands I commend my spirit.

Leader: Let your face shine upon your servant; save me in your kindness.

Take courage and be stouthearted, all you who hope in the LORD.

All: Father, into your hands I commend my spirit.   Based on Psalm 31:2, 6, 12–13, 15–16, 17, 25; Luke 23:46

Leader: We go forth to honor Jesus' sacrifice by following his teachings of love.

All: We shall follow his teachings of love. Amen.

▶ *Sing or play "Take Up Our Cross"*

Meeting Jesus with Joy

♥ Let Us Pray

Leader: Lord Jesus, by your Cross and Resurrection, you have set us free.
You enable us to say,

"God indeed is my salvation,
I am confident and unafraid." Isaiah 12:2–3

All: I am confident, Lord. Amen.

📖 Scripture

Peter proceeded to speak and said:
"You know what has happened all over Judea, beginning in Galilee after the baptism that John preached, how God anointed Jesus of Nazareth with the Holy Spirit and power. He went about doing good and healing all those oppressed by the devil, for God was with him. We are witnesses of all that he did both in the country of the Jews and in Jerusalem.

They put him to death by hanging him on a tree. This man God raised on the third day and granted that he be visible, not to all the people, but to us, the witnesses chosen by God in advance, who ate and drank with him after he rose from the dead.

He commissioned us to preach to the people and testify that he is the one appointed by God as judge of the living and the dead. To him all the prophets bear witness, that everyone who believes in him will receive forgiveness of sins through his name." Acts 10:34a, 37–43

Have you ever thought...

- Why does Jesus' Resurrection take away our biggest fear?
- How does believing in eternal life change the way you live this life?

© Our Sunday Visitor

Catholics gather as the processional begins during an Easter Sunrise Mass

The Center of Our Beliefs

When you were younger, you probably considered Christmas the primary religious holiday. It was easy for you to understand the happiness that came with the birth of a baby, and the traditions that came with the holiday made it even more memorable.

Now that you are older, you can understand why the Easter season, which runs from Easter to Pentecost, is the primary season of the liturgical year. Yes, it is important that God became man in Jesus Christ. What the Easter season celebrates, though, is the entirety of the Paschal Mystery: that Jesus suffered, died, rose, and ascended to Heaven.

When we celebrate Easter, we see the Ris[en] Lord, who is glorified after his horrible suffering for our sake. We celebrate that he has returned from the dead and that he wi[ll] teach us for a little longer. We recognize th[at] he must return to his Father. We are happy that he sends the Spirit to sustain our faith. He tells the disciples, and us, "Peace be with you" (John 20:19).

During this season, we sing "Alleluia!" often It is one way we express the joy we find in the risen Christ.

> How does an appreciation for Easter reflect a more mature view of your faith?

> What does "Alleluia!" mean to you?

♥ A Prayer of Praise

Pray the Sign of the Cross together.

Leader: We give thanks as we joyfully celebrate Christ's victory over death.

All: Alleluia!

Leader: Give thanks to the LORD, for he is good,
for his mercy endures forever.
Let the house of Israel say,
"His mercy endures forever."

All: This is the day the Lord has made;
let us rejoice and be glad.

Leader: In danger I called on the LORD;
the LORD answered and set me free.
The LORD is with me; I am not afraid;
what can mortals do against me?

All: This is the day the Lord has made;
let us rejoice and be glad.

Leader: "The right hand of the LORD has struck with power;
the right hand of the LORD is exalted.
I shall not die, but live,
and declare the works of the LORD."

All: This is the day the Lord has made;
let us rejoice and be glad.

Leader: The stone which the builders rejected
has become the cornerstone.
By the LORD has this been done;
it is wonderful in our eyes.

All: This is the day the Lord has made;
let us rejoice and be glad.
Based on Psalm 118:1-2, 16-17, 22-23, 24

Leader: Let us go forth to celebrate the Easter Season with joy.

All: Alleluia! Amen.

 Sing or play "Come to the Water"

Ascension

♥ Let Us Pray

Leader: Lord Jesus, you returned to your Father. Of you it is said,

"God has gone up with a shout."   **Psalm 47:6**

All: We give you thanks for your great glory. Amen.

📖 Scripture

When they had gathered together they asked him, "Lord, are you at this time going to restore the kingdom to Israel?" He answered them, "It is not for you to know the times or seasons that the Father has established by his own authority. But you will receive power when the holy Spirit comes upon you, and you will be my witnesses in Jerusalem, throughout Judea and Samaria, and to the ends of the earth."

When he had said this, as they were looking on, he was lifted up, and a cloud took him from their sight. While they were looking intently at the sky as he was going, suddenly two men dressed in white garments stood beside them. They said, "Men of Galilee, why are you standing there looking at the sky? This Jesus who has been taken up from you into heaven will return in the same way as you have seen him going into heaven."   **Acts 1:6-11**

Have you ever thought...

• Was Jesus sad to leave his disciples?

• Was Jesus worried that his disciples would be lost without him?

♥ A Prayer of Mercy

Pray the Sign of the Cross together.

Leader: In you, O LORD, I take refuge;
let me never be put to shame.
In your justice rescue me.

Into your hands I commend my spirit;
you will redeem me, O LORD, O faithful
God.

All: Father, into your hands I commend my
spirit.

Leader: For all my foes I am an object of
reproach,
a laughingstock to my neighbors, and a
dread to my friends;
they who see me abroad flee from me.

I am forgotten like the unremembered dead;
I am like a dish that is broken.

All: Father, into your hands I commend
my spirit.

Leader: But my trust is in you, O LORD;
I say, "You are my God.

In your hands is my destiny; rescue me
from the clutches of my enemies and my
persecutors."

All: Father, into your hands I commend
my spirit.

Leader: Let your face shine upon your
servant;
save me in your kindness.

Take courage and be stouthearted,
all you who hope in the LORD.

All: Father, into your hands I commend
my spirit. **Based on Psalm 31:2, 6, 12–13, 15–16,
17, 25; Luke 23:46**

Leader: We go forth to honor Jesus' sacrifice
by following his teachings of love.

All: We shall follow his teachings of love.
Amen.

 Sing or play "Take Up Our Cross"

Meeting Jesus with Joy

♥ Let Us Pray

Leader: Lord Jesus, by your Cross and Resurrection, you have set us free. You enable us to say,

"God indeed is my salvation,
     I am confident and unafraid."   Isaiah 12:2–3

All: I am confident, Lord. Amen.

📖 Scripture

Peter proceeded to speak and said: "You know what has happened all over Judea, beginning in Galilee after the baptism that John preached, how God anointed Jesus of Nazareth with the Holy Spirit and power. He went about doing good and healing all those oppressed by the devil, for God was with him. We are witnesses of all that he did both in the country of the Jews and in Jerusalem.

They put him to death by hanging him on a tree. This man God raised on the third day and granted that he be visible, not to all the people, but to us, the witnesses chosen by God in advance, who ate and drank with him after he rose from the dead.

He commissioned us to preach to the people and testify that he is the one appointed by God as judge of the living and the dead. To him all the prophets bear witness, that everyone who believes in him will receive forgiveness of sins through his name."   Acts 10:34a, 37–43

Have you ever thought...

- Why does Jesus' Resurrection take away our biggest fear?

- How does believing in eternal life change the way you live this life?

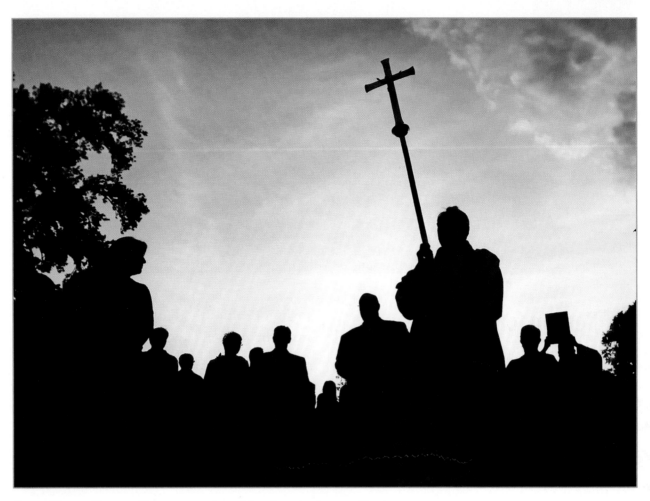

Catholics gather as the processional begins during an Easter Sunrise Mass

The Center of Our Beliefs

When you were younger, you probably considered Christmas the primary religious holiday. It was easy for you to understand the happiness that came with the birth of a baby, and the traditions that came with the holiday made it even more memorable.

Now that you are older, you can understand why the Easter season, which runs from Easter to Pentecost, is the primary season of the liturgical year. Yes, it is important that God became man in Jesus Christ. What the Easter season celebrates, though, is the entirety of the Paschal Mystery: that Jesus suffered, died, rose, and ascended to Heaven.

When we celebrate Easter, we see the Risen Lord, who is glorified after his horrible suffering for our sake. We celebrate that he has returned from the dead and that he will teach us for a little longer. We recognize that he must return to his Father. We are happy that he sends the Spirit to sustain our faith. He tells the disciples, and us, "Peace be with you" (John 20:19).

During this season, we sing "Alleluia!" often. It is one way we express the joy we find in the risen Christ.

> How does an appreciation for Easter reflect a more mature view of your faith?

> What does "Alleluia!" mean to you?

Our Reason for Joy

There is much to be joyful about at Easter. All of nature echoes the joy of the season, with greenery, blossoms, and new life. If we quietly contemplate the season, we will experience inner **joy** as well.

If we have been diligent during Lent and Triduum, we have been serving God and our fellow humans with love. We have denied ourselves pleasures in order to develop self-control. We have given alms and time to worthwhile causes to increase our charity to others. Those self-giving acts have opened us up to Christ's sacrifice and the Easter joy of his presence in our lives.

Joy is a Fruit of the Holy Spirit. It comes from the growing awareness that God and his love are with us no matter our personal circumstances or achievements.

Now that we are in the habit of serving with love, we will want to continue to share Christ's joy with others. Then it will grow even more.

Fruits of the Holy Spirit

The twelve **Fruits of the Holy Spirit** are qualities that can be seen in us when we let the Holy Spirit work in our hearts. This season we are focusing on **joy**.

WRITE

Write a short reflection on your own reasons for feeling Easter joy. Include observations on nature, your relationships, or ways you have changed for the better during Lent.

_____

_____

_____

_____

A Prayer of Praise

Pray the Sign of the Cross together.

Leader: We give thanks as we joyfully celebrate Christ's victory over death.

All: Alleluia!

Leader: Give thanks to the LORD, for he is good,
for his mercy endures forever.
Let the house of Israel say,
"His mercy endures forever."

All: This is the day the Lord has made;
let us rejoice and be glad.

Leader: In danger I called on the LORD;
the LORD answered and set me free.
The LORD is with me; I am not afraid;
what can mortals do against me?

All: This is the day the Lord has made;
let us rejoice and be glad.

Leader: "The right hand of the LORD has struck with power;
the right hand of the LORD is exalted.
I shall not die, but live,
and declare the works of the LORD."

All: This is the day the Lord has made;
let us rejoice and be glad.

Leader: The stone which the builders rejected
has become the cornerstone.
By the LORD has this been done;
it is wonderful in our eyes.

All: This is the day the Lord has made;
let us rejoice and be glad.
Based on Psalm 118:1-2, 16-17, 22-23, 24

Leader: Let us go forth to celebrate the Easter Season with joy.

All: Alleluia! Amen.

 Sing or play "Come to the Water"

Ascension

♥ Let Us Pray

Leader: Lord Jesus, you returned to your Father. Of you it is said,

"God has gone up with a shout."   **Psalm 47:6**

All: We give you thanks for your great glory. Amen.

📖 Scripture

When they had gathered together they asked him, "Lord, are you at this time going to restore the kingdom to Israel?" He answered them, "It is not for you to know the times or seasons that the Father has established by his own authority. But you will receive power when the holy Spirit comes upon you, and you will be my witnesses in Jerusalem, throughout Judea and Samaria, and to the ends of the earth."

When he had said this, as they were looking on, he was lifted up, and a cloud took him from their sight. While they were looking intently at the sky as he was going, suddenly two men dressed in white garments stood beside them. They said, "Men of Galilee, why are you standing there looking at the sky? This Jesus who has been taken up from you into heaven will return in the same way as you have seen him going into heaven."   **Acts 1:6-11**

Have you ever thought...

- Was Jesus sad to leave his disciples?
- Was Jesus worried that his disciples would be lost without him?

Changes for Us All

The Ascension celebrates a major transition for Jesus—and for us. For most of Jesus' ministry, he had been with us on Earth. For a few brief days—Good Friday evening to Easter Sunday morning—he was out of our presence. Then he returned and taught for another forty days.

But then, things changed. His teaching was done, and he was returning to the Father. The Gospels don't tell us how much notice Jesus gave his followers that this would happen. Clearly, they were astonished as he ascended and disappeared from sight. They were so surprised that two men dressed in white had to interrupt their gazing and explain that Jesus had gone up into Heaven. There is a second part to their message, too. They told us that he would also return to us.

The Ascension challenges Catholics to be faithful. It shows us what Jesus has left us: the Holy Spirit, his teachings, the Church, and one another. We are to make use of all of these resources as we wait in hope for his return.

After the Ascension, the early Church community was left with the promise of the coming of the Holy Spirit, who would strengthen them to continue the work of Christ, to spread the Good News and build the Kingdom of God. The Holy Spirit did come to Jesus' followers at Pentecost, and in the Sacraments of Baptism and Confirmation, Catholics receive the Holy Spirit as well. We are strengthened by the Spirit to bring the Good News to others through evangelization: talking to others

Study for a mural of the Ascension,
Hans Felbusch

about our faith, sharing how our faith influences us, using our gifts and talents to help others, and sharing what we have with those who are in need.

In the United States, Ascension Thursday is a Holy Day of Obligation. On the Feast of the Ascension, the priest wears white vestments to signify it is a feast of Jesus. The Church as a whole is reminded on this day of her mission to serve the world.

> **What important lesson do we learn from the Ascension?**

> **What can you do to prepare for Jesus' return?**

Peace from Within

The Easter Season is almost over when we celebrate the feast of the Ascension, but we live as an Easter people all year long. Christ's Death and Resurrection are made present at every celebration of the Eucharist. He is present with us always, even though he has returned to his Father in Heaven.

We are at **peace,** the Fruit of the Holy Spirit in which we experience freedom from worry as God's love fills our hearts. We strive to act as Christ, resolving conflicts respectfully and with kindness. It gives us a sense of calm, but not of complacency. It provides resolve and a sense of mission.

And we do still have a mission to fulfill. Jesus has returned to Heaven, but we are still on Earth. We are here to do his work. It is our responsibility to help prepare the world for his Second Coming. We do that by sharing the Gospel, and by encouraging everyone to long for and share with others the peace of Christ. We do that by being good models of virtue for younger children. We do that by living in peace—trusting in our inner calm and letting the world know that calm comes from living God's will.

Fruits of the Holy Spirit

The twelve **Fruits of the Holy Spirit** are qualities that can be seen in us when we let the Holy Spirit work in our hearts. This season we are focusing on **peace**.

BRAINSTORM

Work in groups to identify what is necessary for peace in our homes, schools, community, and world. Record your top 5 ideas here. Then choose one thing necessary for peace and describe what Jesus teaches us about it.

1. _____

2. _____

3. _____

4. _____

5. _____

♥ A Prayer for Peace

Pray the Sign of the Cross together.

Reader 1: Brothers and sisters,

I, a prisoner for the Lord, urge you to live in a manner worthy of the call you have received,

with all humility and gentleness, with patience, bearing with one another through love,

striving to preserve the unity of the spirit through the bond of peace: one body and one Spirit, as you were also called to the one hope of your call;

one Lord, one faith, one baptism;
one God and Father of all,
who is over all and through all and in all.

Reader 2: But grace was given to each of us according to the measure of Christ's gift. Therefore, it says:

He ascended on high and took prisoners captive; he gave gifts to men.

What does "he ascended" mean except that he also descended into the lower regions of the earth?

The one who descended is also the one who ascended far above all the heavens, that he might fill all things.

All: And he gave some as apostles, others as prophets, others as evangelists, others as pastors and teachers, to equip the holy ones for the work of ministry, for building up the body of Christ, until we all attain to the unity of faith and knowledge of the Son of God, to mature manhood, to the extent of the full stature of Christ.   **Ephesians 4:1–13**

Leader: May we use our gifts to bring peace to all people and to lead them to Christ.

All: Our Father …

Leader: Let us offer each other the sign of peace.

 Sing or play "Go Ye Out"

REVELATION

How does Divine Revelation help us live as children of God?

CHURCH HISTORY TIMELINE

70 The first Gospels written

400 Saint Jerome publishes Vulgate Latin Bible

1455 Johannes Gutenberg prints Bible on newly invented press

1545 Council of Trent convenes to consider matters of faith

Go to page 348 for more

Our Catholic Tradition

- Out of nothing, God created the heavens and the earth, and made humans in his image and likeness. We can come to know God through all that he has created and through human reason. (CCC, 46)

- God speaks to us and tells us about himself and his plan for us. God is the author and inspiration of the sacred words of Scripture that humans have recorded under his guidance and direction. (CCC, 134–136)

- Jesus is the fulfillment of the law, and he perfectly reveals God the Father to us. He has a close and intimate relationship with the Father, and invites us to share in that relationship as God's sons and daughters. (CCC, 65)

Our Catholic Life

- The creation accounts in Genesis reveal a number of truths about God and his creation, including that he created the world from its beginning, for humans to live in harmony and to oversee his gifts of creation. (CCC, 306–307)

- Scripture has an important role in our lives, as God's Word is proclaimed in the liturgy, read and studied personally and in religion class, turned to for wisdom and guidance, and prayed. (CCC, 132–133)

- The many titles of Jesus teach us about him, his mission, and his relationship with God and each of us. (CCC, 429)

CHAPTER 1

The Mystery of God

♡ Let Us Pray

Leader: Your wonderful works surround us, O God. All creation praises you.

"The heavens declare the glory of God;
    the firmament proclaims the works of
    his hands." **Psalm 19:2**

All: God our Father, you have given us so much. We are a grateful people.

📖 Scripture

The works of God are all of them good;
    he supplies for every need in its own time.

At his word the waters become still as in a
    flask; he had but to speak and the reservoirs
    were made.

He has but to command and his will is done;
    nothing can limit his saving action.

The works of all humankind are present to him;
    nothing is hidden from his eyes.

His gaze spans all the ages:
    is there any limit to his saving action?

To him, nothing is small or insignificant,
    and nothing too wonderful or hard for him.

No cause then to say: "What is the purpose
    of this?"
    Everything is chosen to satisfy a need.
    The Wisdom of Ben Sira (Sirach) 39:16–21

Have you ever thought...

- What was it like at the first moment of creation?

- How did we get here, and why we are here?

Getting Started

In this chapter, you will learn about how we come to know God and how we are made in his image and likeness, and how we fit into his plan. You will also explore some of the things we do know about God and about how he makes it possible for us to know him and share in his qualities.

In each box below, write one thing that you have learned about God through Sacred Scripture, and what account or passage helped you to know it.

What I've Learned

Catholic Faith Words

- Divine Revelation
- mystery
- image of God
- eternal

IDENTIFY

ID a Creation Connection Take a few minutes to reflect on the past couple of weeks. Choose two days and identify a simple "creation connection" for each. Write about one way you experienced God's presence. Where or when did you experience a connection with God's creation? For example, perhaps you saw evidence of the "works of God" (**The Wisdom of Ben Sira [Sirach] 39:16**) when you saw the sun rise or went for a walk. Be sure to explain how you gave praise to God.

_____

_____

_____

_____

_____

_____

_____

_____

_____

_____

_____

_____

_____

_____

_____

_____

Coming to Know God

How do we come to know who God is?

Most people can't help but have a sense of awe and wonder at the beauty and order of the stars, planets, and galaxies, especially when they look at some amazing satellite images. Looking at pictures of the universe can sometimes make us aware of how human beings are a part of "the big picture." And at some point in our lives, most of us ask ourselves what's the reason for it all, and what role do we play in that bigger picture.

The creation accounts in the Book of Genesis tell us something wonderful: Even though humans are a small part of the universe, they have a special place in the eyes of God. And God shows that he wants all humans to know and love him.

Scripture

"In the beginning, when God created the heavens and the earth … the earth was without form or shape . . ."   Genesis 1:1–2

Go to the Source

Read *Genesis 1:1–2:4* to find out more about why God created the world and humans.

Seeing God in the Works of Creation

From the beginning of our time on Earth, the natural world has helped humans recognize and acknowledge God. People felt God's power in the forces of wind, fire, and water. They saw God's beauty in the trees and flowers. They got a sense of God's generosity as he gave them the responsibility to be caretakers of his many gifts of creation.

Adam and Eve were able to see these aspects of God because he had given them the gift of human reason. Like all of us, they were given an intellect—the ability to think and make connections. With this gift, we can grow in knowledge and search for the meaning of the things we experience. When we use reason, we discover the power and presence of God even in the most basic parts of his created world.

> What aspects of nature help you see God as the Creator?

> How do you experience God's presence in the world?

The Vatican Observatory at Castel Gandolfo, Lazio, Italy

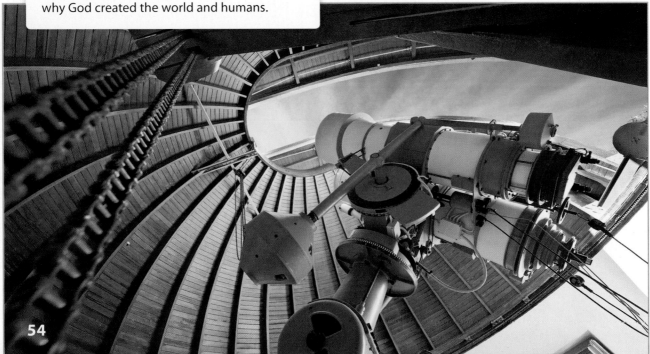

Beyond Words

The works of creation are only one way people can learn about God. We can discover more of who God is through the ways he acts in the world and in our lives. Some things we can only come to know because he chooses to reveal them, or make them known to us. We call the process of God gradually revealing himself to us, **Divine Revelation**. In creating Adam and Eve, also referred to as our first parents, God showed his great generosity and love. He made them in his own image so that they could be like him, free to think and choose, able to love, and experience friendship. Out of love God made himself known to them.

Although he shows himself in so many ways through creation and through his relationship with people, God cannot be fully or completely known. Whether we see God in creation or in relation to a human person, what we see is only a small aspect of who God is.

This is why we call God a **mystery**, because the depth of who God is cannot be seen or fully understood by humans. Human expressions of God are limited because we are human. We will never know all about God's nature while on Earth. We will only know God completely when we know him in Heaven.

Catholic Faith Words

Divine Revelation the process by which God makes himself known. The chief sources of revelation are Sacred Scripture and Sacred Tradition.

mystery a truth of faith that cannot be fully understood but that is believed because God has shown it in Scripture, in the life of Jesus, or in the teachings of the Church

REFLECT

List some ways we come to know God. What are some questions you have about God and creation?

_____

_____

_____

_____

Who or what do you think can help you answer your questions?

_____

_____

_____

_____

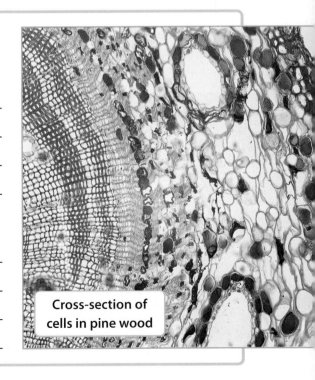

Cross-section of cells in pine wood

God's Plan for Us

How do humans fit into God's plan?

Our first parents reflected the goodness and glory of God. They were created in harmony with one another and with God. And when they freely chose to turn from God and to sin, God did not abandon them. Humans did not completely lose what made them like God—their ability to be good, to love, to be holy, to think, and to be free. In fact, we are each created in the **image of God**, his Divine likeness. Human nature remained basically good, but weakened, inclined to sin.

God remained with humans and promised to restore, or bring back, the human family to its original glory so that all can once again share life fully with him.

- The accounts in Genesis show that God wanted to lead all people to know his love.

- With Noah, God made a lasting covenant, or sacred, binding agreement, to bring all creation back to the harmony he had originally intended it to have. (See Genesis 9:1–17.)

- God made Abraham the "father of all nations," and promised that through Abraham's descendants, all nations would be blessed. (See Genesis 15:1–21.)

- In spite of her old age, God blessed Sarah with a son. She and her husband Abraham shared in God's blessing and promise. (See Genesis 17:15–19; 21:1–3.)

God planned from the beginning of creation to give his only Son, Jesus Christ, to the world so that humans would be restored to the place that they enjoyed originally. The promise of salvation was planted in the hearts of the Israelites, God's Chosen People. This hope gave them the courage to face hardship and even exile.

Go to the Source
Read *1 John 4:6* and *1 John 1:5* to see how John speaks about God, who is Truth and Light.

Moses crossing the Red Sea, artist unknown

The story of God's relationship with the Israelites is recorded in the Old Testament. Throughout their history, God's Chosen People had indications of the salvation that would one day be brought into the world by Christ. For example, when the Israelites fled from slavery in Egypt, God helped them navigate their way across the Red Sea (see Exodus 14:21–31). This liberation foreshadowed, or prefigured, the salvation that Christ would bring us, helping us navigate our way toward the plan God the Father has for all humans. We see in this example how the Jewish faith, unlike other non-Christian faiths, is a response to God's Revelation in the old covenant.

> **What do you think God's plan has to do with you?**

> **What signs of God's plan exist in the world?**

Catholic Faith Words

image of God the Divine likeness in all human beings that comes from being made by God and includes the ability to think, choose, be free, love, and be in relationship with God and others

NOTICE, CONNECT, PRAY

How do you pay attention to the world around you?

- Name two things that surprise you as being signs of God's presence or his action in our lives.

  1. _____

  2. _____

- What could you do with your friends, class, or family to connect to what you've noticed, such as taking care, showing other people, using it?

- What do you want to say to or ask from God because of this? Compare your answer with a classmate.

Jesus said "I go and prepare a place for you…. Where I am going, you know the way" (John 14:3–4).

Revealed Truths

What are some of the things that we know about God?

Because of the way humans think, it's hard to understand anything that does not have a beginning or origin that can be easily explained. Yet, the accounts of creation show us that "God is" and "has always been," even before the beginning of time, and will be forever. This is what it means to say that God is **eternal**.

God alone created the Heavens and the Earth. He didn't need to create anything at all, not the Heavens and Earth or any human persons. He is complete in himself. He isn't lonely. Yet God chose freely to show himself by creating out of nothing all that we see around us today.

God Is Truth

God is Truth itself. He will never deceive us or lead us in the wrong direction. Whatever God makes known about himself is true, and the words that he speaks are always true. God is faithful to his Word. His promise to bring salvation to all people is a promise that we can count on.

> When have you counted on someone to tell you the truth—and they did? When has someone counted on you to tell them the truth—and you did?

> What does all this tell you about the power of truth?

Catholic Faith Words

eternal the term that means "God is" and "has always been," even before the beginning of time, and will be forever

God Is Love

Have you ever been hurt and felt like getting back at someone to "punish" that person? This natural reaction is part of what it means to be a human being who is imperfect. But we strive to grow more like God. One of the reasons people stand in awe of God is because he is strong and consistent in showing love for his People. God's love is perfect.

In the Old Testament, we find a God who never stops showing his love to the Israelites in powerful ways. When they were in captivity in Egypt, he led them to freedom. When they grumbled in the desert, he fed them and gave them water. Over and over, the people who belonged to God would fail to act like it, but God's response would always be the same: a forgiving and compassionate love.

The Attributes of God

○ God is **living**,	in the Heavens and on the Earth.
○ God is **steadfast love**,	always faithful and trustworthy.
○ God is **holy**,	a mystery only vaguely known to us now.
○ God is **eternal**,	without beginning and without end.
○ God is **truth**,	for he is incapable of deception.
○ God is **merciful and gracious**,	always ready to forgive.
○ God is **almighty**,	ruling over and capable of everything.
○ In God **there is only light**;	in him there is no darkness.

1. Highlight the attribute of God that best describes the way you relate to him now.

2. Place a check mark by the attribute you find most comforting.

IN SUMMARY Catholics Believe

We can come to know God through all that he has created and through human reason.

- Out of nothing, God created the Heavens and the Earth, and made humans in his image and likeness, making it possible to know him and share in his Divine qualities.

- God promised to restore the human race to the harmony and perfection for which he originally created us, and throughout history he has shown himself and his plan in many ways.

- From the Genesis creation accounts and the world around us, we come to know God and get a sense of his attributes—eternal, truth, love, merciful, holy, living.

Our Catholic Life

As we learn more about God, we also learn more about ourselves. We get a sense of who God calls us to be and what he wants for us. We can be sure that he wants to know and love each of us. He speaks to us, calling us to be with him, to respond in some way. This dialogue between God and us takes place in prayer.

We have many forms and expressions of prayer. One is a **prayer of adoration**, which honors our Creator, acknowledges we are his creatures, and holds high his greatness. Adoration is traditionally a prayer of respectful silence in which we adore God who made all things. It humbles us, reminding us that the we are dependent upon God, who is eternally good, loving, merciful. We can trust that he hears our prayers and knows what we need.

> When have you noticed and acknowledged God's greatness? What was it like to do so?

People of Faith

Our Lady of Fátima, 20 B.C.–45 A.D.

Mary, the mother of Jesus, is known by many titles, some of which come from places where she has appeared and given a message of hope and love. In 1917, three children from Fátima, Portugal saw the Blessed Virgin Mary. Mary revealed three "secrets" to the children and encouraged them to tell people to pray the Rosary. Sometimes Mary is called Our Lady of Fátima because of that. The Church celebrates her feast day on **May 13**.

For more, go to
aliveinchrist.osv.com

IDENTIFY

List the names of three friends or family who, through their actions, reflect attributes of God.

_____

_____

_____

_____

Choose one and write a concrete example of what he or she has done, or does, to live in God's image.

_____

_____

_____

_____

♥ Celebration of the Word

Leader: Our God is amazing and awesome, beyond our understanding, but here right now—here in our midst.

Let us prepare to hear God's Word to us about his creation.

A reading from the Book of Genesis.

Read Genesis 1:1–31.

The word of the Lord.

All: Thanks be to God.

Leader: There is a single and wonderful source of life.

Let us turn in prayer to God the Creator.

Respond to each petition with these words:

Hear us, O Lord.

Reader 1: O God, you have created the Earth and the Heavens, and in your goodness, you created us.

Help us treasure and respect all you have created.

All: Hear us, O Lord.

Reader 2: O God, at times it is hard to imagine that there is a Creator who could envision all the beauty we see around us.

We thank you for all you have given to us.

All: Hear us, O Lord.

Reader 3: O God, with love and generosity you created all we see.

Help us to accept the love you have for us, And to share that love in the way we live.

All: Hear us, O Lord.

Leader: O God, in your infinite wisdom you have given us life.

In the wonders of nature, through the seasons of the year and the seasons of our lives, we thank you and praise you with every breath we take.

All: Amen.

 Sing or play "Our God Reigns"

Go to **aliveinchrist.osv.com** for an interactive review.

A **Work with Words** Circle the letter of the choice that best completes the sentence.

1. Because the depth of who God is cannot be seen or understood by humans, God is ___.
   a. a mystery   c. one
   b. a spirit   d. eternal

2. Because God was, is, and always will be, he is ___.
   a. spirit   c. eternal
   b. love   d. truth

3. Because God is ___, we can believe in his promise to bring salvation to all people.
   a. faithful   c. truth
   b. holy   d. spirit

4. Out of nothing, God created the Heavens and the Earth, and made humans in his ___.
   a. creation   c. image and likeness
   b. care   d. love and affection

5. Our first parents, Adam and Eve, were able to see the reflections of God through his creation because he gave them the gift of ___.
   a. human reason   c. salvation
   b. communion   d. his likeness

B **Check Understanding** Complete each sentence with the correct term from the Word Bank. Not all terms will be used.

compassionate love	Old Testament
God's attributes	salvation
Theological Virtues	communion
Heaven	Divine Revelation
Original Sin	

6. God's relationship with his Chosen People is told in the _____.

7. The exodus of the Israelites from slavery in Egypt foreshadowed the _____ that Christ would bring.

8. We will only fully know and understand God when we are in _____.

9. Even when we disobey him, God shows us _____.

10. The process of God gradually making himself known to us is called _____.

C **Make Connections** Write a one-paragraph response. Name and describe three attributes of God. Include examples of how you see or experience these attributes in your life today.

_____

_____

_____

_____

_____

_____

CHAPTER 2

The Word of God in Sacred Scripture

♥ Let Us Pray

Leader: O Lord, your Word is alive in our hearts. It is our guide, a light on our journey to you.

"You will show me the path to life,
abounding joy in your presence." **Psalm 16:11**

All: God, we want to know you better. May your Word light our paths.

📖 Scripture

Indeed, the word of God is living and effective, sharper than any two-edged sword, penetrating even between soul and spirit, joints and marrow, and able to discern reflections and thoughts of the heart."

Hebrews 4:12

fada · forte domini electionis numer⁹
compleretur : ſicꝗ paulus cōſumma=
tionē apoſtolicis actibꝫ daret · quē diu
cōtra ſtimulū recalci...
ſet. Quod et legentib...
deū · et ſi per ſingula expediri a nobis

Have you ever thought...

- How is the Word of God living?
- How can you learn more about God?

63

Getting Started

In this chapter, you will learn about how God speaks to us and tells us about himself and his plan for us. God is the author and inspiration of the sacred words of Scripture, and he continues to speak with us today through his Word that we proclaim at Mass, pray with, learn from, and share.

Catholic Faith Words

- Sacred Scripture
- Divine Inspiration
- canon of Scripture
- Gospel
- Evangelists

In the chart below, describe some people, places, and events you already know from both the Old Testament and the New Testament.

Who, Where, and What in the Bible

People	• _____ • _____ • _____
Places	• _____ • _____ • _____
Events	• _____ • _____ • _____

Let God's Word into Your Heart Look up the following Scripture passages and use these questions to guide your reflection.

Hebrews 4:12 How is God's Word alive in the things I do?

_____

_____

_____

_____

_____

_____

Psalm 118:6 How is this passage meaningful to me now?

_____

_____

_____

_____

_____

_____

Ephesians 5:8 In what ways has God's Word helped me live as a disciple of Jesus?

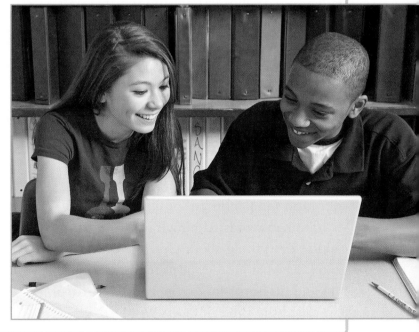

_____

_____

_____

_____

_____

_____

_____

_____

_____

_____

Holy Spirit's direction and guidance. This direction and guidance is known as **Divine Inspiration**.

Scripture records the story of the relationship between God and his People and the communication that he had with them through history. By the Holy Spirit's action, the authors of Scripture faithfully wrote what God wanted to reveal and taught without error the truth about his plan for us.

Interpreting Scripture

The Church accepts and honors a set number of books as being inspired by God. This body of sacred texts is called the **canon of Scripture**. It includes forty-six books in the Old Testament and twenty-seven books in the New Testament. "The Old Testament prepares for the New and the New Testament fulfills the Old; the two shed light on each other; both are true Word of God" (*Catechism of the Catholic Church*, #140).

The Old Testament tells the story of God's relationship with Abraham and his descendants. It includes the laws, history, and stories of the Israelites.

After Jesus' Resurrection, many different people wrote about his life and ministry.

God Speaks in Human Words

What are some of the ways that God speaks to us?

When we meet someone for the first time, our ideas about the way that person talks or looks can sometimes get in the way of understanding him or her. But once we start to hear that person's story, we have a better understanding of him or her. In a similar way, once we get to know God's story, our friendship with him grows.

God Inspires

God wanted humans to get to know him, so he gradually made himself known to us over time. God chose to speak to his People with human words. Although no word can capture everything about God, these words do tell us what God want us to know about him and his hopes for us. **Sacred Scripture**, also called the Bible, is God's Word to us written by humans acting under the

Catholic Faith Words

Sacred Scripture the Word of God written by humans acting under the Holy Spirit's inspiration and guidance; another name for the Bible

Divine Inspiration the gift of the Holy Spirit which assisted the human authors in writing the Bible to ensure it contained the truths God wanted us to know

canon of Scripture the Church's complete list of inspired books included in Sacred Scripture

The New Testament begins with the Gospels, which tell us about Jesus' ministry and teachings. It includes many Epistles, Letters written by Saint Paul and other disciples so the early Christians could learn about Jesus.

Because God is the author of Scripture, the interpretation of Scripture should help us understand what he wants to tell us in the Biblical text and what he desires for us. The Holy Spirit helps the Church to interpret and apply Scripture.

The Bible contains a variety of literary forms. A literary form is the way something is written. Knowing the form of a written work helps us to understand the meaning of what is being said.

Literary Forms in the Bible

• **Narrative stories** recall in a straightforward way something about God's relationship with the world.	See Matthew 2:1–12
• **Parables** are short stories Jesus told, using examples from everyday life or nature, to illustrate moral or spiritual truths.	See Mark 4:1–20
• **Teaching** enlightens people to understand how to live the Christian life.	See Luke 6:20–36
• **Miracle stories** teach how God's power and healing transform people.	See John 4:46–54
• **Laws** portray the rules of conduct that God has set for us in living in right relationship with him and others.	See Mark 12:28–34 and the Books of Exodus, Leviticus, Numbers, and Deuteronomy
• **Hymns and psalms** show the joy and struggle of being in relationship with God.	See the Book of Psalms
• **Proverbs** are short sentences of wisdom.	See the Book of Proverbs
• **Apocalyptic literature** reflects the expectation of decisive intervention of God in history, especially at the end of the world.	See the Book of Daniel

OUTLINE

Working with a classmate, create an outline for a screenplay or podcast on "The Story of God and His People." The story must span from creation to the present time. Choose what you think are the main points, and outline them here.

_____

_____

_____

The Importance of the Gospels

How do the senses of Scripture help us understand its message?

Scripture is so rich in expressing Divine truth that there are many senses, or layers, of Scripture. Two layers of meaning that can be seen in Scripture are the *literal sense* and the *spiritual sense*.

The literal sense of Scripture refers to the actual words that have been recorded. Understanding the literal sense involves studying the culture in which the words were written—the meaning of those words to the people of that time and place.

The spiritual sense has three subcategories:

- The allegorical sense shows how certain events pointed to Christ, even before his birth. The crossing of the Red Sea, for example, is a sign of Christ's victory over death.

- The moral sense gives instruction on how to live justly before God.

- The anagogical sense shows how human events and realities are signs of our heavenly future. The word *anagogical* comes from the Greek word *anongoge*, which means "leading." The Church, for example, is understood as leading to the New Jerusalem of Heaven.

Christ the Good News

The word **Gospel** means "good news." The four Gospels according to Matthew, Mark, Luke, and John contain the Good News of God's Kingdom and his saving love. They have the central place in Scripture because they present Jesus' life, ministry, and teaching. We revere the Old Testament, too, because the events recorded in it point to the salvation that God would bring when he sent his only Son to become man.

When the author of the Gospel according to John wrote that the Word was with God and the Word was God, he meant the living Word that is Jesus Christ (see John 1:1). Jesus Christ is the single Word through whom all the other words in Scripture have their meaning. Because Jesus himself is the living Word of God, the Gospels present the ultimate truth of Divine Revelation. Jesus is the fulfillment of God's Word and of God's promise.

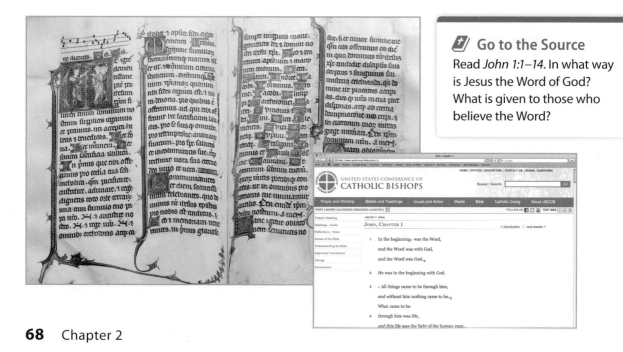

Go to the Source

Read *John 1:1–14*. In what way is Jesus the Word of God? What is given to those who believe the Word?

A Different Emphasis

Inspired by the Spirit, all four **Evangelists** center their writing on Christ, and emphasize different aspects of his life or mission.

> Think of a time when you heard a single story told by more than one person. Why do you think there can be differences in the way two people tell the same story?

The Gospels and their Authors

Matthew addresses a Jewish audience and wants to show them that Jesus is the fulfillment of the Old Testament accounts and promises of a Messiah. This Gospel emphasizes Jesus as the new covenant who fulfills the old covenant.

Mark, in a brief but detailed way, stresses the announcement of God's Kingdom. Mark shows how the disciples did not always understand Jesus, and only gradually came to know who he is. When they did, they were ready to proclaim him to the world.

Luke focuses on practical and ordinary things so that people will be open to Jesus' message of salvation in their life. Written for Gentiles (Greek Christians), this Gospel emphasizes Jesus as a Savior who helps us overcome the evil of sin, suffering, and death. He often shows Jesus in prayer.

John focuses on spiritual things, and readers can see they are entering into an intimate relationship of love with God. In this Gospel, Jesus is shown answering questions that people pose to him. When they misunderstand his answers, he tells them more so that they can understand his truth.

Catholic Faith Words

Gospel a word that means "Good News." The Gospel message is the Good News of God's Kingdom and his saving love.

Evangelists the four inspired human authors of the Gospels: Matthew, Mark, Luke, and John

READ AND DISCUSS

In a small group, read a passage from one of the Gospels. Write about what it means to you. Then, as a group, discuss the meanings each member found in the passage.

- What do you learn about God's Word when you see the way different people respond to it?

_____

_____

_____

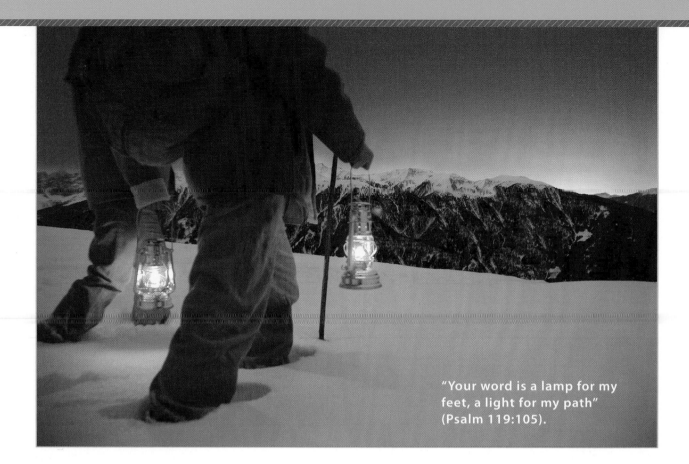

"Your word is a lamp for my feet, a light for my path" (Psalm 119:105).

Conversation With God

How does God speak to us today?

To this very day, God continues to speak to his People. When the Word of God is proclaimed at Mass, it is the voice of God that the assembly hears. This Word proclaimed from the Scriptures is Jesus Christ, a living Word. Even though human readers proclaim this Word, God speaks through them.

The proclamation of the Scriptures at Mass takes place during the Liturgy of the Word. This is just one way in which Catholics today dialogue with God. Through Psalm responses, the homily, and silent reflection, we respond to God and commit ourselves to follow his Word. The worship of the Church relies on God's Word, as do the personal prayer life of Catholics and our growth in virtue, modeled by Jesus.

The Word as Light

When the prophet Isaiah spoke of God's goodness to the Hebrew people, he said that a "people who walked in darkness have seen a great light" (Isaiah 9:1). In a similar way, Jesus explained that people who walk in the darkness will stumble, because people in darkness cannot see where they are going. This is why the Word of God is a light to all people.

Scripture

"You are the light of the world. A city set on a mountain cannot be hidden. Nor do they light a lamp and then put it under a bushel basket; it is set on a lampstand, where it gives light to all in the house. Just so, your light must shine before others, that they may see your good deeds and glorify your heavenly Father."

Matthew 5:14–16

Following the Light

By listening to the Word of God, you develop a conscience—the God-given ability that helps us judge right from wrong—that makes it possible for us to live a right and just life. A conscience formed by God's Word

- challenges us to live a good life and avoid evil.
- helps us judge between choices that are right or wrong, good or bad.
- strengthens us to put God's Word into action and to be signs of his goodness.
- gives us the confidence we need to live with faith. God speaks to followers of Christ through their conscience and the teachings of the Church.

CATHOLICS TODAY

Scripture plays an important role in our lives.

- We proclaim and reflect upon it in communal worship.
- We discover more about Jesus and his message as we read it by ourselves and in religion class.
- We discuss its message for us today in Bible study.
- We pray with it personally and with our families.
- We turn to it for wisdom and for guidance.

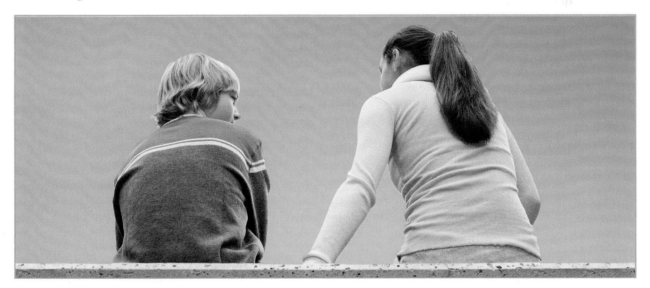

IN SUMMARY   Catholics Believe

God speaks to us and tells us about himself and his plan for us.

- God is the author and inspiration of the sacred words of Scripture that humans have recorded under his guidance and direction.
- The four Gospels, which developed over the course of time after Jesus' Resurrection, are the center of the Bible because they record

the truth of the life, teaching, and saving actions of Jesus.

- God continues to speak to us today through the Scriptures, as we proclaim them at Mass, reflect on them personally, rely on them for making choices, and study them to learn more about the life and teachings of Jesus.

Our Catholic Life

Sacred Scripture is a rich source of **wisdom** that can guide you in all aspects of your life. As one of the seven Gifts of the Holy Spirit, wisdom helps us see God's purpose and plan for our lives. Wisdom leads us to see things as God sees so that we might live holy lives. When you have a difficult decision to make, think about how some people you have read about in Scripture may have acted. How were they open to God's direction in their lives?

One easy way to begin to find wisdom and hope in Scripture is to pray one of the Psalms. You may want to use a concordance or index in your Bible to find a Psalm that speaks to what's going on in your life. Read it a few times. Then pray your chosen Psalm and see what help you gain from it.

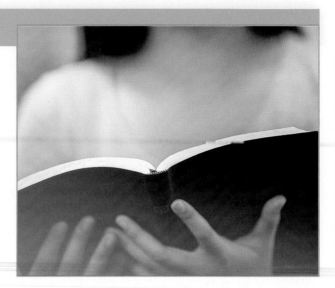

> What wisdom can you learn from Scripture?

People of Faith

Saint Matthew, first century

As a tax collector, Matthew worked for the Roman governor, the enemy of the Jewish people. Fellow Jews saw Matthew as a traitor, but Jesus called him a close friend. Matthew saw the miracles Jesus performed and witnessed his Resurrection and Ascension. His Gospel was written to convince Jews that Jesus was the promised Messiah. His writings tell how God established a spiritual Kingdom for his Son. Some believe that Matthew died a martyr's death. The Church celebrates his feast day on **September 21**.

For more, go to
aliveinchrist.osv.com

RESEARCH

Choose one of your favorite Scripture passages. Write what the Scripture is about, or what it means to you. (Some examples are relating to a new person, choosing values you want to live by, or dealing with conflicts.)

What does it mean?

_____

_____

_____

_____

How does it affect my life?

_____

_____

_____

❤ Prayer of Petition

Leader: Let us now pray, asking God our Father to help us hear, see, listen, live, and learn from the wisdom of Scripture.

Reader: A reading from the holy Gospel according to Luke.

Read Luke 4:16–22.

The Gospel of the Lord.

All: Praise to you, Lord Jesus Christ.

Side 1: God of love, open our ears to always hear your voice—fill us with your Word.

All: Fill us with your Word.

Side 2: God of light, open our eyes to always see your path—fill us with your Word.

All: Fill us with your Word.

Side 1: God of wisdom, open our hearts to always act as we should—fill us with your Word.

All: Fill us with your Word.

Side 2: God of goodness, open our hands to always reach out and serve—fill us with your Word.

All: Fill us with your Word.

Leader: Loving Father,

You alone have the words of everlasting life. Send us your Spirit and give us the grace so that we always welcome your Word, your wisdom and guidance, and your love.

May the gifts we have received be gifts we freely share with others. We ask this through your Son, who is Jesus Christ, our friend and brother.

All: Amen.

 Sing or play: "God Has Chosen Me"

Go to **aliveinchrist.osv.com** for an interactive review.

A **Work with Words** Complete each sentence with the correct term from the Word Bank. Not all terms will be used.

Sacred Scripture	Apostles
Sacred Tradition	Gospels
canon	Divine Inspiration
Evangelists	conscience

1. _____ records the story of the relationship between God and his People.

2. The complete list of sacred texts accepted by the Church as inspired by God is called the _____ of Scripture.

3. The authors of the Gospels, called _____, wrote about Jesus' life and ministry.

4. It is important for us to know God's laws so our _____ can help us make good decisions.

5. The _____ present Jesus' life, ministry, and teachings.

B **Check Understanding** Indicate whether the following statements are true or false. Then rewrite false statements to make them true.

6. Even though the Bible was written by humans, God is the author because he inspired the writers. **True/False**

_____

_____

7. When John writes in his Gospel that the Word was God, he is referring to the Holy Spirit. **True/False**

_____

_____

8. The primary sense of Scripture refers to the actual words that have been recorded. **True/False**

_____

_____

9. The spiritual sense of Scripture includes the allegorical sense, showing how certain events pointed to Christ. **True/False**

_____

_____

10. The Letters of Paul are the central books of Scripture because they present Jesus' life, ministry, and teaching. **True/False**

_____

_____

C **Make Connections** Write a one-paragraph response to the question. Each Gospel presents the life and teaching of Jesus, but each places emphasis on a different aspect of Jesus. Choose one of the four Gospels and explain how it fulfills Jesus' command to spread the Good News.

_____

_____

_____

_____

_____

_____

CHAPTER 3

Jesus, Sign of God's Love

♥ Let Us Pray

Leader: Wondrous God, you did not forget your promise to us. You showed us your unconditional love by sending your Son, Jesus. We want to know and love you.

"Come and see the works of God, awesome in deeds before the children of Adam." **Psalm 66:5**

All: Holy God, you sent your Son Jesus to show us the way to you. Be with us through the Holy Spirit as we try to love others unconditionally.

📖 Scripture

"Here is my servant whom I uphold,
my chosen one with whom I am pleased.

Upon whom I have put my spirit;
he shall bring forth justice to the nations.

He will not cry out, nor shout,
nor make his voice heard in the street.

A bruised reed he will not break,
and a dimly burning wick he will not quench.

He will faithfully bring forth justice.

I, the LORD, have called you for justice,
I have grasped you by the hand;

I formed you, and set you
as a covenant for the people,
a light for the nations,

To open the eyes of the blind,
to bring out prisoners from confinement,
and from the dungeon, those who live in darkness." **Isaiah 42:1–3, 6–7**

Have you ever thought...

- What promise did God fulfill in Jesus?
- How would God define love?

Getting Started

In this chapter, you will reflect on how we know God through Jesus Christ and recognize Christ as a sign of the Father's love. When we follow God's laws, we show our love for him and grow in our understanding of his love. His Commandments help us choose what is good so we can live as his People.

Catholic Faith Words

- covenant
- *abba*
- natural moral law
- Ten Commandments
- New Commandment

In the spaces below give examples of some things Jesus said and did that showed his love or the love of God the Father. Draw a star next to the example that has made the strongest impression on you.

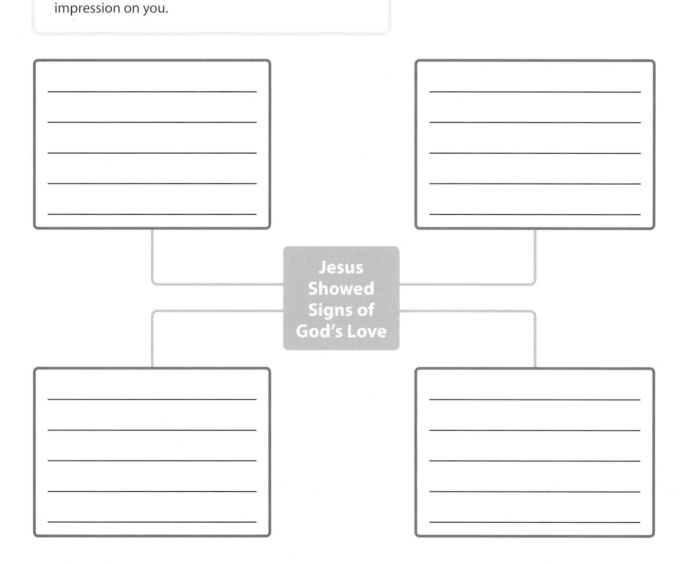

Jesus Showed Signs of God's Love

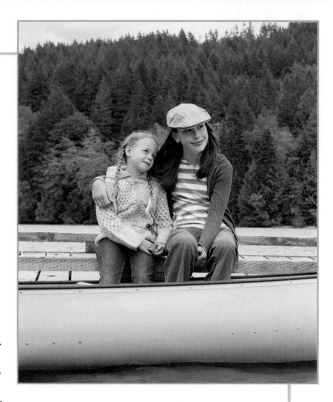

Rank It! Rank the following definitions for love by what you think are the most accurate (1) to the least accurate (5). In the space provided below, explain your reason for the ranking.

____ to have an affection for someone

____ to have a strong liking or attraction to someone

____ to care for another with dignity and respect

____ to need or require someone

____ to worship or adore someone

_____

_____

_____

How do you define love? Write your definition below. Then share with a classmate one way you have witnessed or experienced your definition of love.

_____

_____

_____

_____

_____

_____

_____

_____

_____

_____

_____

_____

_____

_____

_____

Jesus: God's Own Love

How does God show his love for us?

Being loved is great, but sometimes it can be complicated. Sometimes people will show their love only if we behave in a certain way. At other times, people do love us, but they have a hard time expressing it. Plus, we have to build up trust and friendship with new people in our lives before we get to the point where we love them.

God's love is different, because he loves us without any conditions. God showed how much he loved us by sending his only and much-loved Son into the world.

Go to the Source

Read *Matthew 26:26–30*. What does Jesus give us to celebrate and commit ourselves to the new covenant with God?

Jesus: The Way to the Father

The relationship between God the Father and God the Son is the most intimate and loving relationship possible. But God the Father did not keep his Son for himself. Instead, he chose to share him with the world: "For God so loved the world that he gave his only Son, so that everyone who believes in him might not perish but might have eternal life" (**John 3:16**).

In Jesus Christ, God showed us everything he could about himself. What God told us about himself first through creation and history, and then through his Chosen People, the Jews in the Old Testament, he revealed in the most perfect way in Jesus Christ. With the coming of Jesus, there is no further revelation. In Jesus Christ, God has taught us everything there is to be revealed.

Even though God the Father has fully revealed himself in Christ, our understanding of him continues to grow as we discover new things about what God has shared with us. Our limited human minds cannot understand God the first time we learn about him. It takes years of growing into understanding. New experiences and continually being taught more about God help us come to know him more and more, but we'll never fully understand God because he is a mystery.

> **How many times have you heard a story or seen a movie twice, and realized you missed something the first time?**

Jesus: Given to Us

As many passages of the Old Testament testify, God made a covenant with his people and said he would never forget his promise. A **covenant** is a binding agreement, in this case, a sacred promise or agreement between God and humans to remain in a relationship of love together.

God showed the depth of his love when he made a new covenant in Jesus Christ, one that would last forever. At the Last Supper, Jesus and the Apostles were celebrating God's original covenant when Jesus explained that now he was going to be the Father's new covenant. God the Father made that covenant present in the world through the gift of Jesus' own Body and Blood. In Luke 22:20 we read, "This cup is the new covenant in my blood." By pouring out his blood, Jesus offered forgiveness for sins so that all people would be reconciled with God. All four Gospels record the Last Supper, and we celebrate this sacrifice in the Eucharist at Mass.

> **Imagine that you were asked to give away, or say goodbye to, the person you love the most. How hard would that be for you? Could you do it?**

Catholic Faith Words

covenant a sacred promise or agreement between humans or between God and humans

EXPLAIN

What is one of the hardest sacrifices you've made because of your love for a family member, friend, or God? Explain the situation and tell how your decision made a difference in someone's life.

_____

_____

_____

_____

_____

_____

_____

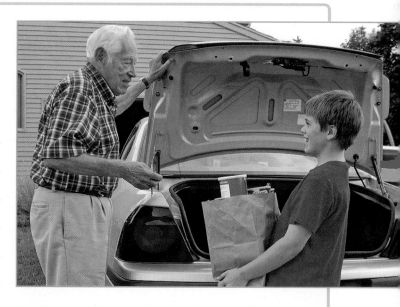

Jesus Shows Us the Father

How do we see God through Jesus Christ?

Sometimes we meet people who say all the right things, but we might wonder if they live the way they talk. With Jesus, there is no doubt that everything about his life is true. He not only talked about God the Father, but he also showed us who God is in the way he lived. He did this because he is God. We call Jesus *God*, like we call God the Father, *God*, and God the Holy Spirit, *God*.

One with the Father

We always appreciate it when someone remembers our name when we haven't seen that person for a long time. On the other hand, people are sometimes embarrassed when they can't remember the name of someone they should know. In the Hebrew tradition, knowing a person's name implied a close relationship between the two people.

The Hebrew people thought of themselves as being unworthy to utter God's name. This is why they were shocked when they heard Jesus address God in the most intimate of ways. When he taught the disciples the Lord's Prayer, he began with the Aramaic word **abba** (See Luke 11:2–4). The English equivalent of this word is "Daddy" or "Papa."

Jesus invited his disciples to address God in the same way, as we do today when we pray "Our Father." By being baptized in Christ, Catholics share that close relationship with God. We become adopted children of God, sons and daughters who can count on God's love at all times. (See Galatians 4:6.)

> **What are some ways you call on God?**

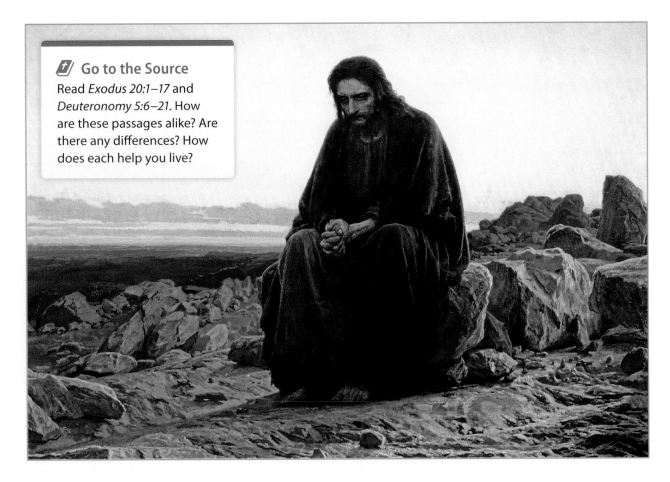

📖 Go to the Source

Read *Exodus 20:1–17* and *Deuteronomy 5:6–21*. How are these passages alike? Are there any differences? How does each help you live?

What We Learn from Jesus

In every way, Jesus Christ is the fulfillment of God's own revelation. Everything about Jesus points to God and the coming of his heavenly Kingdom on Earth.

- In **prayer**, Jesus shows us how trustworthy God is, how God listens and cares for each of us.

- In **miracles**, Jesus shows us God's desire to heal us physically and spiritually and help us change our lives for the good.

- In **his love for the poor**, for children, and for sinners, Jesus reveals that God cares for every single human being.

- By **accepting death on the Cross**, Jesus shows that following God's plan is the best, even when it involves sacrifice.

- In the **Resurrection**, Jesus makes it known that God's heavenly Reign and Divine life can be a part of our human existence.

> Underline which description gives you your clearest picture of Jesus as God. ✱

Catholic Faith Words

abba the Aramaic word with the English equivalent of "daddy" or "papa"

DESCRIBE

Read the Lord's Prayer (see Luke 11:2–4 and page 383 of the Our Catholic Tradition section of your book). Describe several personal ways that you address God in your own prayers. How do your names for God show how you feel about him?

- _____
- _____
- _____
- _____
- _____

Jesus Speaking in the Treasury, **James Jacques Joseph Tissot**

Laws That Point to God

How do laws lead us to God?

When we study the world and the universe, we find a marvelous order to it in the movement of the heavenly bodies, in the cycle of time and seasons, in the fruitfulness of all creation, in the cycle of birth and death, in the relationship of man and woman, and in the laws that are inscribed in our hearts.

This order is created by God. The laws of nature are like building blocks that form the foundation for all life. This **natural moral law** consists of precepts about goodness that are written by God in our hearts and are accessible through our God-given reason. Natural law requires us to do good and avoid evil. Our awareness of natural law can be clouded by the disorder caused by Original Sin.

> **What are some other positive natural laws that you can think of?**

God's Revealed Law

Besides the natural moral law, God has revealed ways that help us live in covenant relationship with him. God's revealed law was evident when he gave us the **Ten Commandments** through Moses. (See page 373 of the Our Catholic Tradition section of your book.) These laws helped to make clear God's hope for the way all people are to live in relationship with him and one another. God's revealed law continued in the Old Testament and led to the Gospels and the fulfillment of God's revealed law in Christ.

Jesus, the New Law

Jesus not only confused some people by his close relationship with God the Father, but he also surprised people in the way he spoke of the Law. He did not want them to follow God's Law only because they feared punishment. Instead, he wanted them to rely on the love of God that had been planted within their hearts.

He explained it all in the Sermon on the Mount (see Matthew 5:3–10), when he said that those who would be blessed are the poor, those who mourn, the meek, the merciful, and the peacemakers. He showed the positive side of the Law.

Jesus gave his followers a new law, a **New Commandment**—to love one another as he has loved them (see John 13:34). Christ poured out his life for us, and his Holy Spirit dwells within us. God's Spirit within us deepens whenever we gather with fellow Catholics to pray and participate in the Sacraments. We are called to live holy lives, not primarily because of external laws, but because of the law of love that exists within our hearts.

> **How is it different when you are doing something because you were told to, and when you are doing something because, in your heart, you know it is right?**

Catholic Faith Words

natural moral law precepts about goodness that are written by God in our hearts and accessible through our God-given reason

Ten Commandments the ten fundamental moral laws given by God to Moses, and recorded in the Old Testament, to help his People live by the covenant

New Commandment Jesus' command for his disciples to love one another as he has loved us

WRITE

Write some other signs of God's love, and describe how you can be a sign of that love, too.

_____

_____

_____

_____

_____

_____

_____

_____

_____

IN SUMMARY Catholics Believe

Jesus is the fulfillment of the Law and he perfectly reveals God the Father to us.

- We know God through Jesus Christ and recognize Christ as a sign of God's love.

- Jesus has a close and intimate relationship with the Father, and he invites us to share in that relationship as God's sons and daughters.

- The natural and revealed laws help us choose what is good and live as God's People; by pouring out the Holy Spirit, Jesus plants within our hearts a New Commandment.

Our Catholic Life

Living in love and friendship with Jesus is in many ways similar to living in love and friendship with those you see every day at home, at school, in church, on teams, in clubs or other extracurricular activities. **Friendship** takes work, but it is some of the best work we can do, and the most fulfilling. Through our friendship, we show our love for people.

There are several ways to get closer to Jesus, all of them important now and later in our lives. They include reading accounts of Jesus in the Gospels and reflecting on how he acts and why it matters, receiving Holy Communion and spending time in prayer with Jesus, seeing Jesus in the faces of those you meet, learning from the example of others, and being grateful for the love that people show you.

> **What is one way you can show friendship with Jesus this week?**

People of Faith

Saint Maria Goretti, 1890–1902

Maria Goretti's family lived near another family who had a son named Alessandro. One day Alessandro tried to get Maria to commit a sin. When she wouldn't, he stabbed her fourteen times. She died the next day, after forgiving Alessandro. After Alessandro was released from jail, he asked Maria's mother for forgiveness, and eventually became a lay brother in a monastery, where he worked until he died. He and Maria's mother were present at Maria's canonization in 1950. The Church celebrates her feast day on **July 6**.

For more, go to
aliveinchrist.osv.com

IDENTIFY

Consider who shows you love, and how, in each of these settings:

At home

_____

_____

At school

_____

_____

In clubs or on teams

_____

_____

In the world

_____

♥ Prayer of Adoration

Leader: Let us pray.

Reader 1: Father, you gave us
your greatest gift—
your Son, Jesus,
who lived and experienced
the same joys and heartaches that
we experience.

All: We love you and adore you, O God.

Reader 2: You sent Jesus to teach us
how to live,
to grow, to learn,
and to know the happiness
that comes from belonging to you.

All: We love you and adore you, O God.

Reader 3: You had Jesus show us the way
to be a servant;
he washed our feet,
he opened his hands,
and offered his life for us.

All: We love you and adore you, O God.

Reader 4: You raised him up again to
new life,
showing us all that we too can share in
your life,
and become who you want us to be.

All: We love you and adore you, O God.

Leader: Loving Father,
Help us to remember your love always.
We ask this in the name of your Son Jesus,
who is your everlasting love.

All: Amen.

▶ *Sing or play "We Ever Will Praise You"*

Go to **aliveinchrist.osv.com** for an interactive review.

A Work with Words **Circle the letter of the choice that best completes the sentence.**

1. God's ___ is a promise to remain in a relationship of love with his People.
   a. covenant
   c. law
   b. word
   d. spirit

2. The Aramaic word ___ can be translated as "Daddy" in English.
   a. *Yahweh*
   c. *abba*
   b. *papa*
   d. *padre*

3. The order in the universe created by God is called ___.
   a. creation
   c. cycle of seasons
   b. cycle of time
   d. none of the above

4. ___ requires us to do good and avoid evil.
   a. Universal law
   c. Laws of nature
   b. Original law
   d. Natural moral law

5. The ten fundamental moral laws given by God to Moses, and recorded in the Old Testament, are the ___.
   a. Miracles
   c. Canon of Scripture
   b. Nicene Creed
   d. Ten Commandments

6. Jesus wants people to follow God's Law out of ___.
   a. fear of the Lord
   c. trust
   b. conscience
   d. love

B Check Understanding **Indicate whether the following statements are true or false. Then rewrite false statements to make them true.**

7. Through Jesus' miracles we see God's desire to heal us physically and spiritually. **True/False**

   _____

   _____

   _____

8. Jesus gives us a New Commandment, to love one another as he loves us. **True/False**

   _____

   _____

   _____

9. God's revealed Law is manifested only in the Ten Commandments. **True/False**

   _____

   _____

   _____

10. At Jesus' birth, God the Father made the new covenant through the gift of Jesus' humanity. **True/False**

   _____

   _____

   _____

C Make Connections **On a separate sheet of paper, write a one-paragraph response to the questions: How might Jesus' relationship to God the Father have been surprising to people of the time? What new law did Jesus give us to help live out that relationship here on Earth?**

A Work with Words **Match the words on the left with the correct definitions or descriptions on the right.**

_____ **1.** New Commandment

_____ **2.** Divine Inspiration

_____ **3.** canon of Scripture

_____ **4.** Evangelist

_____ **5.** covenant

_____ **6.** *abba*

_____ **7.** natural moral law

_____ **8.** image of God

_____ **9.** Gospels

_____ **10.** mystery

_____ **11.** eternal

_____ **12.** Divine Revelation

a. the Church's complete list of inspired books of Sacred Scripture

b. the Divine likeness in all human beings

c. an author of a Gospel

d. Aramaic word that means "daddy"

e. Jesus' command for his disciples to love one another as he has loved us

f. order of the universe created by God

g. God's promise to remain in a loving relationship with his people

h. the gift of the Holy Spirit which assisted the human authors in writing the Bible

i. the process by which God makes himself known

j. a description of God that tells us he was, is, and always will be

k. a truth of faith that cannot be fully understood but that is believed because God has shown it in Scripture, in the life of Jesus, or in the teachings of the Church

l. the central books of Sacred Scripture because Christ is at their center

B **Check Understanding** Complete each sentence with the correct term from the Word Bank. Not all terms will be used.

Word Bank
Ten Commandments
love
literal sense
eternal law
Gospels
human reason
Jesus
salvation
proverbs
Chosen People

13. God gave us the gift of _____, which allows us to grow in knowledge and search for meaning.

14. The Old Testament tells of God's relationship with the _____.

15. The freeing of the Israelites from slavery in Egypt that is described in the Book of Exodus foreshadows the _____ that Christ would bring us.

16. When John writes in the Gospel that the Word was God, he is referring to _____ as "the Word."

17. As a literary form, _____ contain(s) wisdom in short sentences and sayings.

18. Understanding the _____ of Scripture, which refers to the actual words recorded, requires an understanding of the time in which it was written.

19. The _____ are the central books of Scripture because they present Jesus' life, ministry, and teaching.

20. When God gave Moses the _____, he was giving us evidence of his revealed Law.

21. Natural moral law and revealed Law are part of God's _____.

C **Make Connections** Write a short answer to the following questions.

22. Which story about Jesus from the Gospels is your favorite, and why? What does this story reveal to you about God?

_____

_____

_____

_____

_____

_____

23. What are two ways Catholics today enter into conversation with God?

_____

_____

_____

_____

_____

_____

_____

24. How can we connect the way Jesus addressed God with the way we pray the Lord's Prayer?

_____

_____

_____

_____

_____

_____

_____

25. How, in your life today, are you like the Israelites in the desert? In light of how God responded to the Israelites, how do you think God responds to you?

_____

_____

_____

_____

_____

_____

_____

TRINITY

How does Jesus' Incarnation help you to understand the Divine Persons of the Holy Trinity?

CHURCH HISTORY TIMELINE

325 — The First Council of Nicaea convenes

387 — Conversion of Saint Augustine

1265 — Saint Thomas Aquinas begins to write *Summa Theologiae*

1986 — First official World Youth Day is held in Rome

Go to page 348 for more

© Our Sunday Visitor

Our Catholic Tradition

- Believing in the Holy Trinity is central to our Catholic faith. The Father sent the Son and the Holy Spirit to help us know him and to guide us to him. (CCC, 261)

- The Son of God has existed for all time, and through the Incarnation, became fully man while remaining fully God. Because Jesus is truly Divine and truly human, he saves us and brings us back into relationship with the Father. (CCC, 479, 480)

- The Holy Spirit gives the Church life and unites us as one Body of Christ. The Holy Spirit is our Advocate, comforting and strengthening us to know and live by the truth. (CCC, 729, 747)

Our Catholic Life

- Making the Sign of the Cross reminds us of our Baptism into the life of the Trinity. (CCC, 1235)

- In our worship and personal prayer, we call on Jesus using different titles from Scripture—such as Emmanuel, Christ, Lord, and Messiah. (CCC, 452–455)

- The Holy Spirit guides the Church in her Sacred Tradition and her prayer. The Holy Spirit helps us pray at different times, in different ways, and in different circumstances. (CCC, 2650, 2661)

God Is Trinity

💙 Let Us Pray

Leader: O God—Father, Son, and Holy Spirit—always present, always true. Show us the way to you.

"Guide me by your fidelity and teach me,
for you are God my savior." **Psalm 25:5**

All: O God, give us the gift of faith that we may come to know you better.

📖 Scripture

"Father, they are your gift to me. I wish that where I am they also may be with me, that they may see my glory that you gave me, because you loved me before the foundation of the world. Righteous Father, the world also does not know you, but I know you, and they know that you sent me. I made known to them your name and I will make it known, that the love with which you loved me may be in them and I in them."

John 17:24–26

Have you ever thought...

- How is it possible that God's love for his Son is in each of us?

- How much can we ever really understand God?

Detail from the Triptych of the Trinity of Marchiennes, Jean Bellegambe

Getting Started

In this chapter, you will explore how our belief in the Holy Trinity is central to our Catholic faith. The Father sent the Son and the Holy Spirit to help us know him and to guide us to him. You will also learn about God's plan of loving goodness and how the love of the Holy Trinity is a model for our own relationships.

In the web below, record what you know about each Person of the Holy Trinity.

The Holy Trinity

God the Father

_____

_____

_____

_____

God the Son

_____

_____

_____

_____

God the Holy Spirit

_____

_____

_____

_____

Catholic Faith Words

- faith
- Holy Trinity
- grace

REFLECT

Step Deeper into Faith   Reflect on what you know to be true about God. Write down a few ideas. Then consider what you'd like to learn about God.

What I know to be true about God …

_____

_____

_____

_____

_____

_____

What I want to learn about God …

_____

_____

_____

_____

_____

_____

Name a person you know who you believe has a deep faith. What makes you think that?

_____

_____

_____

_____

_____

_____

_____

📖 Go to the Source

For the full account of Jesus' commissioning of the Apostles, read *Matthew 28:16–20*. This gathering took place soon after Jesus' Resurrection. How do you think the Apostles felt about Jesus' words? If you had been with Jesus at this time, what would you have asked him? What does Jesus' promise to always be with us mean to you right now?

God Is Always There

How do we get to know God?

Have you ever ended up with a problem turning around and around in your head, not sure what to do about it? With so much going on in your life, you might not think of turning to a family member for help. You might wonder how others could even understand what you are feeling, much less help you. Sometimes family and friends can help. Different individuals within a family relate to each other in love—over time and through difficult times.

God is always there, even when you don't think your family and friends can help much. The strongest guide through the ups and downs of life is our faith in his presence and in his words.

God Takes the First Step

God created the universe and keeps it going through Jesus Christ, the Word who has existed forever, and through the Holy Spirit, the giver of all life and goodness. We know God because he chooses to show himself to us. If it were left totally up to us, we could never really know the true God, because he is a mystery beyond our own comprehension. Only with faith can we begin to know God.

Fortunately, God doesn't wait for us to make the first move. He has been there from the beginning of time, and he is with us from the first day of our life. He understands us, even when we don't understand him.

On our own, we would be stuck in misunderstanding and confusion. We would never get close enough to God to understand the truth. But he loves us so much he wants us to know the way. God the Father sent us his Son and the Holy Spirit to help us find our way to him. Whenever God sends his Son to us, he also sends his Spirit.

Help from Heaven

The Son of God came down from Heaven to show us the way to God the Father and to bring salvation to all. When his earthly mission was accomplished, Jesus returned to his heavenly Father. Before he ascended, Jesus told his Apostles to continue his work, sharing his message of hope and new life to people everywhere. He instructed them, "Go, therefore, and make disciples of all nations." (**Matthew 28:19**).

Jesus told his Apostles to baptize new disciples in the name of the Father, and of the Son, and of the Holy Spirit. He promised his friends he would always be with them.

Jesus is always with us, too. In the Sacrament of Baptism, we become members of God's family, the Church, and receive the gift of faith. Through **faith**, we can believe in and rely on God, even though we don't completely understand.

So help from Heaven does not stop with Jesus' time on Earth, his public ministry, and his Ascension. Through the Apostles, Christ established the Church. He sent the Holy Spirit as a guide and counselor to the Church.

Since the time of Jesus and the Apostles, believers have proclaimed God as Father, Son, and Holy Spirit.

Catholic Faith Words

faith the Theological Virtue that makes it possible for us to believe in God and the things he has revealed to us. Faith leads us to obey God. It is both a gift from God and a free, human choice.

SHARE

Think about the following questions and share your thoughts with a classmate.

Who or what helps you maintain your relationship with God?

_____

_____

_____

_____

When have you felt closest to God in the last six months?

_____

_____

_____

Three Divine Persons in One God

How can we understand a mystery?

At the beginning of every Mass, we make the Sign of the Cross and say, "In the name of the Father, and of the Son, and of the Holy Spirit." Our belief in three Divine Persons in one God is the center of our celebration. When we pray at Mass, we pray in the name of our Trinitarian God. We base our faith on this central belief.

We speak of God as the **Holy Trinity**, which means that there is only one God in three Divine Persons.

- The Father is God, the First Divine Person of the Trinity, who brings everything into existence by the Son through the Holy Spirit.
- Jesus Christ the Son is God, the Second Divine Person of the Trinity, who was sent by the Father and became man.
- The Holy Spirit is also God, the Third Divine Person of the Trinity, who proceeds from the Father and the Son.

© Our Sunday Visitor

> ## Catholic Faith Words
>
> **Holy Trinity** the mystery of one God in three Divine Persons: Father, Son, and Holy Spirit

The three Persons of the Holy Trinity are distinct from one another, so we can talk about them as God the Father, God the Son, and God the Holy Spirit. But they are inseparable in what they do. Each Person of the Trinity is fully God and has the same Divine nature. There is only one God in three Divine Persons.

The Holy Trinity

We are never going to understand this mystery—until we meet God face to face in Heaven. Meanwhile, the gift of faith assures us that what we know about the Holy Trinity is true.

Being human, we still ask questions and search for answers. As people of faith, we are often guided in our relationships not only by our head, but also by our heart. For example, the love someone feels for family members can grow and spread throughout the family. This love makes families stronger than each person could be individually.

Our relationship with God is something like this, too. God's love is always there. Sometimes we just need to become more aware of it. When we sense God's presence and respond to him in our lives, our

> ### 📖 Go to the Source
>
> Read *John 10:31–38* to find out how some people could not understand the relationship between Jesus and God the Father. If you had been there, what questions would you have asked Jesus about the mystery of the Trinity?

relationship with him and our faith grow stronger. When we place our trust in his love, we feel it in our heart, and we come to believe in it and know it with our mind.

Love is the answer to the mystery of the Trinity. The truth is that the Son loves the Father and the Father loves the Son. The Holy Spirit shares his exact same love with both the Father and the Son.

This love among the Trinity is a model for the connections, affection, and bonds we can make with one another. Families, schools, and groups of friends can mirror the unity of the Trinity.

> **When have you felt really loved by God?**

> **When have you felt out of touch with his love?**

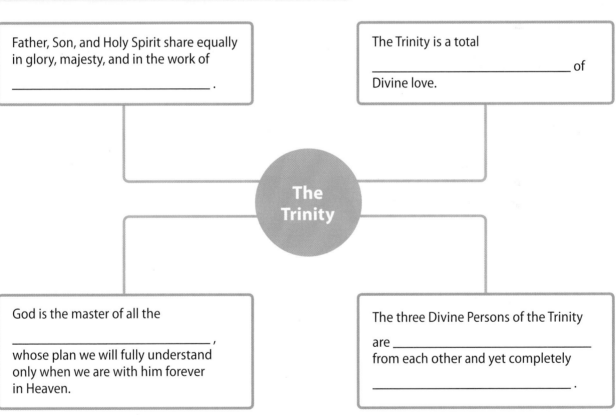

We worship one God, the Trinity. Use the following words to fill in the blanks to complete the statements about God as Trinity: universe, creation, communion, distinct, united

Father, Son, and Holy Spirit share equally in glory, majesty, and in the work of _____ .

The Trinity is a total _____ of Divine love.

The Trinity

God is the master of all the _____ , whose plan we will fully understand only when we are with him forever in Heaven.

The three Divine Persons of the Trinity are _____ from each other and yet completely _____ .

REFLECT

Think about your friendships with three different people, including how each friendship differs from the other two. Is your faith a part of any of these friendships? If so, how? If not, how can you share your beliefs with your friends?

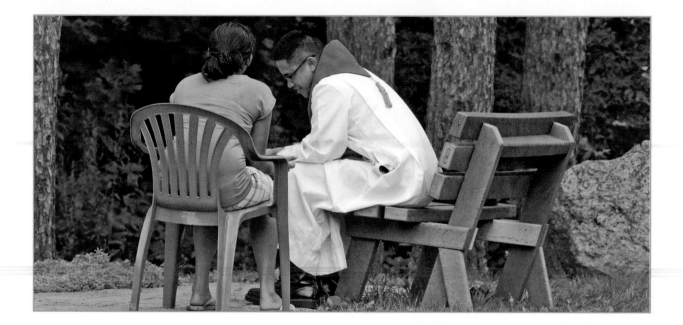

God's Plan for Us

How does the Trinity work?

The three Divine Persons of the Holy Trinity work together through their relationship with each other something like the way a loving family works together for the same goals. The Father sent the Son on his mission of salvation. The Son acted in obedience to the Father to set humans free from sin. The Holy Spirit came to help us be part of a loving relationship as members of the Church.

The work of the Trinity is all about God's plan of loving goodness. God does have a plan for all his children. He wants us to know and share in his love, to bring his goodness and love to others. He desires us to become like him, and so he cares for us and guides us with his wisdom and love. The Father works through the Son, his Holy Spirit, the Church, and the actions of people to help us. God doesn't give up on us. He continues to show his care and act on our behalf.

The unity, love, and goodness within the Holy Trinity radiate outward toward all. Out of this love and goodness the Trinity shares his own life and special help with us. We call this sharing of Divine life, **grace**. God offers us this free, loving gift of his own life and help so we can become his adopted children and do what he calls us to do. Sometimes we are not aware of God's love, even though it's there. Our own actions and stubbornness may block God out or make it difficult to feel his presence. But God's grace is still available to us if we trust in him and his hopes for us.

Home Is Where the Heart Is

The gift of faith is like a compass that points us in the right direction. When our path is directed by faith, our actions build up God's Kingdom. Our lives show Gospel values such as justice, peace, and love.

Catholic Faith Words

grace God's free, loving gift of his own life and help to do what he calls us to do. It is participation in the life of the Holy Trinity.

© Our Sunday Visitor

This is why it is so important to learn and practice what we believe. The teachings of our Catholic Church help us understand and strengthen our relationships with God and others. We are to give our minds, hearts, and lives to God in love and for love. As long as your life is moving in God's direction, you will be journeying into deeper truth, wisdom, and love. You will be on your way home.

> Imagine that your life has been compiled in a book. How has your story followed God's love and the teachings of faith?

> What would you like to change about the way you are living in order to follow the guidance of faith more closely?

WRITE

What does it mean to give your mind and heart to God? Around the illustrations below, write five words or phrases that would describe the mind and the heart of a Catholic. Two examples have been completed for you.

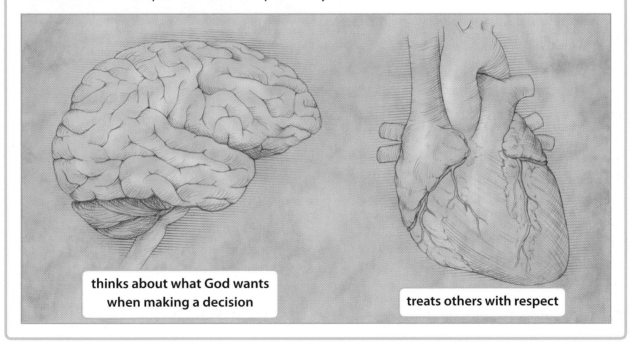

thinks about what God wants when making a decision

treats others with respect

IN SUMMARY Catholics Believe

Believing in the Holy Trinity is central to our Catholic faith.

- The Holy Trinity is a mystery that can never be totally understood by the human mind, but can be approached through faith. The Father sent the Son and the Holy Spirit to help us know him and to guide us to him.

- The love that the Father, the Son, and the Holy Spirit have for each other shows us what our own relationships should be like.

- God has a plan of loving goodness for all his people and offers the gift of grace so that we can become more like him. This sharing in Divine life helps us trust in God, have faith in him, and work for his Kingdom.

Our Catholic Life

In the Catholic Church, we use many gestures with our prayers. Every time we make the **Sign of the Cross**, we are reminded of the Holy Trinity. We bless ourselves in the name of the Father, the Son, and the Holy Spirit, as we were baptized in the name of the Trinity. With the Sign of the Cross, we dedicate ourselves to God and call on him to strengthen us. The movements involve your hand, your head, and your heart. In this way you can be reminded that all blessings come from God, and to treat other people with kindness in what you do, what you think, and what you say. This reflects the love, interest, and care God shows you, and remembering these things helps you to show the same love, interest, and care to others.

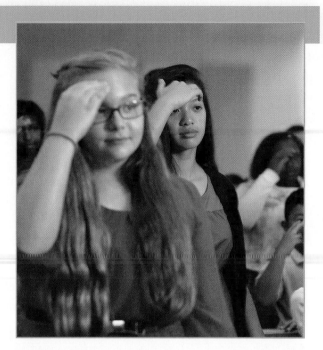

> How would you explain the Sign of the Cross to someone who is not Catholic?

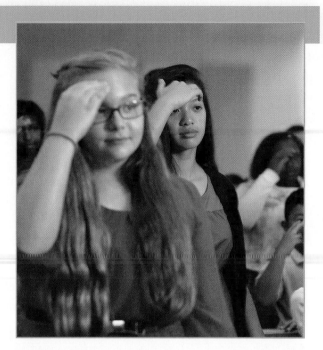
© Our Sunday Visitor

People of Faith

Saint Frances of Rome, 1384–1440

Frances was born in Rome to a wealthy family and married Lorenzo Ponziani, a nobleman. When flood brought disease and famine to Rome, Frances served in hospitals and sold her jewels and clothes to distribute money to the needy. When civil war came, she turned her home into a hospital and homeless shelter. After her husband's death, Frances entered a second vocation as a consecrated religious sister. Her last words were "The angel has finished his task—he beckons me to follow him." The Church celebrates her feast day on **March 9.**

For more, go to
aliveinchrist.osv.com

EXPLAIN

Think of a problem you faced recently and how you resolved it. In the space below, explain how you could see God's care for you in the solution to your problem.

_____
_____
_____
_____
_____
_____
_____
_____
_____
_____

♥ Reflect on the Trinity

Leader: We gather here this day in the name of the Father, and of the Son, and of the Holy Spirit, Amen.

Prepare yourselves to be in Jesus' presence.

Close your eyes and focus on opening your mind and heart to God.

Take a deep, relaxing breath, and enter into the reflection:

Read the following, slowly and in reflection:

Reader 1: O God, our Father, Creator, and maker of all creation, we praise you, and we bless you!

(pause)

We thank you for this good Earth, the air we breathe, the rain that cools our nights, the sun that warms our days, and the life you give to each and every one of us.

(pause)

Reader 2: O God the Son, our brother, teacher, and Savior, we praise you, and we bless you!

(pause)

We thank you for showing us the way to live, to trust in the Father and to love one another, to serve our sisters and brothers, and to take care of the poor and those in need.

(pause)

Reader 3: O God the Spirit, Our holy guide, and friend for the journey, we praise you, and we bless you! We thank you for walking with us, in our struggles, our choosing, our playing, and in our praying.

(pause)

Open your eyes and let us pray together the Lord's Prayer.

All: Our Father, who art in heaven,
hallowed by thy name;
thy kingdom come,
thy will be done
on earth as it is in heaven.
Give us this day our daily bread,
and forgive us our trespasses,
as we forgive those who trespass against us;
and lead us not into temptation,
but deliver us from evil.

Amen.

Go to **aliveinchrist.osv.com** for an interactive review.

A **Work with Words** Complete each sentence with the correct term from the Word Bank.

Holy Trinity	counselor
disciples	Father
miracles	Gospel
Holy Spirit	Apostles

1. Jesus gave his Apostles a command to go and make _____ of all nations.

2. Christ established the Church through the _____.

3. God the Father sends his Son to us; he also sends the _____.

4. God the Father gave the Holy Spirit as a _____ for the Church.

5. The love of the _____ is a model for the connections and love we can have with others.

B **Check Understanding** Circle the letter of the choice that best completes the sentence.

6. ____ makes it possible for us to believe in God and the things he has revealed to us.
   a. Faith
   b. Life
   c. Prayer
   d. a and b

7. The Divine Persons of the Holy Trinity are ____.
   a. Matthew, Mark, and Luke
   b. Jesus and the Holy Spirit
   c. Father, Son, and Holy Spirit
   d. Paul, Silas, and Timothy

8. ____ is God's free, loving gift of his own life and help to do what he calls us to do.
   a. Faith
   b. Grace
   c. Hope
   d. Baptism

9. ____ is the Second Divine Person of the Trinity.
   a. God, the Father
   b. God, the Son
   c. The Holy Spirit
   d. all of the above

10. Through the Sacrament of ____, we become members of God's Church.
    a. the Eucharist
    b. Confirmation
    c. the Holy Spirit
    d. Baptism

C **Make Connections** On a separate sheet of paper, write a one-paragraph response to the questions. What is God's plan of goodness and love? How does grace fit into God's plan of loving goodness?

CHAPTER 5

Jesus, Word of God

♡ Let Us Pray

Leader: O God, from the beginning your Word has brought light and life to our world.

"O Lᴏʀᴅ, our Lord,
how awesome is your name through all the earth!" **Psalm 8:2**

All: O God, let your Word be alive in us.

📖 Scripture

"God greatly exalted him
and bestowed on him the name
that is above every name,
that at the name of Jesus
every knee should bend,
of those in heaven and on earth
and under the earth,
and every tongue confess that
Jesus Christ is Lord, to the glory
of God the Father."

Philippians 2:9–11

Have you ever thought...

- What does it mean to confess that Jesus Christ is Lord?

- How do you really come to have a relationship with Jesus?

Getting Started

In this chapter, you will learn what Catholics understand about the "eternal Word" and how the coming of Jesus changed our relationship with God the Father. You will also see how Mary is a model of trust and discipleship for all of us.

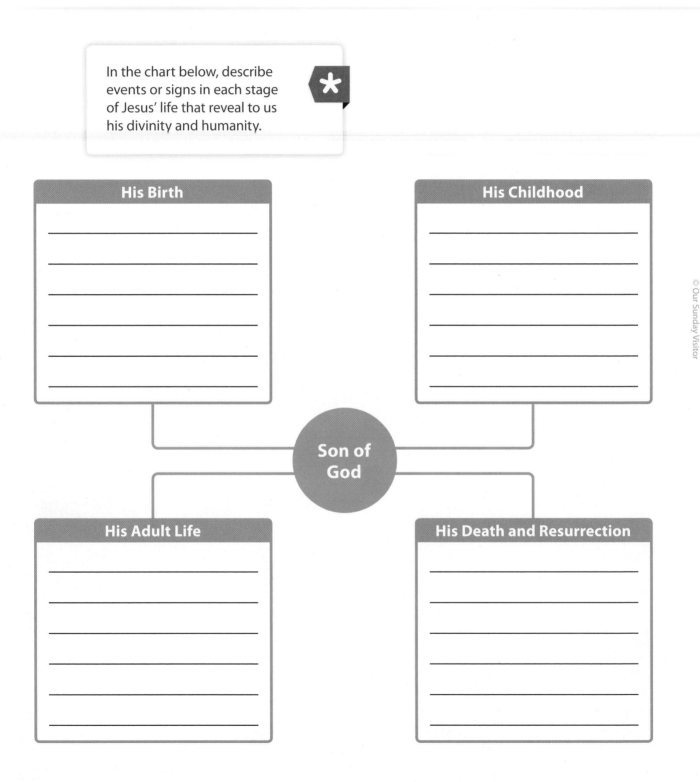

In the chart below, describe events or signs in each stage of Jesus' life that reveal to us his divinity and humanity.

His Birth

His Childhood

Son of God

His Adult Life

His Death and Resurrection

Catholic Faith Words

- Incarnation
- Emmanuel
- Annunciation
- miracle

IDENTIFY

The Name of Jesus Over time, the names of people we know take on deeper meaning as we come to know them better. Think about the name Jesus. On the lines below, describe how your understanding of who Jesus is and what his name conveys has grown as you have gotten older.

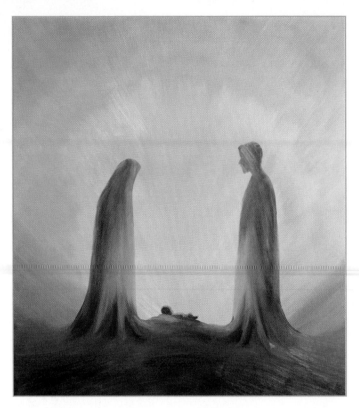

Mary and Joseph look with faith on the child Jesus at his Nativity, Elizabeth Wang

The Eternal Word

What is the "eternal Word"?

As humans, we are called by God to be authentic, which means to be true to who we really are. But our personalities have many different dimensions. We are complex. Sometimes, we are not easy to understand. Other times, we might need to spend some time getting to know ourselves. Because God is our Creator, he knows us best of all. He knows what he made us to be. He even knows us better than we know ourselves! God helps us get in touch with who we really are, and helps us become who we were made to be.

God the Father sent Jesus as our model of being authentic. He was always true to who he was, even when there was a cost. He was fully human and fully Divine at the same time.

© Our Sunday Visitor

Catholic Faith Words

Incarnation the truth that the Second Divine Person of the Holy Trinity, the Son of God, assumed human nature in order to save all people; Jesus Christ is both true God and true man

The Son of God

The Gospel according to John begins differently from the Gospels according to Matthew, Mark, and Luke. Instead of starting with the birth of Jesus or with his ministry on Earth, the author of John goes back to the beginning of time to tell us about Jesus before the world began. That is a side of Jesus we might not think of at first.

Jesus is the Word. He was with God the Father before creation. Then the Son of God became human, like us. What had been invisible, existing above and before all else, became visible. God's loving presence was now in the flesh. Jesus Christ, the only Son of God, is the eternal (everlasting) Word.

Scripture

In the beginning was the Word,
and the Word was with God,
and the Word was God.
He was in the beginning with God.
John 1:1–2

Go to the Source

Read *John 1:1–14*. Why do you think Jesus is called "the Word"? What does belief mean to you?

The Wonder of the Incarnation

The **Incarnation** is what we call the truth that the Son of God took on a human nature and became man. This word means "in the flesh," and shows our understanding that Jesus has two different natures—human and Divine—in one Divine Person. Jesus is like us in all things except sin.

Jesus is the only begotten Son of God. Only Jesus has this unique relationship with God the Father. The Son of God not only has the same Divine nature as his heavenly Father, but also shares in our human nature. Jesus is both truly God and truly man.

What's in a Name?

The name *Jesus* literally means "God saves" (see Matthew 1:21). Jesus entered the world to bring salvation to all people. Jesus is not just a wise prophet or miracle worker; he is the only Son of God. That is why we call him "Lord." In the Gospel according to John, we find Jesus using "I am" statements to teach us about who he is and how he relates to his Father and to us.

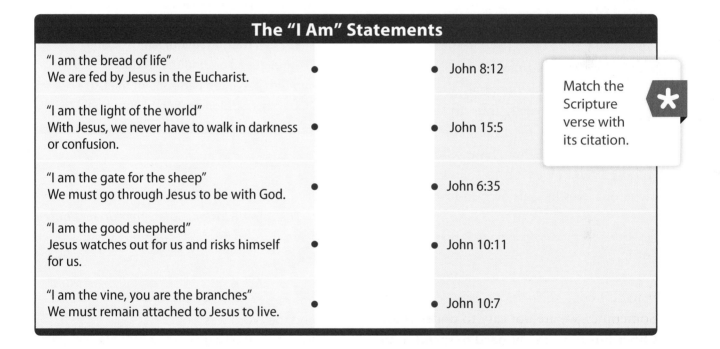

The "I Am" Statements

"I am the bread of life"
We are fed by Jesus in the Eucharist.

"I am the light of the world"
With Jesus, we never have to walk in darkness or confusion.

"I am the gate for the sheep"
We must go through Jesus to be with God.

"I am the good shepherd"
Jesus watches out for us and risks himself for us.

"I am the vine, you are the branches"
We must remain attached to Jesus to live.

John 8:12

John 15:5

John 6:35

John 10:11

John 10:7

Match the Scripture verse with its citation.

CONNECT

Review the "I am" statements above. Which of the images of Jesus do you connect to the most? What other images of Jesus can you think of from Scripture you've heard or read?

_____

_____

_____

God Is with Us

How did Jesus change our relationship with God?

Long before the birth of Jesus, God used the prophets to speak to his People. Then, in an ancient promise God made to the prophet Isaiah, the Lord said the following: "Behold, the virgin shall be with child and bear a son, and they shall name him 'Emmanuel,' which means, 'God is with us'" (Matthew 1:23).

God fulfilled that promise of closeness to his People through the Incarnation of his Son, Jesus Christ. He is called **Emmanuel**, Prince of Peace, Light of the World, and Son of God.

The Incarnation is amazing news for us. It means that God is not at all distant or removed from our daily lives. In the wonder of the Incarnation, God the Father speaks directly to us in his Son, Jesus. Christ lives among us and invites us to follow him, to make our lives like his own in love.

God the Son became human to lead us back into friendship with the Father and harmony with one another. He comes to bring back all things to himself in love. But how does this great truth of the Incarnation happen?

> **When are some times you know that God is with us?**

CATHOLICS TODAY

We profess faith in Jesus' divinity and in the Holy Trinity by reciting together the Nicene Creed when we gather for Mass. There are three major sections in the Creed. Each one pertains to a specific Person of the Holy Trinity. The Creed has been translated into almost 1,300 languages all around the world. For more on the Creed, see page 365 of the Our Catholic Tradition section of your book.

The Annunciation, Salesianerkirche Church

The Holy Spirit Prepares

Jesus is God and shares in the Divine nature. But Jesus came from somewhere—he didn't just show up, already made. He entered the world like any other human being: He was born. However, Jesus' conception is very different from ours. First, Mary was visited by the Angel Gabriel, the messenger from Heaven, who announced to her that she would be the Mother of God and give birth to the Savior.

We call the Angel Gabriel's visit to Mary the **Annunciation**. All of human history hinged on Mary's reply. Because she said "yes" to God's plan, she became the most important woman in history. In conceiving Jesus, Mary helped in God's plan to turn his people back to the life he had always intended for us.

Second, Mary became the Mother of God because God the Holy Spirit made it possible. From before Mary was born, the Holy Spirit was acting in her, so that through her, the Son of God could become man. By the power of the Holy Spirit, not by human means, Mary became pregnant. Jesus Christ was born to Mary and the world, through the power of God.

> **Name someone who has a great devotion to Mary the Mother of God.**

> **How does this devotion seem to be helpful to this person?**

Catholic Faith Words

Emmanuel the name given to the Messiah by the prophet Isaiah, meaning "God is with us"

Annunciation the Angel Gabriel's announcement to Mary that she would be the Mother of God and give birth to the Savior

Mary—Mother of God and Our Mother

By cooperating with God's plan, Mary was already helping her Son, Jesus, in his work as Savior. Before he started his ministry of preaching and healing among the people, Mary became her Son's first and foremost disciple. By saying "yes" to God, Mary anticipated and took part in all the things her Son would do for us.

Mary, Mother of God, is our spiritual mother, also. She received the Lord in her heart before he was conceived in her womb. When he was on the Cross, Jesus gave Mary to his beloved disciple John and to all of us. Just like any mother, she shows us the way to live by her example. Her life shows us the way to Jesus.

Go to the Source

The Angel Gabriel did not just appear to Mary. Read *Matthew 1:18–23*. What was God asking Joseph to do? How did Joseph respond to God's call?

IDENTIFY AND DESIGN

What are some ways we, as Catholics, have been asked to be the disciples of Jesus? Design a motto that explains one way you can follow Mary's example and say "yes" to God.

Signs of Divine Power and Love

How were Jesus' actions signs of God's love?

In his public ministry, Jesus worked miracles. A **miracle** is an event for which there is no scientific explanation because it happened by the power of God. When Jesus worked miracles, it was obvious something extraordinary was happening through him. People experienced God's power in amazing ways that changed their lives and led many of them to believe in Jesus and have faith in him as the Son of God.

Jesus healed people of their diseases. He cast out demons. He restored the dead to life. All four Gospels record this miraculous power in Jesus. For example:

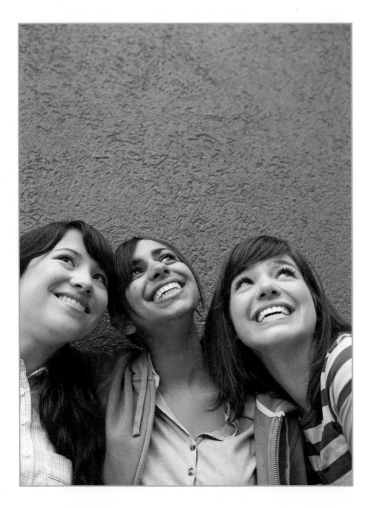

Jesus gave sight to a man who had been blind from birth. Because he did so, the man came to believe that Jesus is Lord. He "saw" Jesus for who he truly is and bowed down before him in worship. (See John 9:1–41.)

Jesus restored the ability to walk to a paralyzed man. As he did so, he performed an even greater healing. He forgave the man's sins. To prove that he has this power to forgive sins, the Lord commanded the man to walk—which the man did. The crowd gave glory to God. (See Luke 5:17–26.)

Jesus raised a widow's dead son to life again. The Lord stopped the funeral procession on its way out of the city gates and commanded the young man to rise. The man sat up and began to speak. At first the crowd was fearful; then, they praised God's power, saying "God has visited his people." **(Luke 7:11–16)**

These miracles, and others like them, show us the divinity of Jesus and the depth of his love. At the same time, they show us the human nature of the Son of God. How? Many of these accounts of Jesus' miracles also tell us about his emotions, like compassion or pity (see Matthew 20:34, Mark 6:34), anger (see John 11:33), and tears (see John 11:35).

> Which do you think was easier: to believe in Jesus after seeing his miracles or after hearing about them from others who saw them?

> Do you agree that seeing is believing? Why or why not?

Catholic Faith Words

miracle an event for which there is no scientific explanation because it happened by the power of God. Jesus worked miracles to help us see the presence of the Kingdom of God.

1. Look up the Scripture passages and summarize what Jesus did in each one.

2. Then discuss how the images we find of Jesus in these passages symbolize each of his natures.

The Two Natures of Jesus Christ: Divine & Human

Jesus worked miracles
(see Luke 5:1–11)

_____

_____

_____

_____

_____

Jesus fed his disciples
(see John 21:7–13)

_____

_____

_____

_____

_____

BRAINSTORM

Think of a problem that you are facing now. Brainstorm some solutions that Jesus Christ could offer you.

_____

_____

_____

_____

_____

_____

_____

_____

_____

_____

_____

_____

_____

_____

_____

_____

_____

IN SUMMARY   Catholics Believe

Because Jesus is the Son of God, truly Divine and truly human, he saves us and brings us back into relationship with God the Father.

- The Son of God has existed for all time, and through the Incarnation, became fully man while remaining fully God.

- Through the work of the Holy Spirit, the Son of God was born to Mary, who is a model

of trust and discipleship for all of us. Her acceptance of God's will brought Jesus into the world.

- Jesus showed that he was Divine in many ways, particularly through the working of miracles, which also gives us a glimpse into his human nature and emotions.

Our Catholic Life

Along with Emmanuel, there are many **titles for Jesus** in Scripture. Some of these titles include Christ (which means "the anointed one" in Greek), Jesus (his common Jewish name, which means "God saves"), Lord (used to acknowledge Jesus' divinity), Messiah (the Hebrew word for "the anointed one"), and Rabbi (which means "teacher"). His early followers used these different names to show their understanding of who he was and what his presence meant to their lives. Throughout her history, the Church has used these titles for Jesus, too. Sometimes we address Jesus by different titles in the same prayers. No matter which name we use to call on Jesus, he responds with the same love and grace.

> **What title for Jesus do you most often use in prayer, at home or in Church?**

People of Faith

Saints Maria, Rosa, and Mary Zhao, d. 1900

In the mid-1800s China was invaded by some of the powerful nations of Europe. At the same time, Jesuit missionaries and others introduced Christianity to China. These missionaries and converts to Christianity were targeted during the Boxer Rebellion. Maria and her daughters, Rosa and Mary, were among them. When the rebels tried to force them to deny their faith, they were defiant. Before they were executed, the family prayed for strength to give up their lives for the faith. The Church celebrates their feast day on **July 9**.

For more, go to **aliveinchrist.osv.com**

DESCRIBE

Write your name on the line below.

_____

Then write three statements that are unique to you and show ways you are living a Christian life.

I am ...

_____

_____

I am ...

_____

_____

I am ...

_____

_____

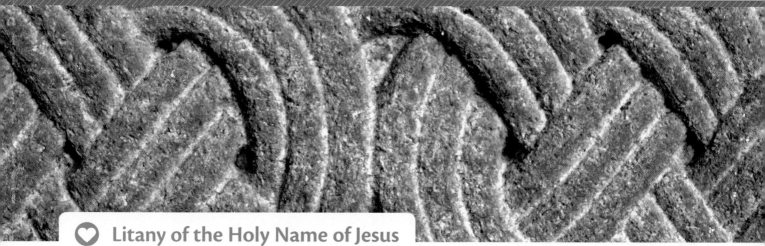

♥ Litany of the Holy Name of Jesus

Leader: We gather here this day in the name of the Father, and of the Son, and of the Holy Spirit.

All: Amen.

Leader: Jesus, Son of the living God . . . have mercy on us.

Jesus, splendor of the Father . . . have mercy on us.

Jesus, brightness of eternal light . . . have mercy on us.

Jesus, King of glory . . . have mercy on us.

Jesus, Son of justice . . . have mercy on us.

Jesus, mighty God . . . have mercy on us.

Jesus, most powerful . . . have mercy on us.

Jesus, most patient . . . have mercy on us.

Jesus, most obedient . . . have mercy on us.

Jesus, author of life . . . have mercy on us.

Jesus, good shepherd . . . have mercy on us.

Jesus, eternal wisdom . . . have mercy on us.

Jesus, our way and our life . . . have mercy on us.

Jesus, Teacher of the Apostles . . . have mercy on us.

Jesus, strength of martyrs . . . have mercy on us.

Let us pray.

Lord Jesus Christ, . . . mercifully listen to our prayers

and grant us the gift of your Divine mercy

that we may ever love you with our whole heart

and never cease from praising you and glorifying your holy name.

All: Amen.

▶ *Sing or play "Jesus, I Trust in You"*

Go to **aliveinchrist.osv.com** for an interactive review.

A Work with Words **Circle the letter of the choice that best completes the sentence.**

1. The ____ is the truth of the Son of God taking on a human nature to save all people.
   a. Incarnation   c. Holy Trinity
   b. Word   d. Annunciation

2. The word *Incarnation* literally means ____.
   a. Son of Man   c. in the beginning
   b. creation   d. in the flesh

3. At the ____, the Angel Gabriel declared to Mary that she would be the Mother of God.
   a. Incarnation   c. Resurrection
   b. Annunciation   d. creation

4. An event for which there is no scientific explanation because it happened by the power of God is called ____.
   a. an Incarnation   c. a miracle
   b. an act of faith   d. an Annunciation

5. "Emmanuel" means ____.
   a. God is with us   c. Lord of all
   b. God who comes   d. the Risen One

6. In the first chapter of the Gospel according to John, Jesus is called the ____.
   a. Incarnation   c. Hope of Mankind
   b. Act of Faith   d. Word

B Check Understanding **Complete each sentence with the correct term from the Word Bank.**

spiritual Mother	Holy Spirit
God	Mary
man	Hope
Jesus	Creed

7. Jesus is both true God and true

   _____.

8. The name _____

   literally means "God saves."

9. Mary became pregnant by the power of the

   _____.

10. Mary is our _____ because when Jesus was on the Cross he gave her to us.

C Make Connections **Write a one-paragraph response to the question: Identify an area in your life where you need to say "yes" to God as Mary did. If you said "yes," how might your life be different?**

_____

_____

_____

_____

_____

_____

_____

CHAPTER 6

Holy Spirit, Comforter and Guide

♥ Let Us Pray

Leader: Most gracious God, wherever we go, whatever we do, you are there loving us, guiding us.

"Where can I go from your spirit?
From your presence, where can I flee?" **Psalm 139:7**

All: Lord, help us see your presence; help us find you in the moments of our day.

📖 Scripture

"Therefore, since we have been justified by faith, we have peace with God through our Lord Jesus Christ, through whom we have gained access [by faith] to this grace in which we stand, and we boast in hope of the glory of God. Not only that, but we even boast of our afflictions, knowing that affliction produces endurance, and endurance, proven character, and proven character, hope, and hope does not disappoint because the love of God has been poured out into our hearts through the holy Spirit that has been given to us." **Romans 5:1–5**

Have you ever thought...

- What keeps you going when things are very difficult?

- What role does the Holy Spirit have in your life?

Getting Started

In this chapter you will learn about God's plan in sending the Holy Spirit. You will also discover the unique and powerful ways the Holy Spirit is present in the Church.

The web below shows three symbols of the Holy Spirit. On the lines below each symbol, explain why it could be associated with the Holy Spirit.

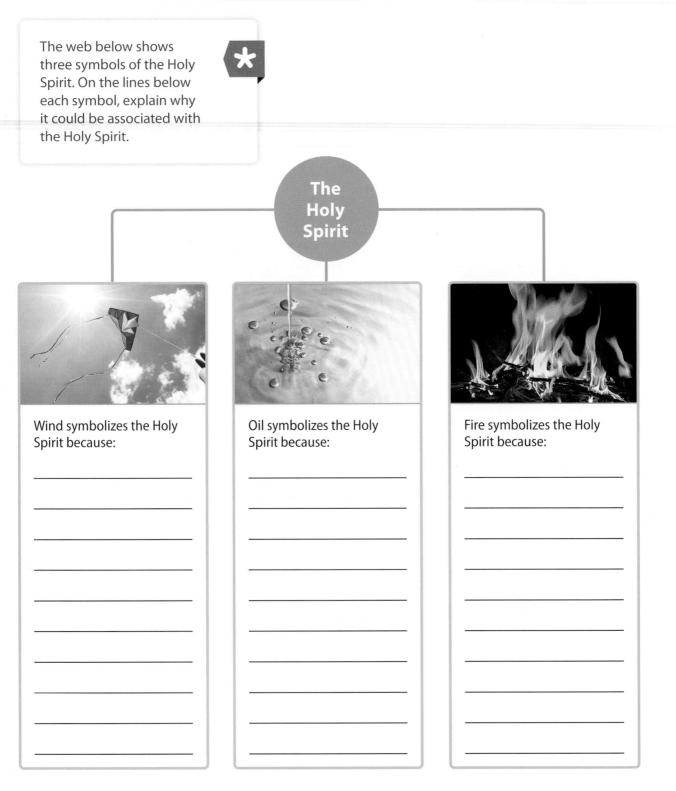

The
Holy
Spirit

Wind symbolizes the Holy Spirit because:

_____

_____

_____

_____

_____

_____

_____

_____

Oil symbolizes the Holy Spirit because:

_____

_____

_____

_____

_____

_____

_____

_____

Fire symbolizes the Holy Spirit because:

_____

_____

_____

_____

_____

_____

_____

_____

Catholic Faith Words

- Advocate
- Saints
- intercession

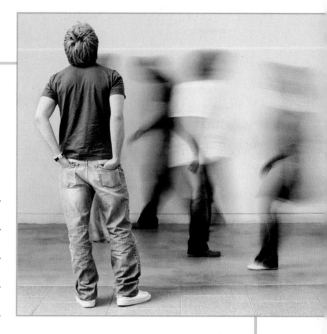

WRITE

Filling the Empty Space Describe an experience when you felt alone. How can the image of the love of God being poured into your heart (see Romans 5:5) fill the empty space of your loneliness?

_____

_____

_____

_____

_____

_____

_____

_____

_____

_____

Write a short prayer to the Holy Spirit that you can pray in times of loneliness.

_____

_____

_____

_____

_____

_____

_____

_____

_____

_____

A Promise Kept

Why did God send the Holy Spirit to us?

It's hard when you can't be with a close friend anymore. He or she might have moved away, or you might be going to a new school. You miss your friend, and things you do are different because that person isn't there. You might feel lonely, wondering why people don't understand you and what's important to you.

Jesus knew his disciples would miss him when he was no longer with them. His followers were going to feel lost without him. His Death would break their hearts. His Resurrection might certainly confuse them. His return to the Father in Heaven would definitely challenge them.

How could the Apostles continue the work they had done with Jesus when he was no longer with them?

Always with Them

Jesus promised his Apostles he wouldn't stop being with them. In fact, he promised them that he would always be with them through an **Advocate**, the Holy Spirit. An advocate is someone who speaks on your behalf.

Scripture

So Jesus said to his disciples at the Last Supper, "'If you love me, you will keep my commandments. And I will ask the Father, and he will give you another Advocate to be with you always, the Spirit of truth, which the world cannot accept, because it neither sees nor knows it. But you know it, because it remains with you, and will be in you.'" **John 14:15–17**

> **How could the Holy Spirit help the Apostles?**

> **How could he help you?**

Catholic Faith Words

Advocate literally means "he who is called to one's side." The Holy Spirit is our Advocate, guiding and comforting us, strengthening us to know and live by the truth.

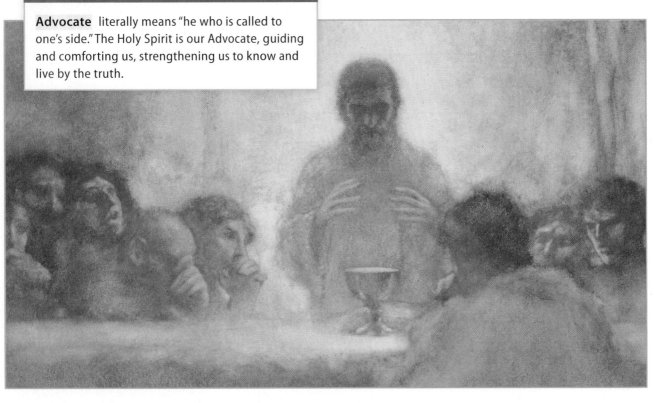

The Soul of the Church

The Church is the Body of Christ in the world. We are the hands and feet of Christ, bringing the truth, joy, and love of the Good News to all people. Our own bodies are more than just a collection of flesh and bones. In the same way that your body is given life by your soul, the Body of Christ comes alive through her soul, the Holy Spirit.

The Holy Spirit keeps the Church going, giving her life. He makes the wonderful diversity of people, places, and cultures in the Church one. He brings us together by our belief in Jesus. The Holy Spirit is the source of the many gifts and talents people bring to the Church.

Underline some of the ways the Holy Spirit acts in the Church.

DESCRIBE AND PRAY

Describe two situations in your life when you wished you had someone who could speak for you and look out for your best interests.

_____

_____

_____

_____

_____

Then pray the Prayer to the Holy Spirit (see page 125 in this chapter or 384 in the Our Catholic Tradition section of your book) and consider ways that the Holy Spirit could fill that role of an advocate for you.

the whistles and cheers of fans he has never met. He feels the support of his coach and teammates. At the same time, he will be alone when he reaches for the rings and performs his routine. He will have to remember everything he has learned in practice and previous meets, and apply all his mental and physical strength to the routine. No one else can do it for him.

The Scripture passage below tells of how, as Jesus prepared himself for the Cross, his friends fell asleep. Twice he returned to find them sleeping and unaware of his pain. How must Jesus have felt?

Have you ever had to do something you knew would be difficult—but you also knew that it was important that you do it? Jesus teaches, ". . . how much more will the Father in heaven give the holy Spirit to those who ask him?" **(Luke 11:13)**.

The Holy Spirit, Comforter

How does the Holy Spirit help us in ways that no one else can?

We May Seem Alone

Often, the support and strength of friends helps us through difficult times. There are times, however, when we must face something all on our own. We might be surrounded by our friends, and they might even offer their help and support. But in the end, whatever it is we must face, we need to do it on our own.

Imagine an Olympic gymnast, about to begin his routine on the rings. He has trained for years to get to this point in his athletic career. He knows that his family and friends are in the arena, watching and sending good thoughts his way. He hears

✝ Scripture

"Then Jesus came with them to a place called Gethsemane, and he said to his disciples, 'Sit here while I go over there and pray.'"

He asked his three friends to sit up and wait. He probably wanted them to be there for him, to support him. Then he said to them, 'My soul is sorrowful, even to death.'

Then, he moved farther into the garden where they could not see him. He addressed his heavenly Father in prayer, asking that the Cross be taken from him, if possible. Jesus prayed, 'My Father, if it is possible, let this cup pass from me; yet, not as I will, but as you will.'"
Based on Matthew 26:36–39

📖 Go to the Source

For more on the Last Supper, read *Matthew 26:26–29*, *Mark 14:22–25*, and *John 13:1–17*.

As you have probably discovered already, none of us can avoid pain and difficulties in life. We will have challenges in our lives that we must face on our own. But we will have the help and special comfort of the Holy Spirit as we face these trials and confront these challenges.

The **Saints** often prayed to God for help, and the prayers they prayed still help people pray effectively today. The Saints poured out their hearts for help from above. We, too, are sure that the Holy Spirit will personally help us. And we call on the Saints to pray for us, asking for their **intercession** on our behalf.

Catholic Faith Words

Saints those whom the Church declares led holy lives and are enjoying eternal life with God in Heaven

intercession a form of prayer that involves praying to God on behalf of another; also called intercessory prayer

We, too, pray a prayer of intercession during the Prayer of the Faithful at Mass.

> **When do you turn to God?**

> **How do you let God know you need him?**

Fill in the chart with one prayer of intercession for each of the groups mentioned.

The Prayer of the Faithful	
We pray for the Church	Our prayer: _____ _____
We pray for the world and world leaders	Our prayer: _____ _____
We pray for the sick and for those who have died	Our prayer: _____ _____

LIST

The work of the Holy Spirit benefits the Church by building up the community of faith, helping people to be faithful, and sanctifying the Church (making her holy). List three things that you do in the Church that benefit your brothers and sisters in faith.

1. _____

2. _____

3. _____

The Holy Spirit, Guide

How does the Holy Spirit help the Church?

A garden grows because someone takes the time and effort to water and weed it. Without weeding, the plants will be choked by unhealthy growth. Without water, the plants in the garden will wither and die.

Similarly, when we raise our minds and hearts to God—which is what prayer is—we cultivate our spiritual garden. Requesting bad things from God will produce in us a spiritual garden full of weeds. Neglecting the time and effort for prayer will produce a withered spiritual garden.

Guidance

We need someone to guide us through life's questions and help us live for God. That guide is the Holy Spirit. He works through the Church and often through the people in our lives.

The Holy Spirit acts through the Church to teach and form us as disciples, guiding the Church in her interpretation of God's Word in Sacred Scripture and Sacred Tradition. This Sacred Tradition is our religious heritage. Sacred Tradition is God's Word to the Church, safeguarded by the Apostles and their successors, the bishops, and handed down verbally—in her Creeds, Sacraments, and other teachings—to future generations. This Sacred Tradition enriches our personal prayer and the prayer life of the Catholic Church, so that we raise our minds and hearts to God in holy and effective ways.

Scripture

"If then there is any encouragement in Christ, any solace in love, any participation in the Spirit, any compassion and mercy, complete my joy by being of the same mind, with the same love, united in heart, thinking one thing." **Philippians 2:1**

A Guide to Prayer

Just like you talk to your friends in different ways depending upon what you have to share, you can talk to God in different ways, too. The Holy Spirit is with you when you pray, guiding you in prayer as you grow in faith. Because you have different needs and different experiences during life, the Holy Spirit gives you a variety of ways to pray.

The Holy Spirit also teaches you to pray. He does this by helping different generations of Church leaders and Catholics pass on the truth of Jesus through the Church's Seven Sacraments, the Creeds, teachings, and devotional practices such as praying the Rosary or the Liturgy of the Hours.

> **When you pray, is it mostly asking God for something, or do you just talk to God as a friend who listens?**

The Ways We Pray

Prayers of **blessing and adoration** bless God for being the source of all that is good and show that we need him. We respond to God's gifts and give respect to God by honoring his greatness.

Prayers of **praise** give honor to God for being who he is. We give him glory as his children not for what he does, but simply because he is.

Prayers of **petition** ask God for something we need for ourselves. We might ask for God's mercy, forgiveness, and guidance.

Prayers of **intercession** ask God for something on behalf of another person. We use intercessory prayer on behalf of others as Jesus intercedes for us with God the Father.

Prayers of **thanksgiving** acknowledge and thank God for all he has given us. We express our gratitude to him for the good things in our lives.

EXPLAIN

One of the symbols of the Holy Spirit at Pentecost is wind. Like the Holy Spirit, we cannot see wind, but we can see what wind does. Look at the Fruits of the Holy Spirit named below. Write the name of a person whom you know has been an instrument of the Holy Spirit in bringing two of these fruits to the world, and explain how they did so.

Fruits of the Holy Spirit: Charity, Kindness, Faithfulness, Joy, Goodness, Modesty, Peace, Generosity, Self-control, Patience, Gentleness, Chastity

_____

_____

_____

_____

_____

IN SUMMARY Catholics Believe

The Holy Spirit is our Advocate, guiding and comforting us, strengthening us to know and live by the truth.

- The Holy Spirit, who strengthened the first disciples to spread Jesus' message and understand his truth, keeps the Church going, giving her life and energy and uniting us as one Body of Christ.

- We all experience difficulties and challenges, some that we must face alone. However, we are never truly alone because the Holy Spirit is with us, comforting, strengthening, and supporting us.

- The Holy Spirit guides the Church in her Sacred Tradition and her prayer. The Holy Spirit helps us pray at different times, in different ways, and in different circumstances.

Our Catholic Life

The Holy Spirit can be a great source of comfort when you feel alone or afraid, as Jesus' followers must have felt after his Death and before the time of Pentecost. Through the strength and wisdom of the Holy Spirit, we are able to lead the life of love Jesus wants us for us. Take the time to **pray to the Holy Spirit** when you need that comfort during a time of difficulty, or when you need guidance in making choices or hard decisions. On the next page you can read the Prayer to the Holy Spirit, but you can address other prayers, either from the Church's liturgy or ones you write or think up yourself, to him. When you pray and listen to what the Holy Spirit is telling you, you allow him to guide you and work in your heart.

> When have you prayed to the Holy Spirit? How did you feel afterward?

People of Faith

Saint Rafqa (Rebecca), 1832–1914

Born in Lebanon as Boutrossieh Ar-Rayes, Rafqa felt a call to religious life at age fourteen and later became a nun. She joined the Order of Saint Anthony of the Maronites (Baladiya Order) in 1871 and took the name of Rafqa (Rebecca).

Blind and near the time of her death, Rafqa asked that her sight be restored for an hour so she could again see the face of her friend Mother Superior Ursula Doumit. The hour of sight was granted. Miracles of healing were later recorded at Rafqa's grave. The Church celebrates her feast day on **March 23.**

For more, go to aliveinchrist.osv.com

CONSIDER

Think of one of your favorite movies in which the main character changes considerably during the film. Why did the change take place? Who supported him or her?

_____

_____

_____

_____

How could the Holy Spirit have been involved in this change?

_____

_____

_____

_____

♡ Prayer to the Holy Spirit

Leader: Come Holy Spirit, fill the hearts of your faithful.

And kindle in them the fire of your love. Send forth your Spirit and they shall be created.

All: And you shall renew the face of the earth.

Reader 1: A reading from the Book of Psalms.

Read Psalm 139:7–12.

Where can I go from your spirit?

From your presence, where can I flee? If I ascend to the heavens, you are there;

if I lie down in Sheol, there you are.

If I take the wings of dawn
and dwell beyond the sea,

Even there your hand guides me,
your right hand holds me fast.

If I say, "Surely darkness shall hide me,
and night shall be my light"

Darkness is not dark for you,
and night shines in the day.

Darkness and light are but one.

The word of the Lord.

All: Thanks be to God.

Reader 2: Come to us, O Spirit of truth, teach us what we need to know, and remind us of all that Jesus did for us.

Reader 3: Come to us, O Spirit of love, walk with us each and every day, and guide us in all we say and do.

Reader 4: Come to us, O Spirit of compassion, be with us when we are lonely and afraid, when we are confused and don't know how to choose.

All: Come to us, O Spirit of wisdom, help us to know that you are always near, help us to know that you will always guide us, help us to know that you are always for us.

▶ *Sing or play "Spirit, Come Down"*

Go to **aliveinchrist.osv.com** for an interactive review.

A **Work with Words** Circle the letter of the choice that best completes the sentence.

1. The Holy Spirit is the Advocate because ___.

   a. he speaks on our behalf

   b. we can't see him

   c. he is the Word

   d. he brings healing

2. ___ is the liturgical feast that celebrates the descent of the Holy Spirit upon the Apostles.

   a. Easter

   b. Christmas

   c. Pentecost

   d. Mass

3. Prayer involves ___.

   a. thoughts about God

   b. raising our hearts and minds to God

   c. guidance by the Holy Spirit

   d. a, b, and c

4. We call on the ___ to pray for us, interceding on our behalf.

   a. clergy

   b. disciples

   c. Saints

   d. shepherds

5. Jesus promised the Apostles he would continue to be present with them after his Death through the ___.

   a. Apostles

   b. Tongues of Fire

   c. Holy Spirit

   d. Creation

B **Check Understanding** Complete each sentence with the correct term from the Word Bank.

ourselves	life and unity
others	intercession
act of faith	Body of Christ
creation	Sacred Tradition
harmony	

6. The Church is the _____ in the world.

7. The Holy Spirit brings _____ to the Church.

8. A prayer of petition asks God for something needed for _____.

9. A prayer of _____ asks God for something for another person.

10. _____ is God's Word to the Church, safeguarded by the Apostles and their successors, the bishops, and handed down to future generations.

C **Make Connections** Write a one-paragraph response to the questions: How are we connected with God? What do you consider the source of your strongest connection to God?

_____

_____

_____

_____

_____

A Work with Words **Match the terms on the left with the correct definitions or descriptions on the right.**

____ **1.** Pentecost

____ **2.** Annunciation

____ **3.** miracle

____ **4.** Holy Spirit

____ **5.** grace

____ **6.** conscience

____ **7.** Holy Trinity

____ **8.** Incarnation

____ **9.** Jesus

____ **10.** Emmanuel

____ **11.** bread

____ **12.** God the Father

a. an event for which there is no scientific explanation because it happened through the power of God

b. the Son of God taking on a human nature to save all people

c. the Third Divine Person of the Trinity

d. the God-given ability that helps us judge right from wrong

e. the outpouring of the Holy Spirit upon the Apostles fifty days after Easter

f. Father, Son, and Holy Spirit

g. the free, loving gift of God's life and help

h. the Angel Gabriel telling Mary that she would be the Mother of God

i. the First Divine Person of the Trinity

j. Jesus described himself in his "I Am" statements as light, a shepherd, a vine, and this

k. A name for Jesus that means "God is with us"

l. the Second Divine Person of the Trinity

B Check Understanding Indicate whether the following statements are true or false. If a statement is false, rewrite it to make it true.

13. When God the Father sends his Son to us, he also sends his Spirit.
True/False

_____

_____

14. Saint Paul is a guide to the Church. **True/False**

_____

_____

15. In the Sacrament of the Eucharist, we become members of God's Church. **True/False**

_____

_____

16. Jesus promised his Apostles that he would continue to be present with them after his Death through the Law. **True/False**

_____

_____

17. A prayer of petition is asking God for something we need for ourselves. **True/False**

_____

_____

18. A prayer of blessing and adoration asks God for something for another person. **True/False**

_____

_____

19. Sacred Tradition is God's Word safeguarded by the Apostles and their successors, the bishops, and handed down verbally to future generations. **True/False**

_____

_____

20. In the opening part of the Gospel according to John, John calls Jesus "the Light of the World." **True/False**

_____

_____

21. The name Jesus literally means "God saves." **True/False**

_____

_____

22. Mary is our spiritual Mother because she shows us the way to Jesus. **True/False**

_____

_____

C Make Connections **Write a short answer to these questions.**

23. As a young girl, Mary made a decision to follow God. In what ways is Mary an example for your life as a young person today?

_____

_____

_____

_____

24. The Church is the Body of Christ. What part of the body are you? Use a part of the human body (hand, foot, eye, etc.) to describe your role in the Body of Christ.

_____

_____

_____

_____

25. How can the Holy Spirit comfort and guide you in your everyday life at home, at school, or at Church?

_____

_____

_____

_____

JESUS CHRIST

When we accept God's gift of salvation in Jesus, why must our lives be formed by his teaching?

CHURCH HISTORY TIMELINE

431	Council of Ephesus
452	Pope Leo I (the Great) meets Attila the Hun
1565	St. Augustine, Florida, becomes first Catholic presence in America
1978	Pope Saint John Paul II is elected Pope

Go to page 348 for more

Our Catholic Tradition

- Jesus Christ is the Son of God who took on human flesh to redeem us from sin and show us the way to the Father. Because he is true God and true man, Jesus gives us the perfect example of how to live the life the Father planned for us. (CCC, 520)

- The Beatitudes challenge us to live by the values of God's Kingdom and understand that true happiness comes from the hope of eternal life with God. (CCC, 1726, 1728)

- Because God the Father loved human beings, he sent his Son, who freely chose to become human and to offer himself in order to redeem us from the effects of Original Sin and our own sins. (CCC, 620, 621)

Our Catholic Life

- We are called to a life of discipleship: this involves accepting Jesus' invitation to believe in and follow him by studying his ways and putting them into practice. (CCC, 2466)

- Listening to and applying the wisdom of Jesus will help us make choices for the good and turn to him in prayer for guidance when making decisions. (CCC, 459, 1787)

- Through his Paschal Mystery, Jesus conquered death and makes it possible for those who have faith to experience new life through the Seven Sacraments. (CCC, 1076)

The Way

♡ Let Us Pray

Leader: Jesus, our brother, you are the Way, the Truth, and the Life. You know our struggles and our joys. Be with us and guide us to know the Father's love.

"Praise the LORD, for he is good;
for his mercy endures forever." **Psalm 136:1**

All: God, help us become our best selves.

📖 Scripture

"Have among yourselves the same attitude that is also yours in Christ Jesus, Who, though he was in the form of God, did not regard equality with God something to be grasped.

Rather, he emptied himself, taking the form of a slave, coming in human likeness; and found human in appearance, he humbled himself, becoming obedient to death, even death on a cross." **Philippians 2:5-8**

Have you ever thought...

- How is Jesus true God and true man?
- What does Jesus being fully human mean for how we live?

Getting Started

In this chapter you will learn that Jesus Christ is true God, true man, the Second Divine Person of the Holy Trinity who took on human flesh. He shows us the way God the Father wants us to live to become more like him.

In the chart below, use words and/or illustrations to show how Jesus is the Way, the Truth, and the Life. How and where does Jesus lead us? What does he teach us? How does he take care of us and give us life?

The Way

The Truth

The Life

- Visitation
- Mediator
- discipleship

WRITE

Fully Alive Saint Iraneaus said, "The glory of God is a human being fully alive." Write a reflection on what you think Saint Iraneaus means.

_____

_____

_____

_____

_____

_____

_____

Think of someone in your life or in the broader community or larger world who you think is "fully alive" and showing God's glory. Describe that person and his or her impact on others.

_____

_____

_____

_____

_____

_____

_____

_____

_____

_____

_____

True God, True Man

How is Jesus like all of us?

At one time or another, everyone wants to excel—to maximize his or her abilities to the fullest. People often say that it's human nature to want to be the best at something. Is that what it means to be "fully human"? But if you fail, is it okay to just remind yourself, "After all, I'm only human" ?

Jesus is "true man and true God," fully human but also fully Divine. He is God. And he is also a human being, a man who walked on Earth, like all of us. He lived the fully human life we are made to live: coming from God and going toward God. So what does that mean for us as his followers?

Sometimes it's hard for us to grasp that Jesus actually lived a human life. Can you picture Jesus as a small child learning to put on his sandals? On sunny days, he might have wanted to go outside and play instead of finishing his chores. Maybe he got tired from too much studying.

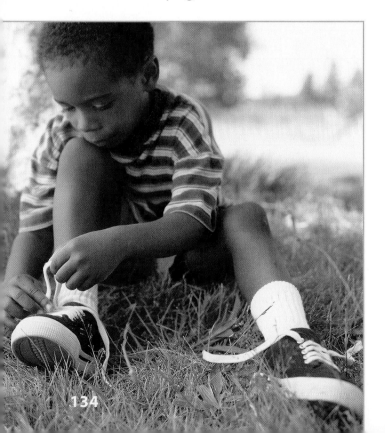

Yet, these kinds of things probably happened. How do we know? They are the kinds of things that happen to all human beings—and in all families. We all face new challenges, feel tired, and become confused. After all, we're human!

> **What are some examples from Jesus' life that show he was fully human?**

The Son of God Became One of Us

Jesus is true man, like us in all things except sin. He is also true God. Jesus has two natures:

- He has a Divine nature. Jesus is the Son of God, the Second Divine Person of the Holy Trinity.
- He has a human nature. He was born of a human mother, and he had to be fed, kept warm, and loved like all other human babies.

The Son of God chose to become a man in order to bring us back to his Father and show us how to live as God intended. Jesus not only brings us closer to the Father, but he also makes it possible for us to become more like him and the Father. God's Son became human to share his divinity with us. Because of that, we can become united with God the Father. When the Son of God became the Son of Man, we also became God's sons and daughters.

God helps us as his children with the grace to live the full lives he calls us to live. When we fail, we need to accept our disappointments with humility. When our thoughts and actions lead us away from God and living his law, we need to turn to God for forgiveness and strength to do better.

The Joyful Mysteries

When praying the Rosary, Catholics remember events from Jesus' and Mary's lives, called the Mysteries of the Rosary. One group of these events is called the Joyful Mysteries. They focus on the great gift of the Incarnation and the joy of the Son of God sharing our human nature.

- The Annunciation—The Angel Gabriel announces to Mary that she has been chosen to be the Mother of Jesus.
- The **Visitation**—Mary, who is pregnant, visits her cousin Elizabeth, who is also pregnant. Elizabeth's son grows up to be John the Baptist.
- The Nativity—Jesus is born.
- The Presentation of the Child Jesus at the Temple—Joseph and Mary present the child Jesus at the Temple in Jerusalem. A man named Simeon had been promised that he would not die before he saw the

Messiah. Simeon recognizes Jesus as the fulfillment of God's promise.

- The Finding of the Child Jesus at the Temple.

Catholic Faith Words

Visitation the event of Mary, who was pregnant with Jesus, visiting her cousin Elizabeth, who was pregnant with Saint John the Baptist

DESCRIBE

In your own words, describe the kind of things you think Jesus expects people your age to do in order to live a full life. Describe what things you think Jesus doesn't expect people your age to do.

What Jesus Expects

_____

_____

_____

What Jesus Doesn't Expect

_____

_____

_____

Jesus Is the Way to God

How does Jesus show us the way?

Before they were called "Christians," the disciples who followed Jesus were called followers of "The Way." Jesus showed them the way to God. He also showed them a new way to live, a way based on truth and love.

Scripture

"I am the way and the truth and the life."
John 14:6

Go to the Source

Jesus used words to describe the Father. Read *Luke 11:9–13* and find out why Jesus spoke about giving a hungry child a scorpion or a snake, instead of an egg or some fish.

The Apostles and disciples of Jesus learned about God in two ways. Jesus talked about God, letting them know that God is Father, and Jesus showed them God the Father

through his life, the life of the Son. Jesus used words to describe what the Father was like, and Jesus used actions to demonstrate what he was like.

Jesus was able to give us a better picture of God—a picture of a loving, gentle, and affectionate Father—a God who takes care of us and gives us what we need, including expectations and rules to keep us safe and help us grow. He is eternal Father and source of all life. Jesus told us, "For everyone who asks, receives; and the one who seeks, finds . . ." (Luke 11:10) Jesus' words and actions still show us the way today.

> **How does "The Way" help you trust in God?**

Catholic Faith Words

Mediator the title given to Jesus because, as true God and true man, he alone is able to reconcile all people to God the Father, bringing us closer to God the Father by his words and saving actions

Titles for Jesus

We call Jesus by many titles that describe who he is and what he does. You're probably familiar with Savior, Lord, Christ, and Lamb of God. How about Mediator and Substantial Image?

A mediator brings together those who might normally be separated or apart, reconciling differences between them. Because of his uniqueness as true God and true man, Jesus alone is the mediator between God the Father and humans. As our intermediary or bridge to God the Father, and by his sacrifice that makes reconciliation possible, Jesus is called the **Mediator**. He brings us closer to the Father by his words and his actions.

When Jesus became man, he remained God. So when we look at Jesus, a human being, we get to see God in living color. He is sometimes called the Substantial Image of the Father. An image is a visible likeness. Substantial implies belonging to its nature. When we say Jesus is the Substantial Image of the Father, we mean that he is a visible image of the true nature of God. In the Son of God, you can see what God the Father is like. Here are some ways Jesus used actions to demonstrate God's love for us:

- healing many people who were sick or injured (see Matthew 8:14−17)
- spending time and eating with people who were unpopular (see Luke 5:30−32)
- feeding people who were hungry (see Mark 6:30−44)

> **What does knowing Jesus better help you to understand about the Trinity?**

Scripture

"For there is one God.
  There is also one mediator between
  God and the human race,
  Christ Jesus, himself human,
  who gave himself as ransom for all."
1 Timothy 2:5−6

SOLVE AND IDENTIFY

In the puzzle find three words to describe Jesus. Write the words on the lines, then share with a classmate why you think they are an accurate description of Jesus. Discuss people you know who can be described in a similar way.

1. _____

2. _____

3. _____

S	S	E	K	G	W	A	Y
J	H	N	Q	U	P	X	N
M	E	D	I	A	T	O	R
J	P	N	Q	B	R	V	Y
W	H	A	M	D	U	R	A
D	E	N	T	F	T	B	Z
B	R	G	N	R	H	L	P
P	D	E	L	I	G	H	T

The Way to Live

What did Jesus want to show us?

Jesus gave his followers many examples of how they could become more like him. When you follow his example, you are acting like he did. The more you do so, the more you can discover the person God intends you to be and live the best life possible.

Jesus' Example
○ taking time to pray; see Mark 6:45–46.
○ having a good relationship with his parents; see Luke 2:51–52.
○ relying on his good friends; see Luke 8:1–3.
○ expressing deep feelings; see John 11:32–37.
○ talking about things with those who disagree; see Mark 12:13–17.
○ listening to others and sometimes changing his mind; see Matthew 15:21–28.
○ taking care of others in need; see Matthew 9:27–31.
○ forgiving his enemies; see Luke 23:33–34.
○ saying no to temptation; see Matthew 4:1–11.
○ standing up for others; see Matthew 21:12–13.

Jesus didn't come to show us the way to play perfect chess or piano, swim, paint, or get straight As. Striving to use the gifts and talents God has given us is a good thing. But, Jesus is most concerned with what importance we give God in our lives, how we treat our families and friends, how we pray, how we care for people we don't know, and how we forgive our enemies. Sometimes these things are a lot harder than doing laps in the pool or practicing scales on the keyboard.

Of all the good that God wants for you, he most wants you to live in his love, to know his happiness, and to become like him. You do all of these things when you follow in Jesus' footsteps and become his disciple.

* Place a check mark beside three ways you have intentionally followed Jesus' example this week.

Discipleship is really what living fully, or being fully alive, is all about. It isn't easy. But we don't follow the path of discipleship alone. God gives us the Church and his grace we need to be the people he has called us to be. The Sacraments strengthen us, and our community of faith journeys with us, guiding and supporting us.

Catholic Faith Words

discipleship accepting Jesus' invitation to believe in and follow him by studying his ways and putting them into practice

DISCUSS AND DECIDE

In a famous address to all the young people of the world, Pope Saint John Paul II called on all young people to take on the "noble and authentic adventure" of discipleship.

Why would discipleship be something "noble" and an "adventure"?

_____

_____

_____

What is one thing we can do together to live this noble adventure?

_____

_____

_____

IN SUMMARY ▶ Catholics Believe

Jesus Christ is the only Son of God, who took on human flesh to redeem us from sin and show us the way to the Father.

- Jesus has two natures. He is fully man and fully God. Jesus is the Second Divine Person of the Holy Trinity.

- Because he is true God and true man, Jesus Christ is "the way" to the Father. Through his words and actions Jesus brings us back to the Father and gives us the perfect example of how to be the people God intended us to be from the beginning.

- Jesus became man to reconcile us to his Father and show us how to live. We need to follow his example and become followers of the Way, disciples who strive to live fully as God's children.

Our Catholic Life

Jesus tells us that discipleship involves praying to God the Father, studying his teachings, participating in the Eucharist, and living the virtues. **Discipleship** also means bringing the Good News of Christ to others. It requires us to understand and live by what we've learned from Jesus and his Church. It is part of the Church's mission to continue Jesus' work, teaching others about him and helping God in his work of spreading his Kingdom. Being a disciple means living a life of compassion, love, justice, and service, for the glory of God. It includes seeing people as our brothers and sisters, no matter their race, nationality, religious beliefs, social group, or income level. We are all made in God's image, and we can all be disciples.

> What is one way the people in your school or parish are examples of discipleship?

People of Faith

Saint Maximilian Kolbe, 1894–1941

When Raymund Kolbe became a priest, he changed his name to Maximilian Maria in honor of Mary. During World War II, he provided shelter for those fleeing the Nazis, including 2,000 Jews. In 1941, Father Kolbe was arrested by the Nazis and taken to the death camp of Auschwitz. While he was there, the Nazis decided to starve some prisoners to death as a punishment. He offered to take the place of a man who had a wife and children. The man whose life he saved was present at the ceremony of his canonization in 1982. The Church celebrates his feast day on **August 14.**

For more, go to
aliveinchrist.osv.com

EXAMINE

Examine your commitment to "the noble adventure of discipleship." How well are you reaching your true potential for discipleship? What is one area that is challenging you right now?

_____

_____

_____

_____

Make some notes as to how you might take some positive steps following "the Way."

_____

_____

_____

_____

_____

_____

♥ Prayer of Thanksgiving

Leader: God, you are our all-knowing and all-loving Creator. We use the words of King David's psalm to praise and thank you for your goodness.

Side 1: LORD, you have probed me, you know me:
> you know when I sit and stand;
> you understand my thoughts from afar.

Side 2: God and Father, you really understand each of us and how we're made. You know how we long to reach our full potential, to be "the best" at something, to make our mark. You see that we are driven and motivated, sometimes in the wrong ways for the wrong reasons.

Side 1: You sift through my travels and
> my rest; with all my ways you are familiar.

Even before a word is on my tongue,
> LORD, you know it all.

Side 2: Loving Father, you understand the pain we feel when we fall short and can't meet our goals. You see how disappointed and how broken we often are. Gently, you touch us to comfort, console, and show us how wonderful we are in your eyes.

Side 1: You formed my inmost being;
> you knit me in my mother's womb.

I praise you, because I am wonderfully made;
> wonderful are your works!

My very self you know.

My bones are not hidden from you.

When I was being made in secret,
> fashioned in the depths of the earth.

Side 2: Our Father, you graciously sent your Son Jesus to live and die for us. He shows us what great plans you have for us. You want us to live in your love and share that love with others. You know what will make us happy. You made us!

Side 1: Probe me, God, know my heart;
> try me, know my thoughts.

See if there is a wicked path in me;
> lead me along an ancient path.
> **Psalm 139:1–15**

Side 2: God, our all-loving Father, you know our strengths and weaknesses as no one else does or can. Deliver us from evil of every sort. Give us the strength to develop the gifts you've given to us. Help us to follow your Son, Jesus.

Leader: Let's conclude our prayer in song.

▶ *Sing or play "Behind and Before Me"*

Go to **aliveinchrist.osv.com** for an interactive review.

A **Work with Words** Circle the letter of the choice that best completes the sentence.

1. ____ is a special prayer form in honor of the Blessed Virgin Mary.
   a. The Rosary
   b. The Creed
   c. Our Father
   d. all of the above

2. Mary's visit to her cousin Elizabeth is known as the ____.
   a. Annunication
   b. Nativity
   c. Visitation
   d. Presentation

3. The Nativity refers to ____.
   a. the birth of Jesus
   b. Elizabeth's visit to Mary
   c. the Angel Gabriel's visit to Mary
   d. Jesus at the Temple

4. Jesus is called the Substantial Image of the Father because ____.
   a. he brings us closer to God
   b. he communicates with us
   c. he is human and Divine
   d. in him we can see what God the Father is like.

5. Disciples of Jesus were first called the followers of the ____.
   a. Trinity
   b. Nativity
   c. Way
   d. Creed

B **Check Understanding** Complete each sentence with the correct term from the Word Bank.

Mediator	the Holy Spirit
words and actions	natures
the Gospels	inspiration
discipleship	human

6. The disciples learned about God through the _____ of Jesus.

7. Jesus is the _____, the intermediary or bridge between God and humans.

8. Jesus has two _____, human and Divine.

9. Being fully _____ means becoming the person God meant you to be.

10. _____ is the process of accepting Jesus' invitation to believe in and follow him by studying his ways and putting them into practice.

C **Make Connections** Write a one-paragraph response to the question: Jesus is both true God and true man. Which aspect of Jesus is harder for you to identify with? Explain why.

_____

_____

_____

_____

_____

CHAPTER 8

Model of Wisdom

♡ Let Us Pray

Leader: Loving God, we praise and thank you for your presence with us. Teach us and heal us. Fill our hearts with your wisdom that we may always live within your peace.

"Teach us to count our days aright,
    that we may gain wisdom of heart." **Psalm 90:12**

All: God, we need your Good News. Give us your wisdom!

📖 Scripture

After three days they found him in the temple, sitting in the midst of the teachers, listening to them and asking them questions, and all who heard him were astounded at his understanding and his answers.

When his parents saw him, they were astonished, and his mother said to him, "Son, why have you done this to us? Your father and I have been looking for you with great anxiety."

And he said to them, "Why were you looking for me? Did you not know that I must be in my Father's house?" But they did not understand what he said to them. He went down with them and came to Nazareth, and was obedient to them; and his mother kept all these things in her heart. And Jesus advanced [in] wisdom and age and favor before God and man." **Luke 2:46–52**

Have you ever thought...

- Did Jesus always know he was God's Son?

- How does knowing God's plan help us to be happy?

Getting Started

In this chapter you will reflect upon the need for wisdom in our daily lives and how Jesus' wisdom answers that need. In the Sermon on the Mount, especially the Beatitudes, we discover the wisdom of Jesus that he calls us to live by.

Catholic Faith Words

- wisdom
- Kingdom of God
- parable
- Sermon on the Mount
- Beatitudes

Fill in the chart with words or phrases that describe Jesus and his teachings. Use the letter at the beginning of the line as the first letter of your word or term. One is done for you. ✳

	Jesus and His Wisdom
W	_____ _____ _____
I	Invited all people to make God the priority in their lives and to trust in the Father's will
S	_____ _____ _____
D	_____ _____ _____
O	_____ _____ _____
M	_____ _____ _____

© Our Sunday Visitor

Words to Live By The dictionary defines wisdom as an understanding of what is true, right, or lasting; common sense; or learning. As people of faith, wisdom is more. It involves seeing as God sees.

In your own words, write a definition for wisdom from a Catholic perspective.

_____

_____

_____

_____

_____

_____

_____

Who in your life has been a source of Catholic wisdom?

_____

_____

_____

_____

_____

_____

What are some words of wisdom you live by?

_____

_____

_____

_____

_____

_____

Christ with the Doctors. S. Luke 2.

Jesus, the Wise Teacher

What made Jesus different from other teachers?

When Jesus started teaching, the people listening to him probably had questions: "Who will help us know God's will? Who can make life better?" Jesus gave the answers to these questions, and more!

📖 Scripture

"Rabbi, we know that you are a teacher who has come from God, for no one can do these signs unless God is with him."
John 3:2

A Teacher Like No Other

Once people heard Jesus' words, they realized he was different. He spoke the truth, even when it was difficult to hear. He encouraged people to follow God's ways, even when it wasn't easy. He spoke across social barriers. He astounded the crowds with authority given to him by his Father.

We know that Jesus possessed definitive **wisdom**, the spiritual gift that helps us to know about the purpose and plan of God. Wisdom leads us to see things as God sees so that we might live holy lives. Jesus challenged the commonly accepted understanding of his time. He did not accept stereotypes or judge others by their social or economic status. He spent time with women, children, people who had undesirable jobs, and those who were poor, sick, or in special need. Jesus got to know those most ignored in society. In all of these ways, he showed the dignity of every person he met.

> **Think of someone you believe sees things and people as God does. What is this person like?**

Ordinary Words, Extraordinary Meaning

Jesus knew things were not perfect in the lives of the people. They needed to turn to God and work on their relationships with one another. They needed forgiveness.

Those who heard Jesus sensed that he was different. He was connected to what was important and truly right. He encouraged people to change how they lived. Jesus wanted his followers to know the true meaning of forgiveness and the way to live by God the Father's will. He spoke often about God's rule in people's lives and hearts, harkening people to the **Kingdom of God**—

God's rule of peace, justice, and love. Jesus talked about things that were difficult to describe, so he often taught using parables.

A **parable** is a short story Jesus told using examples from everyday life or nature to illustrate moral or spiritual truths. Parables sometimes end with a twist or a surprise, and people didn't always understand the meanings. He used examples from everyday life to give a religious or moral lesson, or to emphasize God's love.

Sometimes Jesus spoke in parables when he was challenged by someone who wanted to trap him in his words. In the Gospel according to Luke a scholar tried to test Jesus. He asked, "Who is my neighbor?" to clarify the law, "love your neighbor as yourself." In response, Jesus told the parable of the Good Samaritan (see Luke 10:30–35). This parable would have surprised Jesus' listeners. The Jewish people and Samaritans of Jesus' time had religious and ethnic differences. They would not have expected the Jewish men to ignore one of their own, or the Samaritan to help a man considered to be the enemy.

There are more than thirty parables in the Gospels, including the well-known parables of the Mustard Seed, the Sower, the Lost Sheep, the Rich Fool, and the Prodigal Son.

Catholic Faith Words

wisdom the spiritual gift that helps us to see God's purpose and plan for our lives. Wisdom is also one of the seven Gifts of the Holy Spirit.

Kingdom of God God's rule of peace, justice, and love that exists in Heaven, but has not yet come in its fullness on Earth

parable a short story Jesus told using examples from everyday life or nature to illustrate moral or spiritual truths

READ AND REFLECT

Choose a parable with which you are not very familiar. Locate, read, and reflect on it. Then use your own words to describe its meaning.

The parable:

_____

_____

Its meaning:

_____

_____

_____

_____

A Unique Message

How are Jesus' words surprising and challenging?

Jesus taught everywhere he went. He preached in homes and synagogues, in boats, on the road as he walked, and on the shores. He gathered with his disciples on hilly areas as the crowds followed him, hoping to hear his message or to receive his healing touch. He offered words of wisdom throughout his public ministry, and in the Gospel according to Matthew, many of these teachings are collected into what is known as the **Sermon on the Mount**.

Words and Actions

Have you ever been told that actions speak louder than words? Or that you need to not only say what's right, but also do what's right? Jesus tells us something similar.

Jesus said if you listen to his words, and you pattern your actions on his words, you will have a good foundation. It's like building a house on solid rock. The winds will blow, and the rains will fall, but the house will stand. The strong foundation of Jesus' words will hold up your actions that are based on hearing and believing those words.

WHERE IT HAPPENED

The Gospels do not tell us exactly where Jesus gathered his disciples and the crowds in Galilee. The geography of this part of Galilee contains elevated hills with many associated level places. Some archeologists and people who study the Bible think parts of the Sermon on the Mount took place at Mount Eremos, overlooking the Sea of Galilee. It is often called the Mount of Beatitudes.

Go to the Source

Read *Matthew 7:24–29* and think about why the analogy of a house's foundation ended the Sermon on the Mount.

But if you don't listen to the words of Jesus, it will be like building your house on sand. Your life will have no foundation. The winds and rain will knock it down easily. (See Matthew 7:24–29.)

> **What can you do to become a person who connects your words and your actions?**

Catholic Faith Words

Sermon on the Mount the summary of key teachings of Jesus found in the Gospel according to Matthew

Teachings from the Mount

• You are the salt of the earth.	• When you give to the poor, don't brag about it.
• You are the light of the world.	• Ask and you will receive.
• Our Father is in Heaven; how holy is his name.	• Seek and you will find.
• When you pray, don't use loud and fancy words.	• Knock and the door will open.
• When you fast, don't try to look glum and hungry.	
• Where your treasure is, your heart is, too!	Underline which of these teachings you think people most need to hear and act upon today. Draw a star next to the teachings that are hardest for you to hear or act on.
• Don't judge others harshly, or you will be judged harshly.	

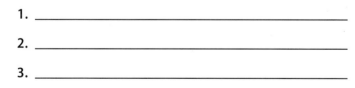

NAME

Name three words or phrases to describe Jesus' wisdom found in the Sermon on the Mount.

1. _____

2. _____

3. _____

What question would you ask Jesus about the points he made in these teachings?

_____

_____

Divine Words for Wise Living

What do the Beatitudes teach us about our relationships with God and others?

The part of the Sermon on the Mount that people are perhaps most familiar with is the **Beatitudes**, Jesus' teachings on the meaning of and path to true happiness. The word *beatitude* means "happiness or blessedness." In the Beatitudes, Jesus asks us to align our spirit and our will with God. Only when we rely on God's grace and the guidance of the Spirit, can we find the eternal blessedness, or holiness, to which God calls all of us. In the Beatitudes, Jesus sets forth for us a path of discipleship, with expectations of how to live in relationship with one another. In the Beatitudes we find the values of the Kingdom of God, and the attitudes and behaviors of Christians living in God's Kingdom now and always.

The Beatitudes are recorded in two Gospels: Matthew and Luke. The two accounts are similar, but different.

Catholic Faith Words

Beatitudes Jesus' eight teachings about the meaning and path to true happiness; they depict the way to live in God's Kingdom now and always, working toward the eternal holiness or blessedness to which God calls all people

Fill in the missing words based on the passages in both Matthew and Luke.

The Beatitudes	
The Words in Matthew 5:3–12	**The Words in Luke 6:20–26**
Blessed are:	Blessed are you:
• the _____ in spirit	• who are poor
• those who mourn and the _____	• who are hungry now
• those who _____ and thirst for righteousness	• who _____ now
• the merciful and the _____ in heart	• when people _____ you, on account of the Son of Man
• the peacemakers	**Woe to you:**
• those who are persecuted for righteousness	• who are _____
• you when people revile you because of _____	• who are full now
	• who are _____ now

📖 Go to the Source
Read both versions of the Beatitudes to find out how each of these groups of people will be blessed.

The Message

The account in the Gospel according to Matthew focuses on the spiritual and religious virtues of God's Kingdom. Luke's account emphasizes the social and economic inequality of the time. In both, we find Jesus' teaching that happiness comes from trusting in God no matter what is happening now. We will know true happiness when God's Kingdom has come in its fullness. In the meantime, being obsessed with material things or current good fortune will keep us from seeing and living the real values of God's Kingdom.

WRITE

The Beatitudes assure those who are in need of God's help and compassion and our trust that God will make all things good and that we can receive eternal happiness with him in Heaven, regardless of our current circumstances. Write two Beatitudes for adolescents that address their suffering or needs. For example, "Blessed are those whose neighborhoods are filled with violence and fear, trusting that God will bring you peace."

1. _____
   _____
   _____
   _____

2. _____
   _____
   _____
   _____

IN SUMMARY ▸ Catholics Believe

As Catholics, we turn to Jesus as our source of wisdom.

- Jesus' wisdom came from being the Son of God; he looked at the world with that perspective.

- He taught through his words and actions. In his Sermon on the Mount, he gave advice and specific direction that emphasize just living, honoring God, and making our actions reflect our beliefs.

- Jesus' Beatitudes challenge us to live by the values of God's Kingdom and to understand that true happiness comes from the hope of eternal life with God.

Our Catholic Life

Jesus is a model of wisdom for us. To gain some of that wisdom and apply it to our own lives, we need to take the time to learn Jesus' teachings, and pray for guidance when making decisions. There are **steps you can take** to find the right answer to hard questions, including: giving yourself plenty of time to think about what you should do, listening to your conscience, considering what the Bible and the Church teach, asking for help and courage in prayer, and being confident in your decision once you've thought and prayed about it. Wisdom helps you make the right choices, and that helps strengthen your relationship with God and others.

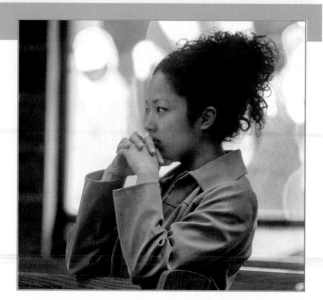

> When have you relied on God's wisdom to help you make a decision? How did it feel?

People of Faith

Saint Gerard Majella, 1726–1755

One day, Gerard Majella was visiting a family and dropped his handkerchief. When one of the daughters tried to return it, Gerard told her to keep it because she might need it some day. Years later, after Gerard had died, the girl was pregnant and her baby was in danger of dying. Remembering the handkerchief, she prayed to Gerard to help her. She gave birth to a healthy baby! Many pregnant women began to pray to Gerard and many miracles occurred. To remind himself of what God wants from us, Gerard kept a note that read: "Here the will of God is done, as God wills, and as long as God wills." The Church celebrates his feast day on **October 16**.

For more, go to **aliveinchrist.osv.com**

IDENTIFY

Think of an important decision or difficult situation you or someone you know is facing right now. What would the wisdom of the world lead you to do?

_____

_____

What would the wisdom of Jesus found in the Beatitudes or Sermon on the Mount lead you to do?

_____

_____

How could you see things differently, as God does?

_____

_____

♥ Prayer of Petition

All: Lord God, Creator of all things, true source of light and wisdom, graciously let your light give me understanding.

Leader: Lord God, send your wisdom through our parents and families, our teachers, our pastor and church. Help us too, to find that light in the example of your Saints. May we welcome this light and the wisdom it brings.

All: Give me the eyes to see your plan for a good and meaningful life in a world that can be disordered and sinful.

Leader: Lord, sometimes it seems that darkness overwhelms us. We live in a world where there is often violence and disrespect for human life and dignity. Sometimes, we contribute to that darkness. Too often, we're selfish or say mean things that hurt others. Help us to see everyone as you see them. Let your light overcome the darkness.

All: Help me to remember the gift of your truth that I have learned as a child, and help me to understand your will more each day so that I may make choices that reflect your love.

Leader: God, help us to work hard at learning. Learning about your world, the work of your hands will help us draw closer to you. Let us keep in our hearts Saint Thomas Aquinas' insight that all learning begins in realizing that you are the source of all Truth.

All: Grant me the talent of being clear in my explanations and the ability to express myself with kindness and respect for another's point of view.

Leader: God, sometimes we're careless in the way we speak. We brag, we "stretch the truth," or we say something just to be noticed. Guide us in speaking carefully and thoughtfully, as disciples of Jesus, the Way, the Truth, and the Life.

All: Direct my talents and interests, and help me discover your plan for my life. Give me the perseverance to complete the journey to serve you through my work. I ask this through Christ our Lord. Amen.

Leader: God, you know how often we are tempted to quit trying. Remind us to ask for your help. Encourage us in all we do.

All: Amen.

Prayer for Students by Saint Thomas Aquinas

▶ *Sing or play "You Are the Way"*

Go to **aliveinchrist.osv.com** for an interactive review.

A **Work with Words** Solve the word search to find words that complete the sentences.

H	A	P	P	I	N	E	S	S
J	H	N	Q	U	P	M	N	V
M	L	D	I	A	A	O	R	L
J	I	N	Q	T	R	V	Y	U
W	S	A	T	D	A	R	A	K
D	T	H	T	F	B	B	Z	E
B	E	F	O	L	L	O	W	R
W	N	E	L	I	E	H	T	D

1. The word Beatitude means

   _____.

2. In the Sermon on the Mount, Jesus said you

   need to _____ and

   _____ his words to

   have a strong foundation in life.

3. A short story Jesus told using examples
   from everyday life or nature to illustrate
   moral or spiritual truths is a

   _____.

4. The Beatitudes are found in the Gospels

   according to _____

   and _____.

B **Check Understanding** Complete each
sentence with the correct term from the
Word Bank.

holiness	Kingdom
Good Samaritan	blessedness
truth	Son of God
true happiness	Sermon on the Mount
Prodigal Son	

5. The _____ is the
   summary of Jesus' key teachings found in the
   Gospel according to Matthew.

6. Jesus preached the message of God's

   _____.

7. In the Beatitudes we learn about the meaning

   of and path to _____.

8. God calls each of us to eternal

   _____.

9. Jesus taught with authority because he was

   the _____.

10. Jesus' Parable of the

    _____ is a good
    example of how his wisdom crossed social
    barriers and cultural norms.

C **Make Connections** Write a brief response
to the question: What wisdom does Jesus have
to offer us and how can following it make a
difference in your life?

_____

_____

_____

Christ Our Savior

♡ Let Us Pray

Leader: Jesus, you love us and save us. You bless us with infinite love. We thank you and praise you for your mercy toward us.

"LORD, your mercy endures forever.
Never forsake the work of your hands!" **Psalm 138:8**

All: Jesus, help us to forgive and be forgiven. Help us make things right. Bring us back to the Father's love.

📖 Scripture

"He is the image of the invisible God,
the firstborn of all creation. … For in him all the
    fullness was pleased to dwell,
and through him to reconcile all things for him,
    making peace by the blood of his cross [through him],
whether those on earth or those in heaven.

And you who once were alienated and hostile in mind because of evil deeds he has now reconciled in his fleshly body through his death, to present you holy, without blemish, and irreproachable before him …"
Colossians 1:15, 19–22

Have you ever thought...

- Why are we in need of reconciliation?
- What weakens our friendship with God?

Getting Started

In this chapter you will learn how sin and suffering entered the world, and about God's never ending love for us. You will explore our need for forgiveness and the ways Jesus makes that forgiveness possible.

Catholic Faith Words

- Original Holiness
- Original Sin
- personal sin
- salvation
- Paschal Mystery

On the lines below each term, explain why it is a title or symbol for Jesus.

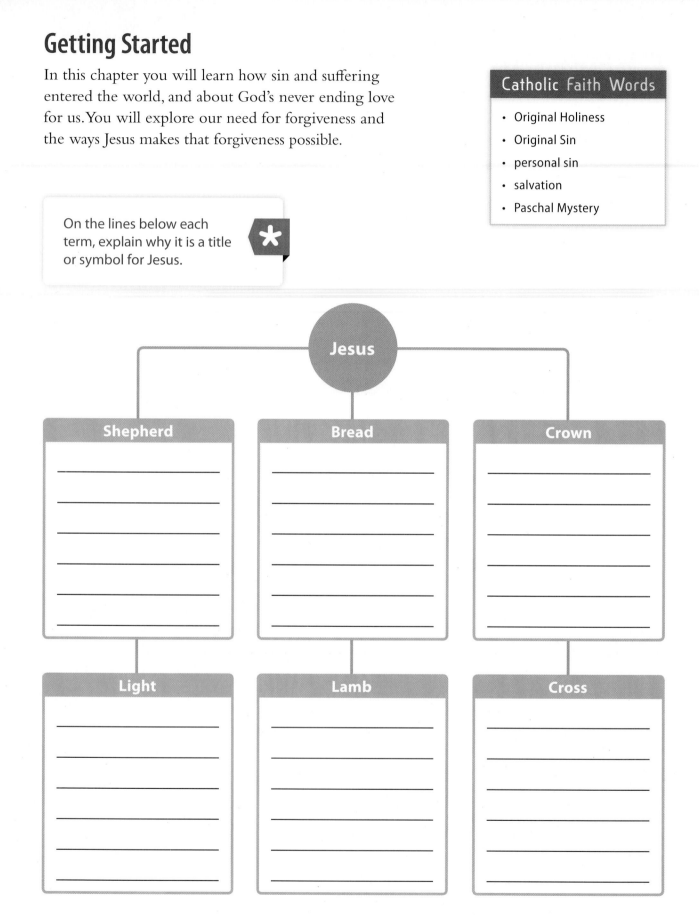

Jesus

Shepherd

Bread

Crown

Light

Lamb

Cross

Redemption What do you think it means to be redeemed? Use the words below to write a definition. Include an example of how you've experienced one or more of these in your own life.

FORGIVE   SAVE   RECONCILE

Definition:

_____

_____

_____

_____

_____

_____

_____

_____

Example:

_____

_____

_____

_____

_____

_____

_____

_____

_____

_____

_____

_____

Original Holiness

How did suffering and sin enter the world?

You've probably heard the accounts of creation many times. What is God telling us in these accounts? Our first parents, called Adam and Eve, initially experienced only good, because sin had not yet entered the world. God made himself known to them, sharing his love. There was no pain or suffering, no arguments or distrust. The Garden of Eden symbolized true paradise, one in which Adam and Eve lived in **Original Holiness** and justice. They were happy in a way that we cannot imagine. This is what God created all humans for: to be free, to be his friends, and to be close to him.

But that's not how things end. Genesis 3 goes on to describe how Adam and Eve took advantage of their freedom and did not turn to God for answers or trust in his word. Instead, they trusted the serpent. He convinced them that if they ate the fruit of the one tree God said not to eat from, they could have the same knowledge as God. They disobeyed the one command God had given them, and they ate the fruit. By doing this, our first parents introduced shame, sin, and suffering into the world.

> **How do you think God might have felt about Adam and Eve's actions?**

Catholic Faith Words

Original Holiness the state of goodness that humanity enjoyed before our first parents, Adam and Eve, chose to sin against God

Original Sin the sin of our first parents that wounded human nature and introduced sin, suffering, and death into the world; all humans are born with Original Sin and are thus tempted to sin

personal sin a deliberate thought, word, deed, or omission that violates the law of God

The banishment from Paradise, engraving from a Pictorial Bible, German school (19th century)

Forever Different

So what happened next? The Book of Genesis tells us that Adam and Eve hid themselves from God, trying to stay away from him because they knew they had sinned. They were afraid. For their disobedience, God expelled them from the Garden.

Everything was different now. The pure happiness and holiness had been lost, not just for Adam and Eve, but for all humans after them. Human nature itself had been harmed. Now, all people suffered because of the choice of our first parents. This disobedience is called **Original Sin**. Original Sin is not something we do; it's something we inherit. Humans can be sad and can suffer because of the sinful actions of others. Humans do not live forever, but die. And all of this is connected to the effects of Original Sin, including the human tendency to commit **personal sin**, to give in to temptation and disobey God. In all of these ways, human nature is affected by Original Sin.

But even though our first parents, and all those who have come after them, disobeyed God, God still loved them. He promised to save them, to bring them back to himself. Throughout history, God sent leaders and prophets to his People, to guide them back to him. Through these people, God promised a Messiah who would bring the people back into the right relationship with God and others, and who would free them from sin.

But why did God allow the physical and moral evil to continue? We do not know the answer to this, but we need to turn to the Son of God whom the Father sent. Jesus Christ died and rose to new life to conquer and defeat evil. In this we must trust.

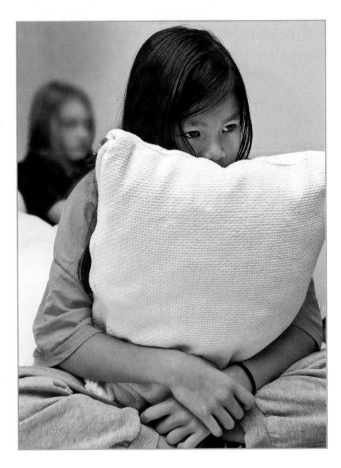

REFLECT

Think of examples of Original Sin in the world—times when the human tendency to be sinful, imperfect, or flawed was evident. What examples have you heard about in the news reporting on current events or social issues, or seen in movies or on TV?

_____

_____

_____

How would the world be different if those stories were replaced with examples of care, honesty, generosity, and humility?

_____

_____

_____

God So Loved the World

Why did Jesus save us?

You might have heard "Jesus is our salvation" and wondered why people need "saving." People need to be restored to the friendship Adam and Eve had with God before Original Sin. Because God created our first parents holy and just, only he can save us from the effects of Original Sin and from our sins. That is what we mean by **salvation**.

For many years, the Jewish people—the People God had chosen to show the whole world his plan of salvation—waited for the Messiah to come and set them free, as their prophets had promised. They lived by the laws of the covenant, but often they strayed. Some thought the Messiah was coming to set them free from the Romans, who had captured their land and taken their religious

freedom. But God wanted to set his People free from the sin that had captured their hearts and all humankind.

"The New Adam"

But how could things be fixed between humans and God? How could the whole human race be redeemed?

✝ Scripture

"In this is love: not that we have loved God, but that he loved us and sent his Son as expiation for our sins. Beloved, if God so loved us, we also must love one another."
1 John 4:10–11

Because God the Father loved human beings, he sent his Son to them. God the Son freely chose to become man and to offer himself in order to redeem us from the effects of Original Sin and from our personal sins. He came into the world as a baby, born from a human mother. Because he did this, no one

Catholic Faith Words

salvation the loving action of God's forgiveness of sins and the restoration of friendship with the Father brought by Jesus Christ

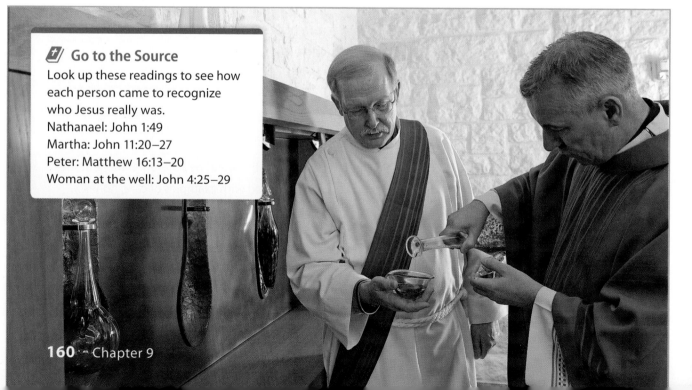

✝ Go to the Source
Look up these readings to see how each person came to recognize who Jesus really was.
Nathanael: John 1:49
Martha: John 11:20–27
Peter: Matthew 16:13–20
Woman at the well: John 4:25–29

could ever say that God didn't understand what it was like to be human and to be tempted by sin.

Jesus is called the "New Adam." Adam was unfaithful to God, but Jesus remained faithful to God, even when he was tempted.

Jesus the Messiah

When Jesus became an adult, many people listened to him tell parables and describe God's love. Jesus came to fulfill the Laws of Moses, called the Mosaic Law, which included the Ten Commandments, and give them deeper meaning. Jesus fulfilled the Law.

Some of Jesus' followers came to believe that he was the Messiah, the one who would save them.

Jesus the King

The Jews before and during Jesus' time used precious oil for anointing. Priests anointed new kings by pouring expensive oil on them as a blessing and sign that God would guide them. Anointing with oil was a symbol of power and authority. It meant the person being anointed was chosen in a special way. At his baptism, Jesus was anointed by the Holy Spirit to fulfill the Father's will.

The Jews were waiting for their Messiah, the one anointed by God himself, not with earthly oil. The Son of God was the one who came to save and redeem the human race. We call Jesus the Christ, the Messiah, our Savior and Redeemer.

Use the following terms to complete the definitions for these titles of Christ:

Redeemer Christ Savior Messiah

Titles of Christ

_____ is a Hebrew word that means "anointed," showing he is chosen and empowered. This word was used by Christians to refer to Jesus as "the Much-Awaited Anointed One from God."

_____ is a Greek word that translates the Hebrew word Messiah. It means "the Anointed One."

In Hebrew, Jesus means "God saves." Jesus is the _____ of the World, the one who saves us from sin and punishment.

Jesus is the _____ of the World. God accomplished once and for all his plan of salvation by Jesus' redemptive Death.

LIST AND DESIGN

What titles would you give to Jesus? List titles you think of for Jesus and what they mean. Then design a poster or bulletin board with the headline "His Name Is . . ." Cut out graphic symbols to write each name on, such as a crown with the title "King of Kings" written on it, or a scroll with the title "Messiah" on it to show that Jesus was the one who came to fulfill the Old Testament prophecies.

This painting of Mary Magdalene at Jesus' tomb by Harold Copping depicts her despair before the Risen Christ appeared to her. (See John 20:11-18.)

Jesus Brings New Life

What happened when Jesus died?

You might be wondering how Jesus actually brought about our salvation from sin. The ultimate result of sin is suffering and death. So another way to ask the question is, how did Jesus conquer suffering and death?

Jesus willingly offered himself on the Cross, which the Church professes in the Nicene Creed every week:

Catholic Faith Words

Paschal Mystery Christ's work of redemption through his Passion, Death, Resurrection, and Ascension

> For our sake he was crucified under Pontius Pilate,
> he suffered death and was buried,
> and rose again on the third day
> in accordance with the Scriptures.

Jesus was free from sin, but he chose to give up his life for the sins of others. He died on the afternoon of what has come to be known as Good Friday. He died for the sins of all people, and we do not hold any one person, or the Jewish people as a whole, responsible for his suffering.

The human and Divine natures are inseparable, and the Son of God suffered, died, and was buried. His redemptive Death won salvation and eternal life in Heaven for all those who had died in God's friendship before him.

His friends saw Jesus die, but no one saw him rise. They found an empty tomb on Sunday morning. However, Mary Magdalene saw the Risen Christ at the tomb. Later, he appeared to many of his disciples. They talked with him and ate with him, before he ascended (went up) into Heaven.

Jesus' redemptive Death was something only God-made-man could do. He was raised to new life, conquering the power of death. His Resurrection was a victory over death. His Death and Resurrection reveal that sin could not keep humans captive forever. Death was not the end, but a passageway to eternal life. This is the salvation that the Son of God won for all who believe in him.

Baptism

Eucharist

Anointing of the Sick

Jesus Continues to Save

The **Paschal Mystery** is the work Christ accomplished principally by his Passion, Death, Resurrection, and Ascension. The Paschal Mystery hinges on the great Easter event of our faith: the Resurrection.

How do Jesus' saving activities continue, since he is no longer with us on Earth? Jesus' saving actions continue through his Church. Jesus makes his Paschal Mystery present in the Eucharist and other Sacraments. In so doing, he continues to offer forgiveness, healing, and new life.

Baptism is the first and primary Sacrament of forgiveness of sins. It unites us to Christ, so we die and rise with him, and gives us the Holy Spirit.

In the name of God, the Church has the power to forgive the sins committed after Baptism. This happens through bishops and priests, normally, in the Sacrament of **Penance and Reconciliation.** We die to sin and rise to renewed life.

The Sacrament of **Eucharist** cleanses us from venial sins and preserves us from future sins. We share in Jesus' suffering and his rising. The Eucharist does not cleanse us from mortal sins. The proper Sacrament for their forgiveness is the Sacrament of Penance and Reconciliation.

The Sacrament of **Anointing of the Sick** also forgives personal sins if the person could not participate in the Sacrament of Penance and Reconciliation.

IN SUMMARY ▶ Catholics Believe

Jesus Christ is our Savior, Redeemer, and Messiah.

- God created human beings with the freedom to live in happiness and harmony with him. By their disobedience, our first parents lost Original Holiness, introduced sin into the world, and became subject to suffering and death.

- God did not abandon his People. He promised them a Messiah who would free them from sin. He sent his own Son to bring that salvation.

- Through his Paschal Mystery, Jesus conquered death and makes it possible for those who have faith to experience new life through the Seven Sacraments.

Our Catholic Life

We worship a God of second chances, who forgives even when we might not expect him to. During his lifetime, Jesus forgave many people in his Father's name. You can give yourself and someone else a second chance. Ask for **forgiveness** when you make a mistake or hurt someone, and forgive others when they do the same to you. Think of a real-life response you can make to someone from whom you are seeking a second chance, or whom you need to forgive.

God is always ready and waiting to forgive. He will always welcome you back. When you turn away from sin and respond to God's love and forgiveness, you experience conversion, which helps you become the person God intends you to be.

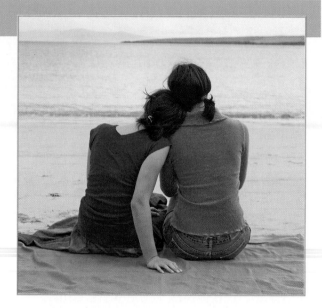

> What second chance do you need right now? Is there someone who needs a second chance from you?

People of Faith

Saint Madeleine Sophie Barat, 1779–1865

Born in France, Sophie was educated by her brother, a priest. She and three companions founded the Society of the Sacred Heart of Jesus in 1800 and started their first convent and school at Amiens. Sister Sophie was appointed Superior General. The Society founded convents and schools in many locations throughout the country. By the time of her death, they had opened 105 schools and convents in twelve countries. The Church celebrates her feast day on **May 25.**

For more, go to
aliveinchrist.osv.com

RECALL AND WRITE

Have you ever learned something "the hard way"? Important lessons can be learned from painful experiences. Recall a time when a good thing came from a "bad" experience. It can be a true report, or a fictional story.

_____
_____
_____
_____
_____
_____
_____
_____
_____

♥ Prayer of Praise

Leader: Blessed be God.

All: Blessed be God forever.

Reader 1: Let us pray.
O Gracious Father,
we praise you, and we thank you for your
endless mercy,
your patience and forgiveness,
your endurance and tolerance,
and the gift of your Son, Jesus,
whom you sent to save us
from all that distracts and keeps us far
from you.

All: We praise you, and we thank you for
your endless mercy.

Reader 2: In you we find a love greater than
any we have ever known.
In you we find hope in the midst of our
darkest act.
In you we find faith in knowing we will
never be alone.

All: We praise you, and we thank you for
your endless mercy.

Reader 3: Be with us in our daily choices.
Guide our hands for service, not for
violence.
Guide our voices for speaking truth, not for
gossip.
Guide our eyes for seeing you in all that we
meet, not for seeking the bad.
Guide our feet to take the "high road," not
for running from responsibility.
Guide our hearts for loving all your people,
not for hating or judging.

All: We praise you, and we thank you for
your endless mercy.

Reader 4: Because we are the young who
search and seek to grow in faith,
remind us always and often that you are on
our side,
that you are for us and never against us,
that you have conquered sin and sadness,
and that through your Son, even in death,
your love is endless.

All: We praise you, and we thank you for
your endless mercy.

 Sing or play "Lord, Your Love Is Everlasting"

Go to **aliveinchrist.osv.com** for an interactive review.

A **Work with Words** Circle the letter of the choice that best completes the sentence.

1. Our human nature is affected by ___, which we inherit from Adam and Eve.
   a. Adam's sin
   b. Reconciliation
   c. Original Sin
   d. Paschal Mystery

2. Jesus came to redeem us—to make it possible for ___.
   a. the Holy Spirit to come
   b. sin to be forgiven
   c. God to become man
   d. man to live a sinless life

3. Jesus is called the "New Adam" because ___.
   a. he was both God and man
   b. he was the son of Adam
   c. he created Adam
   d. he redeemed us from the sin of Adam, the first man

4. The Paschal Mystery refers to ___.
   a. Jesus' Death
   b. Jesus' Resurrection
   c. Original Sin
   d. both a and b

B **Check Understanding** Complete each sentence with the correct terms.

5. When Adam and Eve chose to trust the serpent rather than God, they introduced

   _____ and

   _____ into

   the world.

6. Adam and Eve _____ from God after they ate the fruit in the garden.

7. The words *Messiah* and *Christ* both mean

   "_____."

8. Because of _____, people need salvation.

9. By his Death on the Cross and Resurrection,

   Jesus made _____.
   with God possible.

10. Jesus' _____ is made present to us today in the Eucharist and other Sacraments.

C **Make Connections** Write a one-paragraph response to the questions: What is involved in seeking reconciliation with God? What would this reconciliation mean for you?

   _____

   _____

   _____

   _____

   _____

   _____

   _____

   _____

A Work with Words **Solve the puzzle using the clues provided.**

| Visitation | Nativity | Sermon on the Mount | Rosary |
| Paschal Mystery | Parable | Original Sin | Beatitude |

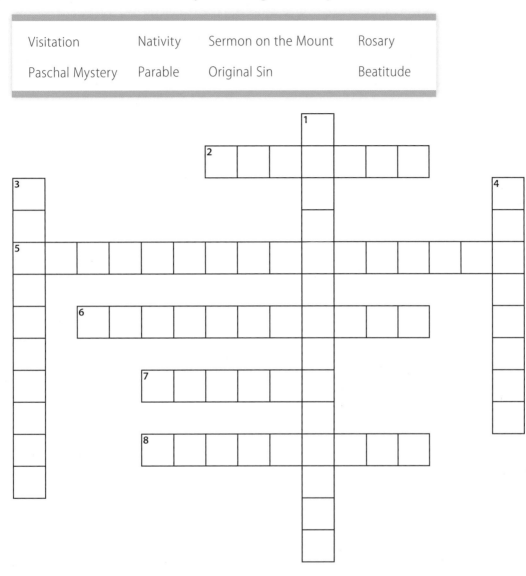

Across

2. A short story told to illustrate moral or spiritual truths

5. Summary of key teachings of Jesus collected in the Gospel according to Matthew

6. The sin that affected human nature, which we inherit from Adam and Eve

7. A special prayer form in honor of the Blessed Virgin Mary

8. Word that means happiness or blessedness

Down

1. Christ's work of redemption through his Passion, Death, Resurrection, and Ascension

3. The pregnant Mary's time with her cousin Elizabeth, who was pregnant with John the Baptist

4. The birth of Jesus

B **Check Understanding** Circle the letter of the best answer to complete the following statements.

9. The words *Messiah* and *Christ* both mean "___".

   a. King
   b. Anointed
   c. Adam
   d. Prophet

10. The disciples of Jesus were first called followers of ___.

   a. The Spirit
   b. The Word
   c. The Way
   d. The Truth

11. Jesus is called the ___ because he is a visible image of the true nature of God.

   a. Substantial Image of the Father
   b. Lord
   c. Messiah
   d. Savior

12. Jesus is ___.

   a. human
   b. Divine
   c. human and Divine
   d. none of the above

13. The ___ are perhaps the most often quoted part of the Sermon on the Mount.

   a. Beatitudes
   b. Psalms
   c. debates
   d. miracles

14. In the Beatitudes we learn that ___ comes from trusting God and living the values of his Kingdom.

   a. righteousness
   b. true happiness
   c. salvation
   d. faith

15. Jesus taught with ___ because he was the Son of God.

   a. authority
   b. parables
   c. the Scriptures
   d. humor

16. Jesus is called ___ because he redeemed us from the sin of Adam, the first man.

   a. Messiah
   b. Savior
   c. the New Adam
   d. the Lamb of God

17. Sin came into the world when Adam and Eve ___.

   a. left the garden
   b. chose to disobey God
   c. were tempted by Satan
   d. from God

18. Because of Original Sin, people need ___ and salvation.

   a. Beatitudes
   b. good works
   c. redemption
   d. the Bible

19. Jesus made eternal life with God possible through ___.

   a. his Death
   b. his Resurrection
   c. his parables
   d. both a and b

C **Make Connections** **Write a short answer to these questions.**

20. How does wisdom make a difference in your life?

_____

_____

_____

21. How are the truths taught by Jesus in the Beatitudes similar
to the values found in today's world?

_____

_____

_____

22. How are they different?

_____

_____

_____

23. God helps us as his children with the grace to live the lives he calls us
to live. How can you become the person God made you to be?

_____

_____

_____

24. In your own words, describe the elements of Jesus' parables.

_____

_____

_____

25. How do you become a disciple?

_____

_____

_____

THE CHURCH

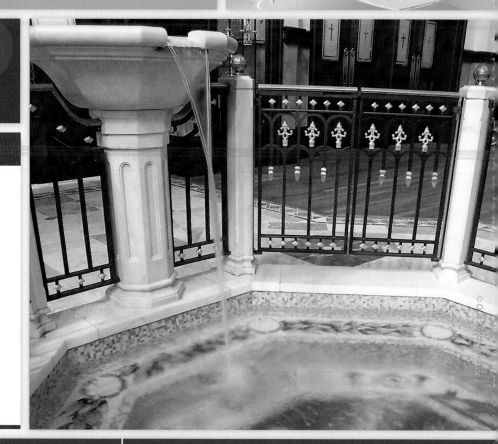

How does the Holy Spirit form us into the Body of Christ sent to proclaim the Good News of salvation?

CHURCH HISTORY TIMELINE

35	Saint Paul's conversion
596	Saint Augustine of Canterbury evangelizes the English
1649	Maryland colony passes Act of Toleration for religious freedom
1769	Junipero Serra establishes first California missions

Go to page 348 for more

Our Catholic Tradition

- We are disciples of Christ together in his Church, following his example by trusting in the Father, learning, praying, and reaching out to others. (CCC, 520)

- The Church is both visible and spiritual, the Mystical Body of Christ united in and to Christ to continue his mission in the world. (CCC, 779)

- The Church has a mission to bring all people to believe in God and to be baptized. She is both a sign and instrument of the communion between God and his People. (CCC, 780)

Our Catholic Life

- Just as Jesus sent the first disciples out, he wants us to be a sign of the Kingdom of God, and to follow Church teachings. (CCC, 941, 942)

- The Church needs the diverse gifts of all members to be a sign of God's Kingdom. We need one another and Christ to bear fruit in the world. (CCC, 791)

- We must have a personal relationship with God nourished by prayer in order to answer our call to bring his love and truth to others. (CCC, 2614)

CHAPTER 10

Disciples in Community

Let Us Pray

Leader: Lord, throughout all ages you have called people to follow you. May we recognize the work of your Spirit among us as we strive to follow your example and be your disciples.

"The LORD is my shepherd;
  there is nothing I lack. …
He guides me along right paths
  for the sake of his name." **Psalm 23:1, 3**

All: Jesus, lead us.

Scripture

"If you will give these instructions to the brothers, you will be a good minister of Christ Jesus, nourished on the words of the faith and of the sound teaching you have followed. … Let no one have contempt for your youth, but set an example for those who believe, in speech, conduct, love, faith, and purity."
1 Timothy 4:6, 12

Have you ever thought...

- What motivated the first disciples?
- Who can you help to follow Jesus?

Getting Started

In this chapter you will reflect on our need for Jesus to lead us and the ways the first disciples responded to him. You will also examine how the Apostles led other disciples, who help us understand what it means to be a disciple today.

The chart below lists different things that take priority in people's lives. In the right hand column, explain how important or unimportant these things are to you.

My Priorities	
Physical Appearance	
Family	
Friends	
Faith	
School	
Sports	
Technology	

Invitation to Discipleship Think back to yourself as a second grader having just received an invitation from Jesus. What are you invited to do? Write what Jesus asked of you then, and how you responded.

You're Invited

_____

_____

_____

_____

Today you have received another invitation from Jesus. What is he inviting you to now? What questions do you have for him?

_____

_____

_____

_____

Jesus blessing children, Carlo De Notaris

A Surprise Invitation

What prompted the first disciples to follow Jesus?

We've probably all known someone who helped us see things differently or to make a commitment. Sometimes that person also leads us to see what matters most in life and to make decisions based on those priorities.

In the time of Jesus, just as today, teachers, politicians, and religious leaders attracted followers. Saint John the Baptist was a preacher whom people followed, but he was preparing the way for the Messiah. When Jesus arrived, John told his followers to follow Jesus. John said, "Now I have seen and testified that he is the Son of God" (John 1:34).

John's followers knew what to expect from him. They must have had to think about leaving the leader they had trusted to follow someone new.

Tell a Friend

Some of John's followers went to see what Jesus was like. After they saw him and heard him speak, they wanted to get to know him better. Many became his **disciples**, and told their friends about Jesus. Jesus asked some to follow him. Other people followed because a friend like Philip told them to come and see Jesus.

📖 Scripture

"Philip found Nathanael and told him, 'We have found the one about whom Moses wrote in the law, and also the prophets, Jesus, son of Joseph, from Nazareth.' But Nathanael said to him, 'Can anything good come from Nazareth?' Philip said to him, 'Come and see.'"   John 1:45–46

📖 Go to the Source

Find out more about who Jesus called to follow him and who came to him through the encouragement of a friend, in these passages: John 1:43–51, Luke 8:1–3, Mark 1:16–20.

Catholic Faith Words

disciples people who learn from and follow the example of a teacher. The disciples of Jesus are those who believe in him, follow his teachings, and put them into practice.

Decisions to Make

Each new disciple already had a family and a job. When Jesus invited them, some people asked if they could have a little time to decide. They wanted to go home and take care of things first. (See Luke 9:61–62.) But Jesus was looking for people who had been looking for his coming and were ready and waiting to go with him. Some people were ready.

Jesus was a vibrant, wise speaker who spoke with authority like only God could do. Some of the things Jesus said confused people. His preaching both challenged and gave hope. Some of the things he did surprised and astounded others. His healing and forgiving of sin brought life and raised questions about his authority. But one thing is certain: people were talking about Jesus in all the towns and villages in the area.

Wouldn't you want to meet a man who was changing people's lives, making things right, and giving people what they desperately needed? Jesus offered the people God's love and compassion, a purpose for living, and hope for renewed life with him and others.

> **When have you had to make a choice that meant changing the way you acted or thought about someone or something?**

> **What are some things about Jesus that surprise or challenge you?**

NAME

Imagine you are living in the time of Jesus. Name three reasons why Jesus would choose you to follow him. What would you do if he invited you?

_____

_____

_____

_____

_____

_____

_____

_____

A Community of Believers

How did the Apostles and their successors lead?

After the disciples had been with him awhile, Jesus gave the Twelve a mission, sending them out two by two. We read in Mark 6:7–13 that they were to announce the coming of the Kingdom of God and were even given the authority to cure some of the sick people they met as they traveled. We also read in Mark 6:7–13 that the Twelve disciples had some important instructions from Jesus. He told them:

- bring no money or food
- do not pack a bag or bring extra clothes
- find a home to stay where the people welcome you
- leave a town that does not welcome you, and shake the dust of that town from your shoes

Jesus wanted his disciples to have total dependence upon God the Father to take care of them. He wanted them to travel light.

> **What do you think this message means for us today?**

We Receive Guidance

We know Jesus had many followers. But Jesus chose twelve men to be his **Apostles** and to share in his work and mission in a special way. The Twelve were Jesus' closest followers. The Apostles continued Jesus' ministry after his Ascension to Heaven.

The night before he died, Jesus said to the Apostles at the Last Supper: "The Advocate, the holy Spirit that the Father will send in my name—he will teach you everything and remind you of all that [I] told you" (**John 14:26**).

Since then and to this day the **Church** has been built on the faith and foundation of the Apostles. This is what we mean when

Go to the Source
You can find the names of the Twelve Apostles in Matthew 10:1–4, Mark 3:13–19, and Luke 6:12–16. For more information, see page 364 in your book.

we say the Church is apostolic. One of the four Marks of the Church—the essential characteristics that distinguish Christ's Church and her mission—is that she is **apostolic**.

The work the Apostles began has been continued down through the ages. The teachings they received from Jesus and his Holy Spirit have been handed on through them to us in the Church today.

How do we know what the Church teaches? How does she hand down the teachings of Christ to everyone? Here is a list of places where Church teaching is found, including **doctrine**, encyclicals and other documents of the Church.

Catholic Faith Words

Apostles the twelve men Jesus chose to be his closest followers and to share in his work and mission in a special way

Church the community of all baptized people who believe in the Holy Trinity and follow Jesus. The word is often used for the Catholic Church because we trace our origins back to the Apostles.

apostolic a Mark of the Church. The Church is apostolic because her teaching authority comes directly from Jesus and his chosen Apostles, handed down through the bishops of the Church, who are direct successors of the Apostles.

doctrine official Church teachings on matters of faith and morals. Catholics are obliged to believe these truths.

MATCH

Match the source of Church teachings with its description.

Where to Find Church Teachings

Sacred Scripture ●	● Records all of the meetings of the Pope and bishops to explain and make decisions abwout the Church
Church Council documents ●	● Presentation of the laws of the Church
The *Catechism of the Catholic Church* ●	● The Old and New Testaments of the Bible
The *Code of Canon Law* ●	● Teachings written by the Pope for all Catholics
Papal encyclicals ●	● Contains the doctrines of the Church
Pastoral Letters ●	● Teachings written by bishops for the Catholics in their dioceses

Archbishop Timothy Dolan debuts his series on SIRIUS XM Radio

Disciples in the Church Today

What does it mean to be a disciple in the Church right here and now?

We have the Church to guide us in all parts of our lives and in everything we do. The Church shows us how to live as Jesus lived. His life and his teachings are light showing us the way to Heaven.

Scripture

Jesus spoke to them again, saying, "I am the light of the world. Whoever follows me will not walk in darkness, but will have the light of life." **John 8:12**

We never have to find our way through life alone. In the Church, we belong to a family of faith, a community of disciples who are following Jesus together. We turn to other Church members for support, guidance, and encouragement. We ask God's forgiveness through the Church. We join with others to help people who are in need. Together we can feed the hungry, shelter the homeless, clothe the naked, visit the sick, and try to change laws and policies that do not protect life and promote human dignity. No one could do as much alone as we can all do together.

A Praying Community

The Holy Spirit also teaches us to pray as disciples of Jesus. We pray alone, and we pray together with the Church in communal prayer and worship. Whether we are praying prayers of blessing, petition, intercession, thanksgiving, or praise and adoration, it is the Holy Spirit who inspires us and calls us to pray.

The most important way we pray together is the celebration of the Eucharist. We are worshipping God together and we are receiving the Body and Blood of Christ.

As we grow in our faith, we learn new ways of prayer. Different ways of praying and living as a disciple, known as spiritualities, have developed over the centuries. In our two thousand years as a Church, many great Saints have guided others in ways of prayer.

There are several "schools" of prayer and Christian spirituality. They are all part of the Church's living Tradition of prayer, and although they are very different, they all come from the Holy Spirit.

When we come together for Mass, we are praying the Church's central and most important prayer.

Schools of Prayer

○ **Spiritual direction:** learning alone from a guide

○ **Prayer groups:** learning to pray with others; Church ministers leading and teaching liturgical prayer

○ **Catechesis:** learning about prayer through classes and ministry involvement; consecrated religious teaching contemplative (wordless) prayer

Place a check mark next to the "schools" of prayer you have already experienced. Name someone who taught you to pray in this way.

＊

IDENTIFY

Look at the "schools" of prayer listed. Choose one of the schools you have not yet experienced, then identify some people you think would be able to teach you how to pray in these ways, and how they could do so.

_____

_____

_____

_____

_____

_____

_____

_____

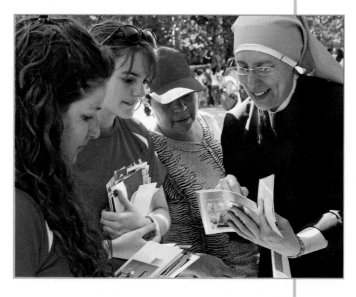

IN SUMMARY   Catholics Believe

We are disciples of Christ in his Church, following his example by trusting in the Father, learning, praying, and reaching out to others.

• Each follower of Christ receives a personal call from him and must choose whether or not to follow Christ.

• Just as Jesus sent the first disciples out, he wants us to be a sign of the Kingdom of God, and to follow Church teachings.

• The Holy Spirit uses many different spiritualties and "schools" of prayer to teach us how to pray.

Disciples in Community   **179**

Our Catholic Life

Prayer connects us with God's love and his plan for us. You may already know about finding a place to pray so you can better speak to and listen to God, but have you thought about finding a quiet prayer space inside yourself? In this chapter, you read about **schools of prayer** and considered ones you have and have not experienced. Contemplative prayer is a special form that establishes a deep connection with God. It is intense and silent, and grows through love and adoration of God's goodness. Choose a time to explore this form of prayer and listen for what God has to tell you.

> How is the experience of contemplative prayer different from other types of prayer?

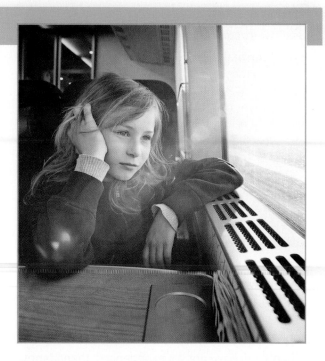

People of Faith

Saint Théodore (Anne-Thérèse Guérin), 1798–1856

After Anne-Thérèse Guérin took her final vows to become a nun, she and other sisters established the Academy of St. Mary-of-the-Woods at Terre Haute, Indiana, the first Catholic women's liberal arts college in the United States. During her nearly sixteen years of ministry in Indiana, Mother Théodore encountered countless hardships, but her faith did not waver. She told the sisters, "With Jesus, what shall we have to fear?" Mother Théodore was canonized by Pope Benedict XVI in 2006. The Church celebrates her feast day on **October 3**.

For more, go to
aliveinchrist.osv.com

LIST

Write down the name of someone you personally know who is a true follower of Jesus. Why did you think of this person? List the qualities of a disciple that you see in this person.

Name

_____

_____

Qualities

_____

_____

_____

_____

_____

_____

_____

♥ Litany of the Saints

Leader: Let us take time to pray to the Saints for their guidance.

Begin with the Sign of the Cross.

Saint Thérèse of Lisieux, you relied on God, not possessions, and knew the comforting embrace of God.

All: Saint Thérèse, pray for us.

Leader: Saint Elizabeth Ann Seton, you suffered many losses and felt the comforting embrace of God.

All: Saint Elizabeth Ann, pray for us.

Leader: Saint Francis de Sales, you treated yourself and others with patience and gentleness.

All: Saint Francis, pray for us.

Leader: Saint Thomas of Villanova, you showed freedom to many slaves and care for many orphans.

All: Saint Thomas, pray for us.

Leader: Saint Genevieve, you showed mercy to prisoners and others in need.

All: Saint Genevieve, pray for us.

Leader: Saint Clare of Assisi, you lived a simple and humble life.

All: Saint Clare, pray for us.

Leader: Saint Francis of Assisi, you sought peace during the Crusades.

All: Saint Francis, pray for us.

Leader: Saint Paul Miki, you preached the Word of God and died on a cross.

All: Saint Paul, pray for us.

Leader: In this great community of the Saints, we find strength and inspiration to seek and to do God's will.

All: Amen.

 Sing or play "Litany"

Go to **aliveinchrist.osv.com** for an interactive review.

A Work with Words **Circle the letter of the choice that best completes the sentence.**

1. The ____ continued Jesus' ministry after his Ascension to Heaven.
   a. Apostles
   b. Samaritans
   c. Jews
   d. Pharisees

2. ____ is the official teaching of the Church that all Catholics are obliged to believe.
   a. Papal Encyclicals
   b. Catechism
   c. Scriptures
   d. Doctrine

3. Ways of praying and living as a disciple are called ____.
   a. spiritualities
   b. church teachings
   c. doctrines
   d. Papal law

4. The ____ are the essential characteristics that distinguish Christ's Church and her mission.
   a. Prayers of the Church
   b. Precepts of the Church
   c. Marks of the Church
   d. Laws of the Church

B Check Understanding **Complete each sentence with the correct terms from the Word Bank.**

Apostles	Pentecost
Old Testament	Last Supper
Church	disciples
Saint John the Baptist	sacramental seal
	apostolic

5. _____ prepared for the coming of the Messiah.

6. The _____ is the community of the baptized who believe in the Holy Trinity and follow Jesus.

7. Jesus called twelve men to be his _____ and to share in his mission and work in a special way.

8. The Church is _____ because her teaching authority comes directly from Jesus and his chosen Apostles and is handed down through the bishops of the Church, who are direct successors of the Apostles.

9. Jesus promised the Holy Spirit to the Apostles at the _____.

10. The _____ of Jesus are those who believe in him, follow his teachings, and put them into practice.

C Make Connections **On a separate sheet of paper, write a one-paragraph response to the question. How is celebrating the Eucharist the most important way we pray?**

Christ Present Among Us

♡ Let Us Pray

Leader: O God of every good gift, help us to love your people by sharing our gifts with each other.

"How good and how pleasant it is,
when brothers dwell together as one!" **Psalm 133:1**

All: Lord, you are the God of all unity.

📖 Scripture

"As a body is one though it has many parts, and all the parts of the body, though many, are one body, so also Christ. For in one Spirit we were all baptized into one body, whether Jews or Greeks, slaves or free persons, and we were all given to drink of one Spirit.

Now the body is not a single part, but many. If a foot should say, 'Because I am not a hand I do not belong to the body,' it does not for this reason belong any less to the body. Or if an ear should say, 'Because I am not an eye I do not belong to the body,' it does not for this reason belong any less to the body. If the whole body were an eye, where would the hearing be? If the whole body were hearing, where would the sense of smell be? But as it is, God placed the parts, each one of them, in the body as he intended."

1 Corinthians 12:12–18

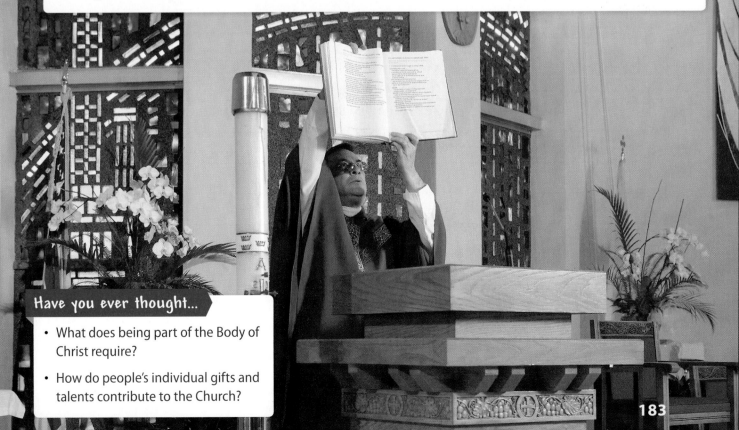

Have you ever thought...

- What does being part of the Body of Christ require?

- How do people's individual gifts and talents contribute to the Church?

Getting Started

In this chapter you will gain a deeper understanding of the Church as the Body of Christ, made up of a diversity of members united by the Holy Spirit. You will also consider how individuals' gifts and talents contribute to the whole Church.

In the web below, name different gifts and talents our Church needs in order to continue Jesus' work.

Gifts and Talents

Needs and Gifts What are three gifts or talents you have? Write about them on the lines below. Then describe how you can use one of your gifts to help meet the needs of another person—such as a family member, friend, classmate, or neighbor—or to help your parish or school.

- _____

_____

_____

_____

- _____

_____

_____

_____

- _____

_____

_____

_____

The Church Is the Body of Christ

How are all the different members of the Church united in one Body?

People gather into groups for many other reasons, but friendship is often the result. It could be that a group forms because there is a job that needs to be done. Sometimes a group forms because of common interests or problems. Some groups become known and visible to others.

Visible and Spiritual

Like Jesus, the Church he founded—our Catholic Church—is both human and divine. The Church is both visible and spiritual. For Jesus told us, "For where two or three are gathered together in my name, there I am in the midst of them" (**Matthew 18:20**).

Visible The word *church* means a "gathering" or an "assembly." Jesus has gathered all who believe in him into a visible group with leaders and members. In our visible gathering as the Church we are the People of God.

Spiritual In Christ we become more than just a visible assembly of people. In the Eucharist Jesus feeds us his own Body, and we become his Body. As a spiritual group, the Church is called the **Mystical Body of Christ**, for Christ is present among us, and through the Church, people come in contact with Christ.

The Church brings us in touch with the sacred, but she is made up of human beings, with all our imperfections and potential.

It is easier to understand the visible part of the Church. You can see how people gather in buildings for worship, for education, and for service. And you can see how the Church is organized into a **hierarchy**, with levels of leadership and membership.

However, the visible part of the Church is not enough. Without the spiritual part, the Church would be like any other organization. Our spiritual part is Christ's presence among us through the power of the Holy Spirit.

> **When are some times people gather together in Jesus' name?**

> **How do you think Jesus makes his presence known among them?**

Catholic Faith Words

Mystical Body of Christ a name for the Church, whose baptized members are all united to Christ and one another through the Holy Spirit, forming one holy people with Christ as her head

hierarchy the organization of the Church into different levels of leadership and membership

One in Christ

Jesus died, but he rose again to new life. Now, through the Holy Spirit, and through his actions in the Eucharist and the other Sacraments, Jesus establishes the Church as his own Body. Christ is the Head of this Body. The Church lives from him, in him, and for him; Christ lives with and in the Church. Here is how Saint Paul, who was also called "Saul," found out that Jesus considers the Church his Body.

Students from LaSalle Catholic High School in Miami celebrate with the late Archbishop Agustin Roman at his street naming ceremony in 2011.

📖 Scripture

"Now Saul, still breathing murderous threats against the disciples of the Lord . . . on his journey . . . a light from the sky suddenly flashed around him. He fell to the ground and heard a voice saying to him, 'Saul, Saul, why are you persecuting me?' He asked, 'Who are you, sir?' The reply came, 'I am Jesus, whom you are persecuting.'"
Acts 9:1–5

📖 Go to the Source

Read 1 Corinthians 12:12–31. What is most comforting to you in this passage? Most challenging?

EXPLAIN

Give some examples of how the Church is both visible and spiritual. Then in small groups make a list of how the Church is visible and spiritual in your school.

_____

_____

_____

_____

_____

_____

_____

_____

_____

Paul realized that he was persecuting Jesus himself by persecuting the Church. In letters he wrote to various groups of early Christians in Ephesus, Rome, Corinth, and Colossae, Saint Paul mentions often that we (the Church) are "One in Christ," or that we are "His Body": "For as in one body we have many parts, and all the parts do not have the same function, so we, though many, are one body in Christ" (**Romans 12:4–5**).

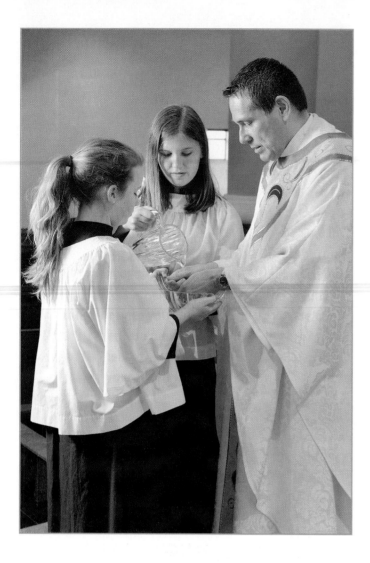

Scripture

[Jesus] said, "Just as a branch cannot bear fruit on its own unless it remains on the vine, so neither can you unless you remain in me. I am the vine, you are the branches. Whoever remains in me and I in him will bear much fruit, because without me you can do nothing."

John 15:4–5

All Parts of the Body of Christ Work Together

There is no use being part of a group if we do not work together with the other members of the group. When even one member of the Church does not participate with the rest of the Church, we are all affected. And when even one member remains faithful and bears the fruit of good works, the whole Church is also affected. All over the world today, the Church is bearing good fruit. The many parts are all connected in Christ. The reception of Holy Communion strengthens the union we have with Christ and others in the Church— locally, nationally, and worldwide. The Eucharist therefore is a sign and a source of our unity.

> **How do you participate in the Church right now? What can you do to improve the role you have?**

Catholic Faith Words

one a Mark of the Church. The Church is one because the power of the Holy Spirit unites all the members through one faith and one Baptism.

One Body, Many Members

What are some signs of our unity as the Body of Christ?

The Church is a body of many members, and each individual is important to the working of the whole Body. Each of us is needed, and we don't lose our individuality as part of the whole. And each member also needs to remain part of the Church and faithful to her mission. We are one Church united in Jesus. Being **one** is another Mark of the Church. The Gospel according to John tells us that Jesus explained it this way at the Last Supper.

Catholics represent many cultures and countries. Still, all Catholics are one. Look at the pictures. List the types of differences and similarities you see.

Differences

1. _____

2. _____

3. _____

4. _____

Similarities

1. _____

2. _____

3. _____

4. _____

Imagine speaking with a member of one of the Catholic Churches in the pictures about what you have in common, and what things about you are different. What would you want to tell this person? Write a few ideas on the lines below.

_____

_____

_____

_____

_____

_____

_____

_____

_____

_____

_____

Ontario, Canada

Réunion Island

Kerala, India

Many Gifts for the Good of All

How are each person's gifts and talents important to the whole Church?

God gave each individual person different gifts. If we were all good at the same things, we would probably all be bad at the same things, too. Some things would not be done well, or at all.

Often people use their gifts to compete with each other. But God did not give us gifts just for competition. As the Church, he wants us to share our gifts to bring Christ to others and to share the message of his Good News with the world.

Because of this diversity, the Church is able to help God build his Kingdom in many ways. The gifts of every member are needed.

In his letter to the Ephesians, Saint Paul tells us that the gifts God gave to his People were "some as apostles, others as prophets, others as evangelists, others as pastors and teachers"

(Ephesians 4:11). God still gives those gifts in the Church today.

> **What would your parish or the whole Church be like without the gifts of all her different people?**

For Those Who Are in Need

Jesus tells a story about the Last Judgment to teach us that we will be judged by how we show our love in the ways we help him. In his story, the people are surprised to hear Jesus say that they are going to be rewarded for helping him on Earth. They wondered when they had helped him. ". . . whatever you did for one of these least brothers of mine, you did for me" (Matthew 25:40). He goes into more detail:

✝ Scripture

I was hungry and you gave me food.
I was thirsty and you gave me drink.
I was a stranger and you welcomed me.
I was naked and you clothed me.
I was in prison and you visited me.
I was ill and you cared for me.

Based on Matthew 25:35–36

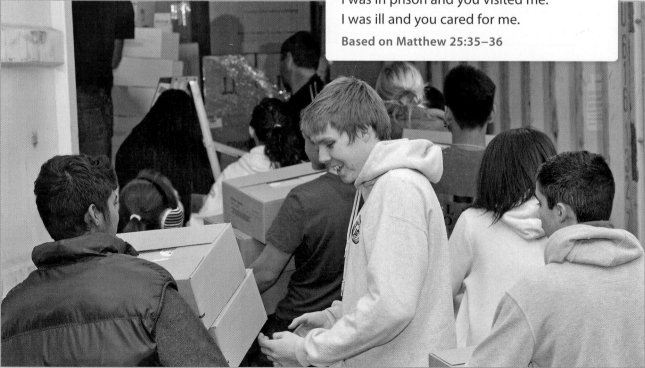

Maybe it was because there were so many different kinds of people and occupations in Ephesus that Saint Paul wrote to the Church there about different gifts. Ephesus was a big, important seaport of ancient Greece, in an area that is now western Turkey. Travelers to Turkey today can see the ruins of the ancient city, including those of the Basilica of St. John, which was built over the alleged burial site of Saint John the Apostle. Travelers can also visit a museum, and a Church shrine to honor Mary.

For more, go to **aliveinchrist.osv.com**

Because we are members of the Body of Christ, everyone in the Church is linked to everyone else, especially to people who are suffering, poor, and persecuted. In these people we can most closely see Jesus, who suffered and died for us. When we reach out to help others who are in need, we are doing what Jesus did and what he told us to do.

You might recognize Jesus' words as the Church's Corporal Works of Mercy, actions that care for the physical needs of people. The complete list adds another work, burying the dead.

LIST

Find a copy of your parish bulletin and identify some of the ways that Church members are using their gifts to be a sign of God's Kingdom and to care for those who are in great need. List some of the ways below, and place a check mark beside two ways you can contribute your own gifts to these efforts.

_____

_____

_____

IN SUMMARY Catholics Believe

The Church is both visible and spiritual, made up of people with many gifts and talents who are united by Christ in the Holy Spirit to continue Christ's mission in the world.

- We call the spiritual part of the Church the Mystical Body of Christ. Jesus is the Head of his Body, the Church.

- Each individual member is united with all members as part of Christ's Body; we need one another and Christ to bear fruit in the world.

- The Church needs the diverse gifts of all members to be a sign of God's Kingdom.

Our Catholic Life

Sharing your gifts and talents is one of the easiest ways to feel part of your parish and school community. As a young person, you can use your **personal gifts** to form friendships, help or mentor younger children, assist in the liturgy by reading, singing, or being an altar server at Mass, or performing some of the Corporal or Spiritual Works of Mercy. But you may wonder about what gifts you have to share. Ask your friends and an adult at your parish or in your school about what they see as some of your gifts, and then think about how you could share them in your community. If you're still not sure about your own gifts or what use they could be, pray to God for guidance. The Church needs the gifts of all her members—including you—to continue Christ's work in the world.

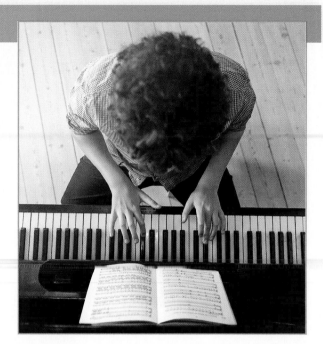

> What is one gift you can share in your community this week?

People of Faith

Saint John Bosco, 1815–1888

At the age of nine, John Bosco of Turin, Italy, began having dreams that would reveal God's plan for his life. John knew that his life's work would be to help troubled children to become more Christ-like. As a priest, he ministered to poor and neglected boys, taking them to Mass, and founded the Salesian Society, which opened homes for young boys to be educated and train for the priesthood. The Church celebrates his feast day on **January 31.**

For more, go to
aliveinchrist.osv.com

IDENTIFY

Explore the hymnbook your parish uses to celebrate liturgies. Make a list of hymns that mention the Body of Christ, our oneness in Christ, our giving of our personal gifts, or our outreach to those in need.

_____

_____

_____

_____

_____

_____

_____

_____

♥ Celebration of the Word

Leader: Let us pray.

O God, of every good gift,

we praise you and we thank you for this time of prayer,

this time of quiet, this time to ask ourselves the question,

"What are the gifts you have given me?"

Reader 1: A reading from the Letter of Paul to the Corinthians.

Read 1 Corinthians 12:4–11.

The word of the Lord.

All: Thanks be to God.

Reader 2: Open our hearts to receive and understand.

Open our minds to trust in your plan.

Open our hands to take hold of all you give us.

Open our lives to share what you offer.

Reader 3: Let us pray to the God who gives us what we need.

Pray aloud your intercessions, one by one.

After each, respond:

All: Lord, hear our prayer.

Leader: Help us see how we all fit together, how each of us offers a different piece, a different gift to strengthen the whole.

Teach us to know the Holy Spirit is with us, guiding us and giving us courage and wisdom.

Help us recognize our gifts and use them with care.

All: Amen.

▶ *Sing or play "Alive in One Spirit"*

Go to **aliveinchrist.osv.com** for an interactive review.

A Work with Words **Complete each sentence.**

1. The word _____
   means a gathering or assembly.

2. As we gather as the Church, we are the
   _____.

3. As a spiritual group, the Church is called the
   _____.

4. The Church is organized into a(n)
   _____ with different
   levels of leadership and membership.

5. The Church is _____
   because the power of the Holy Spirit unites
   all the members through one faith and one
   Baptism.

B Check Understanding **Indicate whether the following statements are true or false. Then rewrite false statements to make them true.**

6. Through the Holy Spirit, Baptism, and the
   Eucharist, Jesus forms the Church as his
   Body. **True/False**

   _____

   _____

7. Jesus taught his disciples that they were the
   roots and he was the branches. **True/False**

   _____

   _____

8. The Church is both invisible and spiritual.
   True/False

   _____

   _____

9. Everyone in the Church is responsible to care
   for those in need. **True/False**

   _____

   _____

10. Jesus taught that people would be rewarded
    at the Assumption for the ways they helped
    him on Earth. **True/False**

    _____

    _____

C Make Connections **Write a one-paragraph response to the question below. What do we need to do so that our efforts "bear fruit" as Jesus instructed?**

_____

_____

_____

_____

_____

_____

_____

_____

_____

_____

_____

_____

_____

CHAPTER 12

Source of Life

♥ Let Us Pray

Leader: God of peace and justice, you call us to be your holy people. May the Holy Spirit open our hearts and minds to you today and throughout our lives. May we be your witnesses to the ends of the Earth!

"Blessed are those who dwell in your house!
They never cease to praise you." **Psalm 84:5**

All: Help us continue your saving work, O Lord.
Hear our prayer.

📖 Scripture

When the time for Pentecost was fulfilled, they were all in one place together. And suddenly there came from the sky a noise like a strong driving wind, and it filled the entire house in which they were. Then there appeared to them tongues as of fire, which parted and came to rest on each one of them. And they were filled with the holy Spirit and began to speak in different tongues, as the Spirit enabled them to proclaim.

Now there were devout Jews from every nation under heaven staying in Jerusalem. At this sound, they gathered in a large crowd, but they were confused because each one heard them speaking in his own language. They were astounded, and in amazement they asked, "Are not all these people who are speaking Galileans?"
Acts 2:1–7

Have you ever thought...

- How does the Holy Spirit strengthen the Church to spread the Good News of salvation?

- How much does faith have to do with everyday life?

Getting Started

In this chapter you will learn about the need for faith and Baptism, and the ways the Church helps us restore our friendship with God. The Church keeps us close to God, showing us how to pray and helping us open our minds and hearts to God.

In the web below, name ways that the Church brings people close to God, and how she is a sign of God's grace to the world.

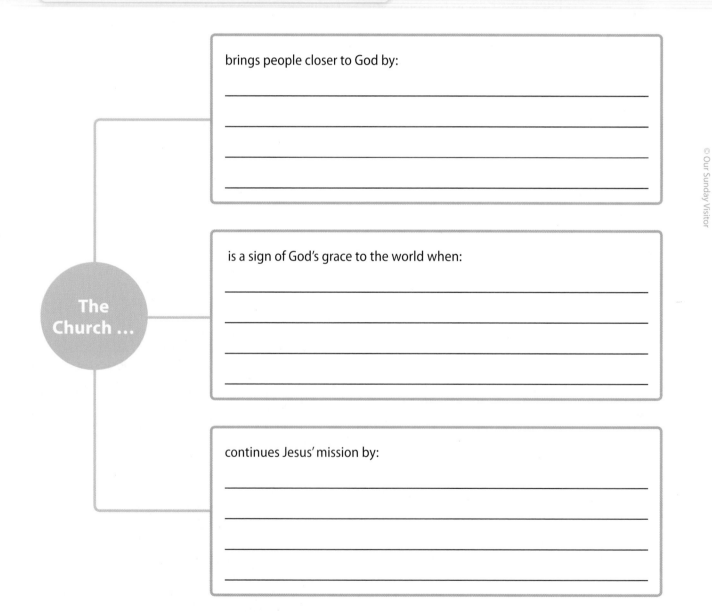

The Church ...

brings people closer to God by:

_____

_____

_____

_____

is a sign of God's grace to the world when:

_____

_____

_____

_____

continues Jesus' mission by:

_____

_____

_____

_____

Live the Good News List five things that your school does to continue
Jesus' work. It could be things within the school or for others in the community.

1. _____

   _____

2. _____

   _____

3. _____

   _____

4. _____

   _____

5. _____

   _____

Then describe how you are or can be involved in one or more.

_____

_____

_____

_____

_____

_____

_____

_____

_____

_____

_____

_____

That All May Have Life

Why does the Church continue Jesus' saving work?

We are made in God's image. And God created us to be with him—completely happy and whole. But, he wanted us to choose to be in relationship with him. So he also created us with **free will**, the ability to act freely in making choices. Because humans are free to choose, and because each person is born with Original Sin, they sometimes choose hurtful, sinful actions. But God can help us learn to use free will to choose what is good. Free will is one of God's greatest gifts to us, but it is very easy to misuse it.

After Jesus died, Saint Paul wrote to the Corinthians about the salvation God offered us through Jesus: "God was reconciling the world to himself in Christ" (2 Corinthians 5:19). If we accept Jesus Christ as our Savior, and

have faith in him, we will be reconciled, or restored, in our relationship with God. But it is our free will to choose. And not everyone accepts Jesus as his or her Lord, not even those who believe in God. Until they do, the world will not be in full communion with God.

> When have you used your free will to decide to do something good?

> When has it been hard for you to choose good instead of evil?

Faith and Baptism

Jesus is the only one who can save us from our sins. When he returned to be with his Father in glory, he left on Earth his Body, the Church, to continue bringing people hope, new life, and salvation. The Second Vatican Council explains that, "all salvation comes from Christ the Head through the Church which is his Body." The Council based this statement on Sacred Scripture and

Sacred Tradition. Christ is the one Mediator who can bring us to salvation. He is present in the world now in his Body, the Church.

We cannot be restored to the right relationship with God without faith. Jesus said, "Whoever believes and is baptized will be saved; whoever does not believe will be condemned" (Mark 16:16). We can see that faith is not enough. We need to be baptized into new life in Christ. We receive **Baptism** in and through the Church, so again we see that the Church is needed for salvation.

But what about those who have never heard of Christ and his Church? Living a good life and following his or her conscience can still save a person who, through no fault of their own, has not heard of Jesus and the Church. And Jesus is still bringing such a person new life. The same is true for those preparing to become Catholic, but who for some reason are not baptized before they die. Some

people die for the faith even though they are not baptized, and they, too, can be saved.

We might also wonder about children who have died without Baptism. It is best for babies to be baptized, but if they die before they are baptized, we can trust our loving God to have mercy on them and save them. That is what we pray for all unbaptized infants and children.

> **What else do we need besides our faith?**

Catholic Faith Words

free will the God-given freedom and ability to make choices. God created us with free will so we can have the freedom to choose good.

Baptism the Sacrament in which a person is immersed in water or has water poured on him or her. Baptism takes away Original Sin and all personal sin, and makes a person a child of God and member of the Church.

NAME

Imagine you have just been asked by an exchange student at your school who is a Hindu to explain what Catholics believe. Name the five most important things you would say about your faith.

_____

_____

_____

_____

_____

_____

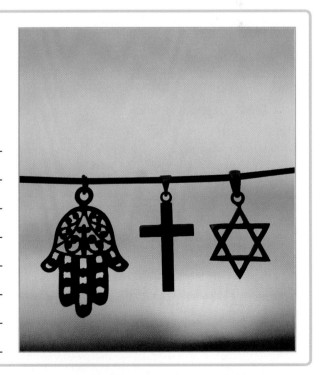

Communion with God

How does the Catholic Church help people be close to God?

The Church is the Sacrament, or sign, of our salvation. She is also the way of getting to know God, or having communion with him. We are in communion with God when we are members of the Church. Only through the Church do we receive the Eucharist, which deepens our union with Christ. The Eucharist is Christ's sacrifice on the Cross. The Eucharistic sacrifice is offered to make reparation for people's sins and to gain both material and spiritual gifts from God.

We celebrate the Holy Trinity, the mystery of one God in three Divine Persons: Father, Son, and Holy Spirit. We celebrate that mystery through, with, and in Christ. We are drawn to God the Father through the Son's sacrifice and the Holy Spirit's action.

On our own we could never even imagine being this close to God. The Holy Spirit

Catholic Faith Words

eternal life life forever with God for all who die in his friendship

catholic a Mark of the Church. The Church is catholic because she is universal, meant for all people in all times and in all places.

brings about this communion between God and all of us in the Church. Jesus has poured out his Holy Spirit on all the members of the Church. This Spirit builds the Church, brings her to life, and makes her holy.

The Church's Treasury

We have a "treasury" in the Church—not a collection of money, but a spiritual treasury of all the holiness and goodness from Jesus, and from the prayers and good works of Mary and all the Saints. There is "an abundant exchange of all good things" among the Saints in Heaven, the souls in Purgatory, and all of us on Earth (CCC, 1475).[1] Jesus gave the Church the authority over this spiritual treasury.

The forgiveness of sins removes eternal punishment, but it is still necessary to be purified, either on Earth or in Purgatory, of the unhealthy attachment of sin. This purification frees us from the temporal punishment of sin. The Church has the power to grant indulgences based on this spiritual treasury. Indulgences, such as particular prayers or actions, allow faithful Catholics who have met certain requirements to avoid some of the temporal punishment that is the consequence of our sin. We can obtain indulgences for ourselves and for souls waiting in Purgatory. This helps us work toward the salvation and **eternal life** that God offers all who respond to his grace.

Pope Francis meets with Hispanic community and immigrants in Philadelphia, PA.

Missionary Church

Another Mark of the Church is that she is **catholic**, or universal. Jesus did not found his Church to exist in only one time or place. He sent her out to all nations to preach the Gospel to everyone. She is the universal Sacrament of salvation.

Scripture

"Go, therefore, and make disciples of all nations, baptizing them in the name of the Father, and of the Son, and of the holy Spirit, teaching them to observe all that I have commanded you. And behold, I am with you always, until the end of the age."

Matthew 28:19–20

Salvation is not meant for just a select few people. God wants everyone to come to him because he loves all human beings. The Church believes in God's universal plan of goodness, salvation, and redemption, so she has to be a missionary Church.

Salvation is found in the truth. Even before people know about Jesus and his Church, or come to faith in God, they are drawn to seek the truth. They have begun to move toward salvation without even knowing it. They are following the promptings of the Holy Spirit.

God has entrusted the truth about himself to the Church. While people are searching, she goes out to bring them the truth.

> Where do missionaries work in the Church today?

> What are some things they do to help bring the truth and Good News about Jesus to people?

IDENTIFY

List some ways that you are close to God. Then think of who or what helps you to be close to him. How can you help others realize that God wants to be close to them?

1. _____

2. _____

The Church Prays

Why is prayer an important part of the Church's life?

We cannot give ourselves a share in God's life. Salvation is a gift from God, not something we can either cause or earn. God uses the Church to give us the hope of life forever with him.

But we do not have to wait until we are in Heaven to be united with God. We can already be in communion with him while on Earth. In the Lord's Prayer, Jesus taught us to say: "your kingdom come, your will be done, on earth as in heaven" (**Matthew 6:10**).

The Lord's Prayer brings us into communion with God the Father, and his Son, Jesus. When we pray it, it is a bit like holding up a mirror—the Lord's Prayer shows us who we are as children of God and members of his Church.

God tirelessly calls each of us individually to meet him and live in his love. He never stops loving individuals and wanting each one to be in communion with him. Salvation history also tells how God has repeatedly called out to individual human beings and how they have answered his call in the quiet of their own hearts.

It is not always easy to pray, so people might be tempted to stop or even to skip praying. We can get distracted while we are praying, but God wants us to stay in prayer even when we are distracted. With practice, we can send distractions out of our minds and pay more attention to God.

Sometimes good feelings come to us in prayer, but not always. Sometimes people feel nothing while they pray, unsure if they are really praying. We don't need to have special feelings when we pray. All we need to have is faith. God will speak to us and listen to us if we remain faithful to have a time of prayer.

> When do you like to pray alone?

> How can you find a certain time of day or a certain place that is best for you?

© Our Sunday Visitor

Go to the Source

Read *Matthew 6:9–13*. What do you think the world would be like if all humans truly desired what we ask for in this prayer?

The Church's Forms of Prayer

In a prayer of **blessing and adoration**, we acknowledge our dependence upon God and respond to his goodness with joy and gratitude.

_____

_____

Prayers of **petition** ask God for something specific, turning to him for help with things we need, such as forgiveness or guidance.

_____

_____

Prayers of **intercession** are requests made on behalf of someone else. For example, you might ask God to bring healing to someone who is ill.

_____

_____

In prayers of **thanksgiving**, we acknowledge God as our Creator and thank him for his goodness. We can also offer prayers of thanksgiving for specific gifts God has given us.

_____

_____

Prayers of **praise** give God honor and glory not for what he does, but simply for who he is.

_____

_____

Write examples of each kind of prayer on the lines below.

DISCUSS

Think about the following questions and discuss your answers with a partner. When do you pray best? What are some things that make it hard for you to pray? What forms of prayer do you find yourself praying most often? How do you feel after you have prayed?

IN SUMMARY Catholics Believe

The Church has a mission to bring all people to believe in God and to be baptized.

- Faith and Baptism are necessary for the freedom and new life that come from salvation.

- The Church is both a sign and instrument of the communion between God and his

People; it is through her actions that people can come to know God and share in his life.

- We must have a personal relationship with God nourished by prayer in order to answer our call to bring his love and truth to others.

Our Catholic Life

The Catholic Church encourages bishops, priests, and others to share her message in many ways. In the United States, most parishes and dioceses have websites that share information with God's People. Blogs, podcasts, and other **forms of social media** can play a positive role in teaching and informing Catholics. In 2013, millions around the world waited for news of the Papal Conclave that elected Pope Francis, and social networks were quick to share his first messages to the faithful. Pope Francis soon counted millions among his followers on social media sites. No matter how the message of the Church is sent out to the world, it is important to present it faithfully.

> How would you present the Church's message through social media?

People of Faith

Saint Lorenzo Ruiz, c. 1600–1637

Saint Lorenzo Ruiz of the Philippines served as an altar boy and later was a helper and clerk-sacristan in his parish Church. In 1636, he was accused of a serious crime. While proclaiming his innocence, he fled to Okinawa, Japan. The Japanese rulers didn't like the Christians. Lorenzo and his companions were taken to Nagasaki and given the choice of renouncing their faith or being executed. All six were tortured, but they refused to deny Christ. In 1981, Pope Saint John Paul II beatified Lorenzo Ruiz along with other Philippine and Japanese martyrs. All were canonized six years later. The Church celebrates Saint Lorenzo's feast day on **September 28**.

For more, go to
aliveinchrist.osv.com

TEXT

You have just been appointed the person in charge for sending out text messages from your parish Church this week. These messages need to tell people about the work that the Church is doing to serve others. Research seven different things you could text for seven days. Remember each message can only be 140 characters!

_____
_____
_____
_____
_____
_____
_____
_____
_____

_____
_____

❤ A Prayer for Peace

Leader: Lord Jesus, Saint Francis of Assisi was just a young man when he responded to a call to become your great instrument. Although we are young, help us to see how we too can be instruments of your peace. Let us pray:

Lord, make me an instrument of your peace.

Where there is hatred, let me sow love;

All: God, help me to sow the seeds of love by…

Leader: where there is injury, pardon;

All: God, help me to sow the seeds of pardon by…

Leader: where there is doubt, faith;

All: Jesus, you understood that even good people have doubts about you. Help me to encourage the growth of faith by…

Leader: where there is despair, hope;

All: God and Father, I am growing up in a world where many people have lost hope. Help me to be instrumental in planting seeds of hope by…

Leader: where there is darkness, light;

All: Jesus, you are "the Light of the World." Give me the courage to reflect your light by…

Leader: and where there is sadness, joy.

All: Jesus, you knew all the joys of life and wanted to share them. Show me how to be your joyful witness by…

All: O Divine Master, grant that I may not so much seek to be consoled as to console; to be understood as to understand; to be loved as to love.

For it is in giving that we receive; it is in pardoning that we are pardoned; and it is in dying that we are born to eternal life. Amen.

Leader: Let's sing the Prayer of Saint Francis together.

▶ *Sing or play "Make Me A Channel"*

Go to **aliveinchrist.osv.com** for an interactive review.

A   Work with Words   Circle the letter of the choice that best completes the sentence.

1. God created human beings with ___, the freedom and ability to make choices.
   - **a.** free will
   - **b.** open will
   - **c.** good will
   - **d.** free choice

2. Along with faith, ___ is necessary for salvation.
   - **a.** Free will
   - **b.** Baptism
   - **c.** Reason
   - **d.** Penance

3. The Church is ___ because she is universal, meant for all people in all times and places.
   - **a.** holy
   - **b.** temporal
   - **c.** apostolic
   - **d.** catholic

4. The Church has a spiritual ___ of all the holiness and goodness from Jesus, and from the prayers and good works of Mary and all the Saints.
   - **a.** inheritance
   - **b.** treasury
   - **c.** library
   - **d.** account

5. When waiting in the state of Purgatory, the soul suffers ___ punishment for sin.
   - **a.** final
   - **b.** earthly
   - **c.** eternal
   - **d.** temporal

B   Check Understanding   Indicate whether the following statements are true or false. Then rewrite false statements to make them true.

6. The Church is a sign or Sacrament of John. **True/False**

   _____

   _____

7. For the world to be in communion with God, all people must have received Communion. **True/False**

   _____

   _____

8. The Lord's Prayer brings us into communion with God the Father and his Son, Jesus. **True/False**

   _____

   _____

9. The Eucharist makes present on the altar Christ's sacrifice on the Cross offered to make reparation for people's sins. **True/False**

   _____

   _____

10. Prayers of petition are prayers that thank God for specific gifts. **True/False**

    _____

    _____

C   Make Connections   On a separate sheet of paper, write a one-paragraph response to the questions. How does the missionary Church bring people into communion with God? How does the prayerful Church do so?

© Our Sunday Visitor

A Work with Words Match the words on the left with the correct definitions or descriptions on the right.

____ **1.** doctrine

____ **2.** indulgences

____ **3.** spiritualities

____ **4.** temporal punishment

____ **5.** Apostles

____ **6.** hierarchy

____ **7.** spiritual treasury

____ **8.** People of God

____ **9.** encyclicals

____ **10.** schools

____ **11.** Church

____ **12.** Mystical Body of Christ

a. ways of praying and living as a disciple

b. image for the Church; first used to refer to God's Chosen People in the Old Testament

c. the purification of a sinner, here on Earth or in Purgatory due because of forgiven sins or the attachment to sin

d. levels of leadership and membership in the Church

e. official Church teachings we are obliged to believe

f. the holiness of Jesus and the good works of Mary and the Saints accounted to the Church

g. the twelve men Jesus chose to be his closest followers and to share in his work and mission in a special way

h. release from some of the punishment for sin

i. a name for the Church, whose baptized members are all united to Christ and one another through the Holy Spirit, forming one holy people with Christ as her head

j. word meaning a gathering or assembly

k. different ways to pray

l. letters written by the Pope to the Church community

MORALITY

Why are practicing the virtues and developing a well-formed conscience necessary?

CHURCH HISTORY TIMELINE

34	Death of Stephen, first Christian martyr
81	Domitian persecution begins
1870	First Ecumenical Vatican Council clarifies papal infallibility
1962	Second Ecumenical Vatican Council convenes

Go to page 348 for more

Our Catholic Tradition

- God made us with a free will, an intellect, and a soul, and we are responsible for our choices. A well-formed conscience—and the help of Christ's teachings, the Church, the Holy Spirit, prayer, and wise people—will guide us to do what is right and good. (CCC, 1711, 1783)

- All human life is sacred and a gift from God. All people possess the human dignity that comes from being made in God's image. We have a responsibility to honor and protect life at all stages, from conception to old age. (CCC, 2319)

- Virtues are good spiritual habits that strengthen us and help us make good moral decisions and guide our conduct. The Theological Virtues make the moral (human) virtues possible. (CCC, 1803)

Our Catholic Life

- Morally good actions require that their object, intention, and circumstance be good; the end does not justify the means. (CCC, 1750–1756)

- We respect the dignity of the human person by respecting the rights of others, taking care of ourselves physically and emotionally, not abusing ourselves or others, and by not leading others into sin. (CCC, 2288–2290)

- The Cardinal Virtues of prudence, justice, fortitude, and temperance can help us respect ourselves and others and act with integrity. Learning about and practicing the virtues can help us live truthful, faith-filled lives. (CCC, 1804–1809)

CHAPTER 13

Freedom and Responsibility

💜 Let Us Pray

Leader: Wondrous God, you have given us the awesome gift of freedom. With that gift comes the responsibility to make choices that show our love for you, each other, and ourselves.

"What is man that you are mindful of him,
   and a son of man that you care for him?
Yet you have made him little less than a god,
   crowned him with glory and honor." **Psalm 8:5–6**

All: Jesus, we want to do what is right. Show us. Teach us. Be with us as we discover how to love you well.

📖 Scripture

"God in the beginning created human beings
   and made them subject to their own free choice.
If you choose, you can keep the commandments;
   loyalty is doing the will of God.
Set before you are fire and water;
   to whatever you choose, stretch out your hand.
Before everyone are life and death,
   whichever they choose shall be given them."
The Wisdom of Ben Sira (Sirach) 15:14–17

Have you ever thought...

- Why did God create us with the freedom to choose?

- How are freedom and responsibility connected?

Getting Started

In this chapter you will gain a deeper understanding of human free will and responsibility for choices and actions, and explore how you can make morally good decisions. You will also learn about forming and informing your conscience.

Catholic Faith Words

- soul
- intellect
- conscience
- mortal sin
- venial sin

In the chart below, record synonyms for "freedom" and "responsibility." With the class, discuss the connection between the two words.

Freedom and Responsibility

Synonyms for Freedom	_____ _____ _____ _____ _____ _____ _____ _____
Synonyms for Responsibility	_____ _____ _____ _____ _____ _____ _____ _____

Everyone's Doing It! Imagine a situation where someone your age is feeling pressured to do something wrong that the group they are hanging out with is about to do. On the lines below, describe that situation.

_____

_____

_____

_____

_____

_____

_____

_____

_____

_____

What might be going through the person's head as he or she decides whether or not to participate?

_____

_____

_____

_____

_____

_____

_____

_____

_____

_____

_____

Living is Thinking and Doing

How can you make good choices?

Every day, you are faced with choices that require decisions. Some decisions seem more important than others, and you might not know how to make the more difficult ones. Just remember, you've been given some important tools to help you.

Scripture

"Do to others whatever you would have them do to you. This is the law and the prophets." Matthew 7:12

Your Decisions

Sometimes other people make decisions for you because they have authority over you. But all those decisions that you make freely are your own responsibility. Something that you decide to do (or not to do) is a decision that belongs to you alone and no one else.

Why is this important? You are not morally responsible for decisions that you have not voluntarily made. Your intentional thoughts, decisions, and actions are yours. Morally, you are responsible for your freely-made decisions, and the action or inaction that comes from them.

Made to Choose

You have the ability to choose to act in a variety of ways. Why? Because God made humans unique from all other creatures.

You have a **soul**—the spiritual part of you that lives forever; **intellect**—that which makes it possible for you to think, reason, and judge; and free will—the God-given freedom and ability to make choices on your own without being forced to choose or act in a certain way. This unique combination makes you an image of God. You are created with the tremendous ability to seek what is good and true, and therefore reach happiness with God in Heaven.

God gives you another important gift to help you make decisions: your **conscience**. Your conscience is like an inner voice, part of your ability to reason, that helps you to judge whether actions are right or wrong.

Conscience is what moves you to know and follow the moral law, to do good and avoid what is evil. It is important for us to know God's laws so our conscience can help us make good decisions. You are called by God to develop an informed conscience.

Choices That Lead You from God

Listening to your conscience leads you along the path that keeps you in the right relationship with God and away from sin—any deliberate thought, word, or action that goes against moral law and offends God. Sin is a deliberate choice to disobey God. It's not a mistake or an accident.

Catholic Faith Words

soul the spiritual principle of a human person that is individual, created by God, and will exist forever

intellect the God-given ability which makes it possible for humans to think, reason, and judge

conscience the God-given ability that helps individuals judge whether actions are right or wrong

mortal sin a grave (very serious) sin by which someone turns completely away from God and breaks his or her relationship with God

venial sin a sin that weakens, but does not destroy, a person's relationship with God

There are two types of personal sins for which someone is responsible. **Mortal sin** breaks a person's relationship with God. The effect of mortal sin, without repenting and being forgiven, is total separation from God forever. For a sin to be mortal, three conditions must be met:

- the matter involved must be very serious;
- the person must know the action is serious and sinful (called sufficient reflection); and
- the person freely chooses or agrees to commit the wrong anyway (full consent of the will to do what is wrong).

The Commandments specify gravely serious matter. But not all sins are gravely damaging or mortal. Less serious sin, called **venial sin**, weakens a person's relationship with God, but does not destroy it. Venial sins lessen the love of God in your heart and make it more difficult for you to resist sin. Venial sins arise from not using moderation or acting without full knowledge, and can sometimes lead to mortal sin.

NAME AND DISCUSS

Name three things someone might do to become more aware of his or her conscience.

1. _____

2. _____

3. _____

How would someone know if his/her conscience has been well formed? Discuss your answers with a classmate.

_____

_____

The Sources of Action

What determines whether an action is good?

How do you know if what you are doing is morally right? Three things determine the morality of a human action:

- the object, which characterizes the action in and of itself.
- the intention, which is the immediate end or purpose the person intends to achieve through the action.
- the circumstances, which surround the action.

"A morally good act requires the goodness of the object, of the end, and of the circumstances together . . . One may not do evil so that good may result from it" (see the *Catechism*, 1755–1756).

Consider this situation: Your older brother is driving Grandma to the doctor using Dad's car with his permission. The *object* of this action is to drive his grandmother to the doctor.

A bike rider loses control and swerves in front of the car. Your brother makes a snap decision and turns the steering wheel, causing the car to jump the curb. There are no pedestrians at the curbside. The object of his action and his intention are to avoid hitting the biker. Your brother's *intention* is not to break the rules of the road or to put pedestrians in danger, but to avoid hitting and hurting the bike rider.

The *circumstances* are that no pedestrians are at or near the curb and that your brother only drove on the curb long enough to avoid the biker. In this case, the immediate object of the brother's action was to avoid the biker. This too was his intention.

The circumstances permitted him to do this without hurting anyone else. Even though he technically violated the law by going off the road, the immediate object of his action was to avoid hitting the biker. The object, intention, and circumstances were good. His was a morally good act.

Go to the Source
Read Matthew 6:2–4 to find out more of what Jesus had to say about good deeds.

When making a choice, you have to consider all three elements: what is the action or object itself; why are you doing it, or not doing it; and what are the pressures, environment, or issues surrounding it that might be affecting your judgment.

> **Why is the brother's action described earlier as a morally good act?**

Consider This

A good intention—such as wanting to help your sister—does not make an object or behavior that is morally wrong—such as lying to your parents—good. A bad intention—such as the desire to boast—can make an object or behavior that is good—such as donating money or time to a worthy cause—morally bad. As Jesus said, "[But] take care not to perform righteous deeds in order that people might see them" (**Matthew 6:1**).

Saint Thomas Aquinas argued that whether an act is good or evil depends on the end result of that action. Human acts are good if they promote the purpose and honor of God. Aquinas taught that by repeating a good action, people develop a moral habit, which allows them to do good easily. He wrote, "An evil action cannot be justified by reference to a good intention." Today we say, "The end does not justify the means." In an extreme example of this belief, if asked what to do in a situation where killing one person would save one hundred other lives, a Catholic person's answer is that murder is wrong no matter how many lives it saves.

The circumstances of an action can increase or decrease the moral goodness of the action. Factors such as fear, ignorance, and pressure are some examples. But circumstances cannot change whether an act is morally good or not, only the degree of its goodness or evilness. Some acts, such as murder, are always wrong no matter the intention or the circumstances because choosing them entails so great an evil that they are against the natural moral law.

THINK AND WRITE

Think about a moral decision you are currently dealing with, or have dealt with recently. Write about the act, the intention, the circumstances, and what your conscience tells you.

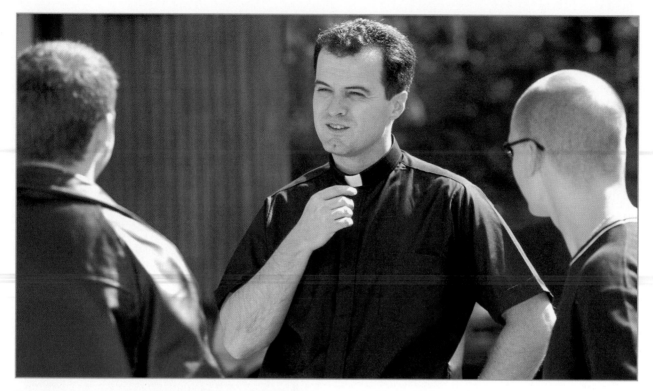

"Listen to counsel and receive instruction, that you may eventually become wise" (Proverbs 19:20).

Formation for Doing Right

How can a well-formed conscience help you?

Athletes know that if a person wants to build up his or her body, he or she has to work at it. He or she has to establish a routine involving exercise and the right food.

Building and shaping a conscience is similar. If you want to make good decisions through life and do the right things, then forming a conscience is critical. If a conscience has been formed well, it will lead you to what is truthful and just. It will help you make sound, rational judgments and follow what is good.

When you have a moral decision to make, your conscience will move you to make a right (morally good) judgment that follows reason and God's law. Or it can lead you to make an incorrect (morally bad) judgment that does not follow reason and God's law.

Conscience Formation

Someone who wants to become a better pianist will seek out a teacher who can introduce skills and guide the student to feel the music as they play. The person will spend a lot of time practicing, and accepting the fact that their development will be ongoing; if you don't use the skills, you'll lose them. The same holds true with building up your conscience. There are a few important ways to do this:

- **Scripture:** What does the Bible tell you?
- **Church teaching:** What does the Church say about it?
- **Getting advice:** Ask for input from family members or trusted adults, study the facts of the situation, and look at the standards of society (e.g., is the action legal?).

> **How can taking one or more of these steps help you?**

When you use these resources to inform your conscience and find that there is a conflict between some of these sources, rely on the wisdom found in Sacred Scripture and the teachings of the Church in Sacred Tradition.

Vices and Virtues

You've probably heard that practice makes perfect, but have you ever thought of it in the reverse? What happens when you keep repeating the same negative, sinful behavior over and over? You create in yourself a vice, a habit or tendency to be more sinful. The Church uses the term *vices* to refer to the seven capital sins that tend to produce other sinful behavior. Vices incline us to actions that are harmful to ourselves and to others. Traditionally, the Church has identified seven capital sins or vices: pride, covetousness, envy, anger, gluttony, lust, and sloth or laziness.

Fortunately the Cardinal Virtues of prudence, justice, fortitude, and temperance are good habits within us that, when strengthened and practiced, help us counter these vices in our daily lives. Virtues help us respond consistently to the situations we face, guiding us to make morally good decisions. The more we intentionally practice the virtues, the more we can rely on them to guide us.

Underline which step you tend to rely on most when making a moral decision. Circle one that you could do more often.

Steps in Making a Moral Decision

Think	Take time to consider your options and the possible consequences to yourself, others, and your relationship with God. Take time to hear what your conscience might be saying.
Compare	How do your options compare to Jesus' Beatitudes, his New Commandment, the Ten Commandments, and Church teachings? If an option contradicts any of these, then it's not really an option anymore.
Talk	Find someone who can understand the situation you are in. Tell him or her what you are thinking and why. Ask for advice.
Pray	Turn to the Holy Spirit in prayer, asking for guidance to make the right decision.
Act	Make your choice and be confident that you have made the right one based upon your conscience.

IN SUMMARY Catholics Believe

We are free to choose, responsible for our choices, and guided in our moral decision-making.

- God made us with a free will, an intellect, and a soul. Our conscience works with these gifts so that we can choose to do good and avoid sin.

- Morally good actions require that their object, intention, and circumstance be good; the end does not justify the means.

- A well-formed conscience will guide us to do what is right and good, and with the help of Christ's teachings, the Church, the Holy Spirit, prayer, and wise people, we can make good decisions.

Our Catholic Life

Your conscience is meant to be maintained and used to guide you in doing what is right and good. You can **inform and strengthen your conscience** by listening with your heart and mind to the Word of God, the teachings of the Church, and the prompting of the Holy Spirit. You can also seek guidance from parents, teachers, and mentors when making big and small choices. You can practice informing your conscience by ending each day with a prayer and an examination of conscience like the one on the next page to think about how you might have helped or hurt others that day, and how you might do more or better the next day.

> What is on your mind that an examination of conscience might help or make clear?

People of Faith

Blessed Aloysius Stepinac, 1898–1960

Aloysius Stepinac was ordained as a priest after World War I, and eventually was appointed Archbishop of Zagreb. During World War II, he raised his voice against the Nazi tyranny. After that war, during the pro-communist regime of Marshal Tito, Stepinac was imprisoned. He was released after five years on the orders of Tito, who wished to meet him. At their meeting, Stepinac told Tito, "I am for the freedom of the people and accordingly I will raise my voice against you every time you should encroach on this freedom." The Church celebrates his feast day on **February 10**.

For more, go to
aliveinchrist.osv.com

PRACTICE

Choose a tough issue you are dealing with in your life and practice informing your conscience by consulting these four resources.

What does God tell you in the Bible?

What does the Church teach?

What do respected and wise figures in your life say?

What are your community's laws and values?

_____

_____

_____

_____

_____

_____

♥ Examination of Conscience

Leader: Jesus, we know that you came into the world to cast out the darkness of sin, ignorance, and death. You are the Light of the World. As your followers, show us how to reflect your light. Let us take a moment to reflect on the times we have not been a sign of your light in the world, and ask the Lord for his mercy and his forgiveness.

Reader 1: Did I take God's name in vain? Did I curse or use bad language?

Reader 2: Did I miss Mass on a Sunday or Holy Day of Obligation without any serious reason?

Reader 3: Did I obey my parents, teachers, or trusted adults?

Reader 1: Was I selfish in how I treated others?

Reader 2: When have I forgiven others? When have I refused to forgive?

Reader 3: Did I look at indecent pictures or videos?

Reader 1: Did I steal or damage another's property?

Reader 2: Did I tell lies?

Reader 3: When have I stopped people from gossip? Did I gossip or make fun of someone through my words, texts, or social media?

Leader: Let us now pray the Act of Contrition as a way to show that we are truly sorry for our failings.

All: My God,
I am sorry for my sins with all my heart.
In choosing to do wrong
and failing to do good,
I have sinned against you
whom I should love above all things.
I firmly intend, with your help,
to do penance,
to sin no more,
and to avoid whatever leads me to sin.
Our Savior Jesus Christ
suffered and died for us.
In his name, my God, have mercy.
Amen.

Rite of Penance

Leader: Lord, teach us to be persistent, to be strong, and to be courageous. Nourish in us a practical desire to build up rather than tear down; to reconcile instead of polarize. Send your Holy Spirit to enlighten us and show us the way.

All: Amen.

 Sing or play "Be Merciful, O Lord"

Go to **aliveinchrist.osv.com** for an interactive review.

A **Work with Words** **Complete each sentence with the correct term from the Word Bank.**

soul	free will
moral law	intention
conscience	circumstances
sin	intellect

1. _____ is a God-given ability that helps you judge whether something is right or wrong.

2. Conscience moves you to know and follow the _____, which directs us to do good and avoid evil.

3. _____ is any deliberate thought, word, action, or omission that goes against moral law and offends God.

4. Every human action is composed of three elements—the object, the _____, and the circumstances.

5. The _____ of an action can increase or decrease the moral goodness of the action.

B **Check Understanding** **Circle the letter of the choice that best completes the sentence.**

6. Your ____ is the spiritual principle in humans that is created by God and exists forever.
   a. intellect   c. soul
   b. free will   d. conscience

7. Your ____ is the God-given ability to think, reason, and judge.
   a. intellect   c. soul
   b. free will   d. conscience

8. The effect of ____, without repenting and being forgiven, is separation from God forever.
   a. venial sin   c. free will
   b. mortal sin   d. moral law

9. ____ weakens, but does not destroy, a person's relationship with God.
   a. Venial sin   c. Free will
   b. Mortal sin   d. Moral law

10. If a(n) ____ has been formed well, it will lead you to what is truthful and just.
   a. intellect   c. free will
   b. conscience   d. soul

C **Make Connections** **Write a one-paragraph response to the question. What types of decisions are people your age currently facing? Write about the process of making a moral decision using the steps *think, compare, talk, pray,* and *act.***

_____

_____

_____

_____

_____

_____

_____

_____

Respecting Life

♥ Let Us Pray

Leader: God of all life, we thank and praise you for the many gifts you have given us. Your care and love for us goes deeper than the human mind can comprehend. Even before we came to be you have loved us. May we choose life!

"Who is the man who delights in life,
who loves to see the good days?" **Psalm 34:13**

All: Lord, thank you for your blessings and the abundance you share with us.

⊕ Scripture

"I call heaven and earth today to witness against you: I have set before you life and death, the blessing and the curse. Choose life, then that you and your descendants may live, by loving the LORD, your God, obeying his voice, and holding fast to him. For that will mean life for you, a long life for you to live on the land which the LORD swore to your ancestors, to Abraham, Isaac, and Jacob, to give to them."
Deuteronomy 30:19–20

Have you ever thought...

- What does it mean to *always* choose life?

- What does it mean to respect and value *all* human life?

Getting Started

In this chapter, you will learn how the Fifth Commandment requires us to value and respect all life, which is sacred because all people have human dignity and worth. You will also explore the Church's teachings about protecting and honoring life at all stages.

Catholic Faith Words

- human dignity
- murder
- abortion
- euthanasia
- scandal

Use the chart below to show what you already know about the dignity and value of human life. First, in your own words describe what it means for all people to have human dignity and worth. Then list actions and attitudes that acknowledge, respect, and honor the dignity of others, and actions and attitudes that do not.

Dignity and Worth

What it Means

_____

_____

_____

_____

What Honors Life and Dignity?

_____

_____

_____

_____

What Does Not Honor Life and Dignity?

_____

_____

_____

_____

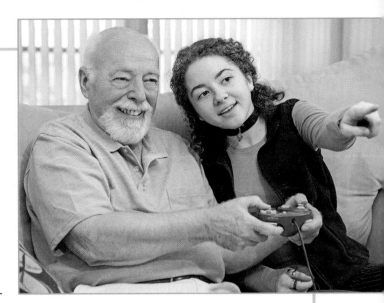

Stand in Another Person's Shoes Think about a person you know who, because of his or her life situation, faces challenges that are different from yours. Maybe this person is a neighbor who is elderly and homebound, or a classmate who has a learning disability. Perhaps this person is physically impaired or has a medical condition. Stand in the shoes of this person. List the challenges you might face.

_____

_____

_____

_____

_____

_____

_____

_____

_____

How can you "choose life" (**Deuteronomy 30:19**) by the way you treat others?

_____

_____

_____

_____

_____

_____

_____

_____

_____

_____

A Sacred Gift from God

Why does human life have value?

If we could choose how we look and what abilities we have, we might change some things. But it's not up to us to choose our challenges. We do not enter this world on our own. Each of us owes his or her life to God. So one life is not more valuable than another. We are all equally valuable because we are each made in God's image.

Human beings are so unique and beautifully made because God designed us. For this reason, the author of the psalm praises God:

Scripture

"You formed my inmost being;
  you knit me in my mother's womb.
I praise you, because I am wonderfully made."
Psalm 139:13–14

Go to the Source

Read *Psalm 139:13–20*. What does this song of praise tell you about your relationship to God—past, present, and future? What good can come from praising God for creating and knowing you?

Now, we really don't know what the man who wrote that psalm looked like or what his limitations were. But he praised God for the way he was made. He believed God had a plan for his life that he was made to fulfill.

Not only are we made by God, but of all the creatures, humans alone have the capacity for "self-awareness"—we know we are individuals, separate from the world around us. We are able to recognize God's presence and to freely choose to know, love, and serve him.

For these reasons, each human life has a sacred value from conception to death. This **human dignity** cannot be taken away or lessened by any condition or situation.

The Creation of Adam in stone, based on Michelangelo

Usefulness

We tend to get rid of things when they're not useful anymore. Usefulness determines their value to us. Human beings, however, are different. Our value is not determined by our usefulness. It comes from God, who made us and for whom we exist. We have that value when we are healthy or sick, young or old. Even when dying, our life has worth. When we die, our existence continues. We continue to fulfill our purpose with our Creator.

We who are sacred should not be discarded, judged useless, or killed. Those decisions are not ours to make. The Fifth Commandment instructs us not to kill another person. **Murder** is the deliberate killing of another person. It is always gravely sinful. It shows the contempt the murderer has for human dignity as well as for the holiness and goodness of God.

Sometimes life is so difficult that people don't feel valued or respected; they may feel helpless, and forget that life is a gift from God, who wants us to stick with this gift. Suicide is never an option because it goes against God's love and our hope, and it's forbidden by the Fifth Commandment. The *Catechism* tells us that suicide "unjustly breaks the ties of solidarity" with humanity (see CCC, 2281). But praying and asking for help is an option.

> **Why do you think some people have so little respect for human life?**

Catholic Faith Words

human dignity the worth each person has because he or she is made in the image of God

murder the deliberate killing of another person when the killing is not in self-defense. It is always gravely sinful.

LIST

Imagine God has asked you to take notes on the creation of human beings. Make a list of how we are different from the rest of creation.

Humans:

_____

_____

_____

_____

The Rest of Creation:

_____

_____

_____

_____

Go to the Source

Read more of the Sermon on the Mount from Matthew 5:38–48. What does Jesus teach about retaliation and loving your enemies?

Honoring Life

What does the Church teach about protecting life at all stages?

In the Sermon on the Mount, Jesus refers to the Fifth Commandment, which bans murder. He then widens the understanding to include anger and vengeance: "But I say to you, whoever is angry with his brother will be liable to judgment . . ." (Matthew 5:22).

Jesus understands human nature and speaks against destructive emotions that can lead to worse things. Anger, hatred, and vengeance tear peoples' lives apart. Jesus didn't preach one message and live another. His actions and behavior show that he lived in a way that valued life. He told the disciples, "But I say to you, offer no resistance to one who is evil. When someone strikes you on (your) right cheek, turn the other one to him as well" (Matthew 5:39).

When Jesus is arrested, he allows his enemies to lead him to an unjust trial and execution. He upholds and honors every human life to the point of not raising a hand against his oppressors or allowing his disciples to take up the sword against them.

The Church Follows Her Master

The Church has taken a stand on life issues, advocating for the rights of others. Over the centuries the Church has established hospitals; outreach organizations; and programs for the poor, immigrants, children, victims of domestic abuse, and others in need.

The Church also confronts today's culture. She gets the message out—through preaching, outreach, papal encyclicals, bishops' letters, media campaigns, and more—that each human life, from conception to natural death, is innately valuable and deserves respect.

Safeguarding Life

A human life still in the womb or a life that is no longer as strong as it once was is to be protected from direct harm.

Because of this teaching, **abortion**, the deliberate termination of a pregnancy by killing an unborn child, is a grave sin. The Church does not believe that human life begins at some arbitrary point later in a pregnancy. An embryo requires the same efforts of care as any human. Life is bestowed by God at conception. We are called to protect the life of the most vulnerable.

In the same way, our lives cannot be considered less valuable because we are older or sick. For this reason, **euthanasia**—the deliberate action or inaction that causes the death of someone who is sick, or dying, or has disabilities—is also a grave sin. We owe tender care to those who, at the end of their lives, are most fragile.

It follows from this principle that sometimes we must defend ourselves, or others, from a person or group of people causing harm. It is legitimate and necessary to defend the lives of others, and this is a serious duty for those who have responsibility for the lives of others.

The late Joseph Cardinal Bernardin, Archbishop of Chicago, described our Catholic beliefs and teachings as a "consistent ethic of life." Catholics should honor, respect, and defend all life. Bernardin taught that Catholics must be consistent in opposing abortion, the death penalty, war, the nuclear arms race, and anything that threatens life. Being consistent in our approach to the sacredness of human life makes the human family, and the Church, stronger.

> **Who helps you to respect the dignity and sacredness of life?**

Catholic Faith Words

abortion the deliberate termination of a pregnancy by killing an unborn child. It is a grave sin.

euthanasia the deliberate action or inaction which causes the death of someone who is sick, dying, or suffering because of disabilities or a debilitating condition. It is a grave sin.

IDENTIFY

Think about the different organizations or people that protect the right to life of people at different stages of life. On the lines below, name one way you can value and honor life at each stage. Then discuss with classmates two ways you can value and honor life, no matter the age.

Seniors _____

Infants _____

Adults _____

Adolescents _____

All ages _____

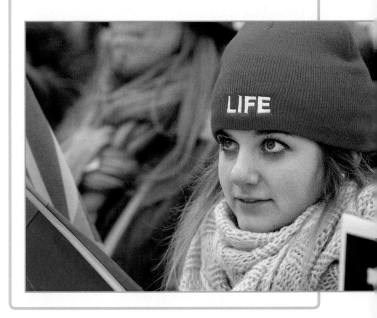

Respecting the Human Person

Why is it important to take care of ourselves and others?

Unkind words are hurtful. They can affect how people think and feel about themselves, and they don't have a positive purpose.

If words can be demeaning and cause damage, think about how much worse it is to allow harmful conditions to continue. Harmful conditions that deny people their rights exist all around us: people living in poverty with no means to change the situation, trapped in unsafe housing, or people who don't have access to an education, health care, or a job.

People need to be able to meet these basic rights in order to grow and mature. Without them, they are constantly using all of their energy merely to survive. They cannot flourish as God would want.

© Our Sunday Visitor

Catholic Faith Words

scandal the destructive behavior by which a person deliberately leads, through his or her own action or inaction, another person to sin

Raising Ourselves Up

A great piece of artwork is meant to be put on display so that everyone can appreciate it and be made better by it. We are God's work of art. The human person is the pinnacle of creation.

We honor the human person, so that all might appreciate and be made better by the creative work of God among us. We avoid all the things that damage the artistry of God at work in the human person, such as overindulgence, extremism, or physical and mental intimidation.

Things that Damage God's Artistry in You

abusing food, alcohol, tobacco, and drugs

sacrificing everything else for the sake of physical perfection

promoting success in school, popularity, and sports without considering those involved

bullying

sexual exploitation or manipulation of another person

pornography

kidnapping, hostage-taking, terrorism, and torture

Add two more examples to the list. *

_____

_____

Care for Others

Harsh words are not the only way people harm others. Another way is to encourage others to do sinful things. Jesus warns his disciples against leading others into sin. He says, "Whoever causes one of these little ones who believe in me to sin, it would be better for him to have a great millstone hung around his neck and to be drowned in the depths of the sea" (**Matthew 18:6**).

Scandal is the name given to the destructive behavior by which we deliberately lead others to sin through our own action or inaction. For example, the sin of scandal is committed when a radio talk show host rallies his listeners to engage in racism.

Those in authority have a greater responsibility to guard against scandal. Teachers and government and business leaders must exercise care for others by not misleading and manipulating them. The *Catechism* teaches that anyone who uses his or her power to lead others to scandal is "responsible for the evil that he has directly or indirectly encouraged" (CCC, 2287). This special responsibility also includes those who influence public opinion because these are areas of life that can promote or hinder how we perceive and care for one another.

© Our Sunday Visitor

IN SUMMARY | Catholics Believe

All human life is sacred and a gift from God.

- All people possess the human dignity that comes from being made in God's image, and we do not have the right to take that life away from others or ourselves.

- We have a responsibility to honor and protect life at all stages, from conception to old age to death.

- We respect the dignity of the human person by respecting the rights of others, taking care of ourselves physically and emotionally, not abusing ourselves or others, and by not leading others into sin.

Our Catholic Life

The Fifth Commandment tells us "you shall not kill." The Catholic Church has always been clear about protecting human life from the moment of conception to natural death. The Church also calls us to provide special protection to the unborn, who are among the most vulnerable and innocent. Through prayer and action, the Church calls governments to protect the **right to life** of all human beings, the unborn as well as the terminally ill and aged. She provides prayer, guidance, and many types of support to people facing challenges in these areas. The Church also protects those who are sick or have serious disabilities. Because God made each of us, the value and human dignity of every human life is an important teaching of the Catholic Church.

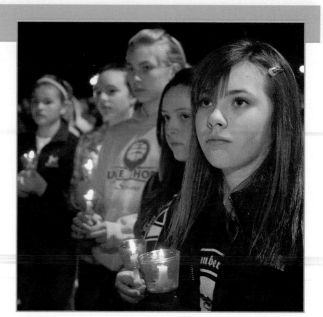

> **How do you show respect for human dignity in your life right now?**

People of Faith

Saint Martin de Tours, 316–397

Saint Martin joined the Roman army at age fifteen. One day while stationed in Gaul (now France), he gave half his cloak to a beggar. That night, Martin dreamed that he saw Jesus wearing half of his cloak. He heard Jesus say, "Here is Martin, the Roman soldier who is not baptized; he has clad me." Martin was baptized when he was 18. He traveled and preached throughout the country and was eventually named bishop of Tours. Saint Martin helped people understand true Christianity and not believe errors, called heresies. The Church celebrates his feast day on **November 11.**

For more, go to
aliveinchrist.osv.com

LIST

Make a list of movies, television shows, books, or songs that encourage respecting life.

_____

_____

_____

_____

_____

_____

_____

_____

As a class, discuss the items you have listed in common, and think about watching or reading some of your classmates' suggestions.

Prayer for Life

Leader: Father and Creator, you are the source of all life. You gave your son Jesus to redeem our fallen world and offer us new life on Earth and in Heaven. When your Angel Gabriel asked Mary of Nazareth to become the Mother of your Son, she graciously accepted. Not knowing what would come with this "Yes" to life, she trusted in you.

Thank you, Mary, the Blessed Mother of the world's Redeemer. Jesus told the world, "I came so that they might have life and have it more abundantly" (**John 10:10b**). Please guide us in honoring the gift of life. Give us courage, the courage of Pope Saint John Paul II, to defend the right to life for all.

All: [recite together slowly]: O Mary, bright dawn of the new world, Mother of the living, to you do we entrust the cause of life. Look down, O Mother, upon the vast numbers of babies not allowed to be born, of the poor whose lives are made difficult, of men and women who are victims of brutal violence, of the elderly and the sick killed by indifference or out of misguided mercy.

Grant that all who believe in Your Son may proclaim the Gospel of life with honesty and love to the people of our time. Obtain for them the grace to accept that Gospel as a gift ever new, the joy of celebrating it with gratitude throughout their lives and the courage to bear witness to it resolutely, in order to build, together with all people of good will, the civilization of truth and love, to the praise and glory of God, the Creator and lover of life.

Prayer of the Gospel of Life, by Pope Saint John Paul II

▶ *Sing or play "Lover of Life"*

📶 Go to **aliveinchrist.osv.com** for an interactive review.

A **Work with Words** Circle the letter of the choice that best completes the sentence.

1. Murder is always gravely sinful because it shows contempt for the ___ of human life as well as for the holiness and goodness of God, the Creator.
   a. dignity   c. love
   b. happiness   d. wonder

2. ___ is deliberately ending a pregnancy on purpose by killing an unborn child.
   a. Euthanasia   c. Suicide
   b. Genocide   d. Abortion

3. Deliberate action or inaction that causes the death of someone who is sick, or dying, or suffering because of disabilities is called ___.
   a. euthanasia   c. suicide
   b. genocide   d. abortion

4. Behavior or attitudes that leads others to sin are known as ___.
   a. disobedience   c. free will
   b. scandal   d. suicide

5. Because humans are made in the ___ and likeness of God, each human life is sacred.
   a. shadow   c. image
   b. mirror   d. awareness

6. The human person is the ___ of creation.
   a. zenith   c. image
   b. pinnacle   d. purpose

B **Check Understanding** Complete each sentence with the correct term from the Word Bank.

abortion	kill
overindulgence	sin
life	self-awareness
love	action
breath	covet

7. The Fifth Commandment instructs us not to _____ another person.

8. We avoid _____ and extremism because these actions can damage the artistry of God at work in the human person.

9. Jesus warns his disciples that it would be better to drown in the sea than to lead others into _____.

10. Not only are we made by God, but we humans alone, of all creatures, also have the capacity for _____.

C **Make Connections** On a separate sheet of paper, write a one-paragraph response to the following questions. Choose a current issue (local, national, or worldwide) in which human life is being valued, respected, or protected. Who are the people involved, and what impact are their actions having on others? How can this be an example of living out the Fifth Commandment?

Being Virtuous

♥ Let Us Pray

Leader: Holy God, you are the source of all faith, hope, and love. These are three gifts you give us so that we can be happy and holy. May your Spirit be our strength and our guide as we strive to love you completely in all we do and say.

"The LORD is just and loves just deeds; the upright will see his face." **Psalm 11:7**

All: Lord, we belong to you.

✝ Scripture

"Put on then, as God's chosen ones, holy and beloved, heartfelt compassion, kindness, humility, gentleness, and patience, bearing with one another and forgiving one another, if one has a grievance against another; as the Lord has forgiven you, so must you also do. And over all these put on love, that is, the bond of perfection. And let the peace of Christ control your hearts, the peace into which you were also called in one body. And be thankful."
Colossians 3:12–15

Have you ever thought...

- How do we "put on love"?
- How can the virtues help us become the people God created us to be?

Getting Started

In this chapter, you will study and identify virtues and understand the importance of becoming the person God has created you to be, by living the virtues in your daily life.

© Our Sunday Visitor

Catholic Faith Words

- virtue
- Theological Virtues
- Cardinal Virtues

In the space next to each symbol, explain why that symbol is used to represent that virtue. In the second chart, share something you know about each of the Cardinal Virtues.

The Theological Virtues

Virtue	Symbol	Explanation
Faith		
Hope		
Charity		

The Cardinal Virtues

Virtue	Description
Prudence	
Justice	
Temperance	
Fortitude	

Holy Habits Good habits are keys to excellence. For example, good study habits are keys to excellence in school and learning. Good eating and exercise habits are keys to excellence for our health.

What are your best habits? How do they help you be a better person?

_____

_____

_____

_____

_____

_____

_____

_____

_____

_____

Good habits are also keys to excellence in our spiritual lives. How do the habits you've identified help you be the person God made you to be?

_____

_____

_____

_____

_____

_____

_____

_____

_____

_____

_____

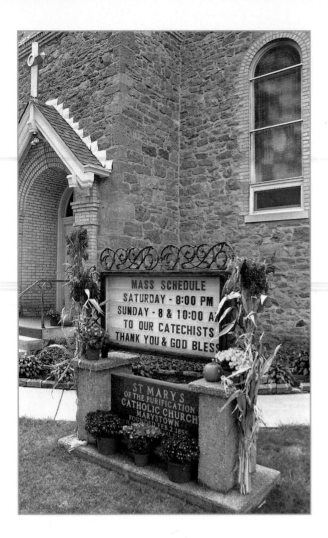

the way you typically relate to others; and how you learn from life experiences and from others.

These things together can be a powerful force to reach your ultimate goal: to be good and holy, to be loving and welcoming, to become more like God, and to one day be with him forever.

But what does being good and holy look like? Saint Paul tells us that we are to help one another strive for those things that are most worthwhile in life.

✝ Scripture

"Finally, brothers, whatever is true, whatever is honorable, whatever is just, whatever is pure, whatever is lovely, whatever is gracious, if there is any excellence and if there is anything worthy of praise, think about these things."
Philippians 4:8

✝ Go to the Source

Read *Philippians 4:13* and think about the ways God gives you the strength that you need, just as he gave it to Paul.

> **If Saint Paul were writing to you and your friends, how do you think he might word his message differently?**

Good and Holy

How do you grow to be the person God made you to be?

The freedom God gives us is meant to be used for doing good. Living a good life requires practice and self-discipline. The truth is, it's not always easy.

Our Truest and Best Selves

God shares his love completely with you. Your response should be just as strong and focused. By responding to his love, you can discover and strengthen your truest, best self.

Many things contribute to who you are and who you can become, such as your individual talents, gifts, and uniqueness;

Helping Habits

Saint Paul's list is pretty challenging. In specific situations, it is sometimes difficult to determine exactly what is true, honorable, and just. All kinds of positive and negative pressures and assumptions can be at play. Some situations require us to really think through how the final outcome will impact everyone.

The virtues help us do this. A **virtue** is a good spiritual habit that strengthens you and enables you to do what is right and good. Virtues develop over time with our practice and openness to God's grace. Virtues guide our conduct and emotions. Faith, hope, and charity (love) are the **Theological Virtues**. They are gifts from God that help us believe in him, trust in his plan for us, and love him as he loves us. We have to respond to God's gift and live out the virtues for them to be strong in our lives.

- **Faith** means believing in God and all that he has revealed to us and believing in all that the Church proposes for our belief.

- **Hope** is a desire, strengthened by trust in Jesus' promises, to do God's will, and achieve eternal life and the graces to make this desire come true.

- **Charity** means we love God above all else, and our neighbors as ourselves.

The Theological Virtues make the human, or moral, virtues possible. These virtues guide the way we act and feel. They help us live according to our conscience, control our passions, and deal with how we respect others and ourselves in light of our faith.

Moral virtues don't automatically appear within us. They grow when we learn about them and are intentional about practicing them, even in the face of struggles. God's grace helps us cultivate virtue. In this way, the virtues that we are growing get strong inside us.

Catholic Faith Words

virtue a good spiritual habit that strengthens you and enables you to do what is right and good

Theological Virtues gifts from God that help us believe in him, trust in his plan for us, and love him as he loves us; they are faith, hope, and charity

DEFINE AND DESCRIBE

Imagine you are writing a dictionary entry for the term virtuous. Write your entry here.
virtuous (adj.)

_____

_____

_____

_____

Now describe how a virtuous person would act. A virtuous person…

_____

_____

_____

_____

A Life of Virtue

Why should you try to live a life of virtue?

People have dreams for themselves and where they want their lives to go. Some people want to be explorers and travel to distant lands. Some people want to be great teachers, influencing others. Dreams are important. They fuel our lives. They provide the motivation for what we learn and how we grow.

Keys to Excellence

In a similar way, striving for excellence is fueled by virtues. They are powerful keys that help to open the doorway into a faithful, reasonable life of excellence. In that sense, they help us to follow the Ten Commandments, Jesus' Beatitudes, and his New Commandment to love one another as he has loved us.

There are some behaviors that do not build up excellence in our life. The Eighth Commandment has identified some that damage our character and integrity:

- **lying**: deliberately saying false things by which we intend to deceive others
- **slander or calumny**: false words or even attitudes that maliciously injure others
- **revenge**: words or actions that return injury to another whom we perceive as having harmed ourselves
- **not living up to our promises**: behavior that shows that we are not worthy of another's trust

These behaviors are sinful. They hurt the person doing them and others. They are signs that a person is not interested in pursuing what is good and beautiful in life.

These behaviors are opposite of the virtue of truth, by which a person shows that he or she is true and honest in words and actions. Truth helps people avoid being deceitful, hypocritical (saying one thing but doing another), or disguising their true intentions.

The Blessing of Children in the Church of the Saviour of Spilled Blood, St. Petersburg, Russia

A Challenge

Pursuing the good life by striving for excellence within ourselves and in our behavior does not necessarily mean that we will have it easy or that life will be comfortable. Just the opposite!

Because society does not always believe as Catholics do, you may end up frustrated that people don't get it. dYou may be tempted to "sit down and go with the flow." You may have to stand up for things or act in ways that your friends or acquaintances don't understand or agree with. Sometimes this will cost you. You may be laughed at or ignored because of it.

Does this sound like the life of someone you know and have learned about? Jesus faced all of these things, but we know that he was happy in the truest sense of the word. He is our model for living a life of excellence. Living a life of virtues brings true inner peace.

DISCUSS

Talk with a classmate about two of the four behaviors that do not build up excellence, listed on page 242. Think of examples of those behaviors and discuss how someone your age could stand up to or address this behavior.

IN SUMMARY Catholics Believe

We are called to strive for what is right, just, holy, and gracious.

- The virtues are good spiritual habits that strengthen us and help us make good moral decisions and guide our emotions and conduct. The Theological Virtues make the moral, or human, virtues possible.

- The Cardinal Virtues of prudence, justice, fortitude, and temperance can help us respect ourselves and others and act with integrity.

- Learning about and practicing the virtues can help us live truthful, faith-filled lives.

Our Catholic Life

The virtues are important habits that give us strength and make it easier for us to do the right things. You can learn more about **virtuous living** by studying Catholic teachings, Scriptures, and the lives of the Saints, and from the good examples of family members, leaders, mentors, and friends who exemplify virtuous living. Charity, or love— the Theological Virtue that directs us to love God above all things and our neighbor as ourselves— may be easiest to see in other people from day to day, but the virtues of faith and hope can be seen, too, sometimes when we least expect it. Make a commitment to practice more of the Virtues in a disciplined way for a period of time to help develop the "muscles" to make this virtue part of your life.

> How can you show the Theological Virtues to yourself and others this week?

People of Faith

Saint Margaret Ward, d. 1588

Father Watson was a priest imprisoned during a time when Catholics in England were persecuted. Margaret Ward, a Catholic, helped him escape by smuggling a rope into the prison, but she was arrested when authorities traced the rope back to her. Even under torture, she refused to tell where Watson was hidden. At her trial, she was told that if she asked for forgiveness and joined the Church of England, she would be pardoned. She refused, saying she had done nothing wrong and that it was against her conscience to join a Protestant church. The Church celebrates Saint Margaret's feast day on **August 30**.

For more, go to
aliveinchrist.osv.com

IDENTIFY

Examine the list of virtues and practices below. How well would you rate yourself (on a scale of 1 to 10) in practicing each virtue? Think about things you could do to become more virtuous.

Gratitude

Prudence

Fortitude

Truth

Abstinence

♥ Act of Hope and Love

Leader: God, come to my assistance.

All: Lord, make haste to help me.

Leader: Glory be to the Father
and to the Son, and to the Holy Spirit,

All: as it was in the beginning
is now, and ever shall be
world without end. Amen.

Leader: A reading from the Letter to the
Ephesians.

Read Ephesians 6:10–20.

Leader: The word of the Lord.

All: Thanks be to God.

Leader: God, source of our faith, hope,
and love,
give us the strength to be the people you
call us to be,
a witness and light for all to see.

All: O God, relying on your almighty
power and your endless mercy and promises,
we hope to gain pardon for our sins,
the help of your grace, and life everlasting,
through the saving actions of Jesus Christ,
our Lord and Redeemer.

O God, we love you above all things,
with our whole heart and soul,
because you are all good and worthy
of all love.
We love our neighbor as ourselves
for the love of you.
We forgive all who have injured us
and ask pardon of all whom we have injured.

O God, we love you because you are
supremely good and worth loving;
and because we love you,
We are sorry with all our hearts for
offending you.
Lord, have mercy on us sinners, Amen.

▶ *Sing or play "I Love You, Lord"*

Go to **aliveinchrist.osv.com** for an interactive review.

A Work with Words **Circle the letter of the choice that best completes the sentence.**

1. A ____ is a good spiritual habit that strengthens you and enables you to do what is right and good.
   a. virtue
   b. discipline
   c. Sacrament
   d. reparation

2. When we attempt to indirectly correct the damage done by sin, we are making amends or ____.
   a. forgiveness
   b. virtue
   c. reparation
   d. justice

3. The ____ Virtues are the four most important moral virtues.
   a. Theological
   b. Divine
   c. Lost
   d. Cardinal

4. The virtue of ____ helps us to dress, talk, and move in appropriate ways.
   a. modesty
   b. chastity
   c. prudence
   d. both a and c

5. The virtue of ____ helps us express sexuality in the right way for our state in life.
   a. modesty
   b. fortitude
   c. chastity
   d. prudence

B Check Understanding **Indicate whether the following statements are true or false. Then rewrite false statements to make them true.**

6. Theological Virtues help us live as children of God and gain life everlasting with God. **True/False**

   _____

   _____

7. Prudence, justice, fortitude, and charity are four of the most important moral virtues. **True/False**

   _____

   _____

8. Temperance is showing courage, having strength to get through difficult times, and not giving up. **True/False**

   _____

   _____

9. Your sexuality affects the way you think and feel about things and the way you are inclined to act. **True/False**

   _____

   _____

10. The Tenth Commandment identifies lying, slander, and revenge as sins that damage our character and integrity. **True/False**

    _____

    _____

C Make Connections **On a separate sheet of paper, write a one-paragraph response to the question: We should think about things that are true, honorable, just, and pure. Think about some movies, music, and magazines. How do they encourage virtue?**

A Work with Words **Use the clues below to complete the crossword puzzle.**

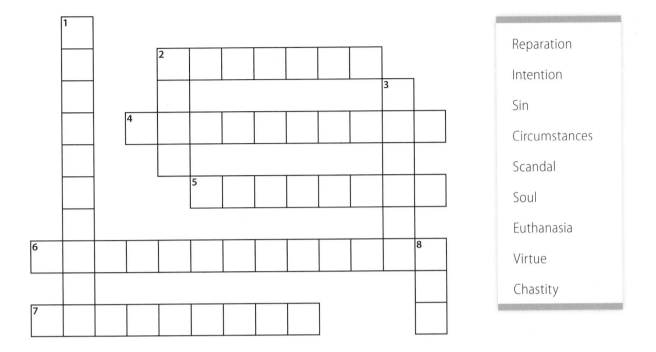

Reparation

Intention

Sin

Circumstances

Scandal

Soul

Euthanasia

Virtue

Chastity

Across

2. Destructive behavior by which we deliberately lead others to sin

4. Deliberate action or inaction that causes the death of someone who is sick, dying, or suffering

5. Virtue that helps you express sexuality and show love in the right way for your state of life

6. The aspect of human action that can increase or decrease its moral goodness

7. The object, the circumstances, and ____ are the elements included in human action.

Down

1. An attempt to indirectly correct the damage done by sin

2. Your unique combination of intellect, free will, and ____ make you an image of God.

3. A good spiritual habit that strengthens you and enables you to do what is right and good

8. Any deliberate thought, word, action, or omission that goes against moral law and offends God.

B **Check Understanding** **Fill in the correct term from the Word Bank to complete the sentences.**

Word Bank:
faith
prudence
human dignity
life
Cardinal
temperance
modesty
thought
Theological
fortitude

9. The _____ Virtues are the most important moral virtues.

10. The virtue of _____ is being discreet in the way you dress and the things you say.

11. Prudence, justice, fortitude, and _____ are four of the most important moral virtues.

12. _____ is showing courage, having strength to get through difficult times, and not giving up.

13. Each human _____ is sacred because humans are made in the image and likeness of God.

14. _____ is believing in God and all that he has revealed to us, and in all that the Church proposes for our belief.

15. The worth each person has because he or she is made in the image of God is called _____.

Indicate whether the following statements are true or false. Then rewrite false statements to make them true.

16. Your free will is the spiritual principle of a human person that is individual, created by God, and will exist forever. **True/False**

_____.

17. The effect of venial sin, without repenting and being forgiven, is total separation from God forever. **True/False**

_____.

18. If a conscience has been formed well, it will lead you to what is truthful and just. **True/False**

_____.

19. We humans, alone of all creatures, have the capacity for self-awareness. **True/False**

_____.

20. Mortal sin breaks a person's relationship with God **True/False**

_____.

C Make Connections **Write a short answer to these questions.**

21. Choose a television show or book whose characters struggle with Eighth Commandment issues. What are the issues, how do the characters choose to act, and what is the impact of their actions?

_____

_____

_____

_____

22. How do self-indulgence and extremism damage the artistry of God at work in the human person?

_____

_____

_____

23. Describe the five steps to making good moral decisions.

_____

_____

_____

_____

_____

24. All human life is sacred. What implications does this statement have for your relationships with others—friends, family, neighbors, and strangers?

_____

_____

_____

25. How is Jesus your model for living a life of excellence?

_____

_____

_____

SACRAMENTS

How do the Sacraments help us to encounter God's presence so to receive the grace to live as Christ's disciples?

CHURCH HISTORY TIMELINE

33 Holy Spirit empowers Apostles to baptize and preach at Pentecost

313 Edict of Milan establishes religious freedom for Christians

1215 Fourth Ecumenical Lateran Council ends

1992 Publication of the new *Catechism of the Catholic Church*

Go to page 348 for more

Our Catholic Tradition

- Christ is a Sacrament because he makes God known to us and makes it possible for us to share in God's life. The Church is a Sacrament because in her we come to know God and share in his life through the Sacraments, which Christ instituted and in which he is always present. (CCC, 775–776)

- As Christ first welcomed and fed his followers, we are welcomed and belong to the Church though the Sacraments of Initiation. (CCC, 1212)

- Jesus shows us that God is compassionate, always willing to forgive and care for those who turn to him and believe. God heals us spiritually, emotionally, and sometimes physically in the Sacraments of Healing. (CCC, 1421)

Our Catholic Life

- Christ instituted the Sacraments so that we would always know and experience his welcoming, forgiving, healing, and nourishing power. (CCC, 1114, 1210)

- In the Eucharist, the Sacrament that we celebrate regularly, we are fed with the Body and Blood of Christ and are brought closer to Christ and one another. (CCC, 1382, 1416)

- In the Sacrament of Penance and Reconciliation, those who are truly sorry for their sins receive God's forgiveness and are reconciled with him and the Church. (CCC, 1424)

CHAPTER 16

God's Masterworks

♥ Let Us Pray

Leader: Father of life, you sent your Son, Jesus, to us so that we could come to know you completely. Jesus' actions have the power to save us and bring us to you.

"You changed my mourning into dancing;
 you took off my sackcloth
 and clothed me with gladness. ...
O Lord, my God,
 forever will I give you thanks."   Psalm 30:12–13

All: Open our hearts to your grace.

📖 Scripture

"For this reason I kneel before the Father, from whom every family in heaven and on earth is named, that he may grant you in accord with the riches of his glory to be strengthened with power through his Spirit in the inner self, and that Christ may dwell in your hearts through faith; that you, rooted and grounded in love ... may be filled with all the fullness of God. Now to him who is able to accomplish far more than all we ask or imagine, by the power at work within us, to him be glory in the church and in Christ Jesus to all generations, forever and ever. Amen."

Ephesians 3:14–21

Have you ever thought...

- Why is it important for faith customs to be passed down through generations?

- Which Church traditions are especially meaningful to you?

Getting Started

In this chapter, you will gain an understanding of how the Holy Trinity is the source of the Sacraments, how Christ instituted each of the Sacraments, and how he is present today in their celebration.

Catholic Faith Words

- Seven Sacraments
- Sacraments of Initiation
- Sacraments of Healing
- Sacraments at the Service of Communion
- Real Presence

1. For each Sacrament identify the category (Sacraments of Initiation, Sacraments of Healing, or Sacraments at the Service of Communion) to which it belongs.

2. Then explain how each relates to its category title.

The Seven Sacraments		
Sacrament	**Category**	**How It Relates**
Baptism		
Confirmation		
Eucharist		
Penance and Reconciliation		
Anointing of the Sick		
Holy Orders		
Matrimony		

© Our Sunday Visitor

Meaningful Traditions How do you mark time, remember important events, celebrate special milestones? Of your traditions, which is your favorite? In the spaces provided, describe in words or symbols one or more of your favorite personal and/or family traditions and favorite Church traditions.

_____

_____

_____

_____

_____

Using two of the traditions you've identified (one personal and/or family tradition, and one Church tradition), explain what these traditions mean to you.

_____

_____

_____

_____

_____

_____

It All Starts with Jesus

How is Jesus the source of the Seven Sacraments?

The best traditions are always about the people who keep the traditions alive with us. If you ever made a card or present for your parents when you were a child, someone else probably provided the materials, cleaned up, and helped you wrap. This is similar to Christ's presence in his Church and our experience of grace, which is God's free, loving gift of his own life and help. We receive this gift of grace directly from God.

The Seven Sacraments

The Church celebrates seven "masterworks of God" (CCC, 1116): the **Seven Sacraments**. The Seven Sacraments are effective signs of God's grace instituted by Christ and given to his Church. In the celebration of each Sacrament, there are visible signs and Divine actions that give grace and allow us to share in God's work.

Every sacramental celebration is a meeting between God's children and their Father, a dialogue in the form of actions and words. We, the People of God, perform the rituals (read, process, sing, anoint) provide the materials (plant wheat and grapes, sew garments, order hosts and candles) and participate in the celebration (choir practice, seminary training, lector workshops).

We do these things to give God our praise and thanks, as well as offer ourselves to him. Yet God took the initiative in sending his Son. We are totally dependent upon God's Divine action in the celebration of each of the Sacraments.

So how do we begin to understand the Seven Sacraments? We start with Jesus Christ. Jesus himself is a Sacrament because he is a visible sign of the mystery of the Holy Trinity. He makes God known to us perfectly because he is God. Jesus said, "Whoever has seen me has seen the Father" (**John 14:9**). Jesus is the Mediator between God and humanity, because he is fully God and fully man.

> **Go to the Source**
> Read *John 14:1–10*. What does Jesus say about God's works?

So his actions have the power to save—whether it is by healing a lame man or carrying his Cross. His whole life, from his Incarnation to the sending of his Spirit, is sacramental: it shows us God, shares God's life with us, and is the source of our salvation and new life.

Through Jesus, we have access to God the Father and God the Holy Spirit; from him, we receive Divine help in becoming God's children.

The Church Is the Sign and Source of God's Life

Every Sacrament always starts with remembering the works of God the Father, and being thankful, and celebrating Christ's presence. God the Holy Spirit helps us remember all that Christ said and did, and everything he taught about God the Father. In fact, the Holy Spirit, working with the Church, makes Jesus' saving work present in the Sacraments. Through the power of the Holy Spirit working in us and in the Church, we not only remember what brings us new life, but that new life is made available to us. The Holy Spirit unites us to the Son of God, drawing us into relationship with the Father as his adopted children.

In this way, the Church herself is "the sacrament of Christ's action at work in her through the mission of the Holy Spirit" (CCC, 1118). The Church is a sign of God's love and action in the world.

Underline what the Holy Spirit does for us in the Sacraments.

Catholic Faith Words

Seven Sacraments effective signs of God's grace instituted by Christ and given to his Church. In the celebration of each Sacrament, there are visible signs and Divine actions that give grace and allow us to share in God's work.

SOLVE

Unscramble the words to discover how what we do in two of the Seven Sacraments connects us to God through Jesus Christ.

Humans plant and grow the **HETWA**

_____ and grapes

for use in the Sacrament of **TRISUECAH**

_____ . We also sew the

RMNGTEAS _____

for the Sacraments of Baptism and Holy

DRORES _____ .

The Foundation of the Seven Sacraments

How did Jesus institute the Sacraments?

At Pentecost, the Apostles became certain that they had to share the Good News of Jesus. They knew they now had the strength from the Holy Spirit to carry out Jesus' command to:

- teach and baptize,
- remember him in the breaking of the bread, and
- continue his work of forgiving and healing.

All the Sacraments are rooted in the life of Jesus and show us something about him and eternal life. They draw us into Christ's Paschal Mystery, connecting us to his suffering and rising to new life. Through the work of the Holy Spirit we are made more like Jesus.

We share in the divine life so that we can have the hope of life forever with God. Jesus wanted future believers to know him as his first followers did. This is why he told the Apostles to baptize, break bread, forgive, heal, and bless in his name. Jesus did not leave manuals with his Apostles, or dictate the words and symbols to be used in each Sacrament. In the Bible, we find the attitudes and actions of Jesus that are still those of the Church today, expressed in the Seven Sacraments.

The **Sacraments of Initiation**—Baptism, Confirmation, and Eucharist—make individuals full members of the Catholic Church. The **Sacraments of Healing**, received when a member is in need of God's healing, forgiveness, or strength, are Penance and Reconcilation, and the Anointing of the Sick. The **Sacraments at the Service of Communion**, celebrated in commitment to the Church and her members, are Matrimony and Holy Orders.

Following Jesus' Command

On Pentecost the Apostles baptized nearly three thousand new believers. From Jerusalem they went out to share the message of Jesus. Everywhere they went, the Holy Spirit worked through them to establish the Church. They gathered to celebrate the Eucharist in the evening after their day of work. They would gather for a meal followed by *eucharistia*, "giving thanks" with bread and wine in memory of Jesus. They still followed the Law of Moses and worshipped in the synagogues on the Sabbath. They were like other Jews, but they believed in the Risen Lord.

256

Peter Baptizing the Centurion Cornelius, **by Francesco Trevisani**

As people spread the Good News, they settled in other areas like Antioch, where "the disciples were first called Christians" (Acts 11:26). The Gentiles—people of non-Jewish cultures—who became believers there wanted to be baptized as well. Eventually Christianity became a separate religion.

Constantine issued the Edict of Milan in A.D. 313, ordering tolerance toward Christians in the Roman Empire after many years of persecution. Sunday became a day of rest, and Christians celebrated the Eucharist on Sunday mornings. More importantly, Christians began to shape the Lord's Day. Their traditions changed to respond to their desire to be a serious part of their Church community.

Catholic Faith Words

Sacraments of Initiation the three Sacraments that celebrate membership into the Catholic Church: Baptism, Confirmation, and Eucharist

Sacraments of Healing Penance and Reconciliation and the Anointing of the Sick. In these Sacraments, God's forgiveness and healing are given to those suffering physical and spiritual sickness.

Sacraments at the Service of Communion Holy Orders and Matrimony. They celebrate people's commitment to serve God and the community and help build up the People of God.

IDENTIFY

Read the following Scripture passages:

- John 2:1–11
- Matthew 8:1–4
- Matthew 16:19
- Luke 22:4–20
- John 21:15–17
- Acts 1:2–4
- Matthew 28:15–20

Identify the Scripture passage that goes with the corresponding action or attitude of Jesus and Sacrament to complete the chart below.

Jesus and the Sacraments		
Jesus' Action or Attitude	**Sacrament that Reflects Jesus**	**Scripture Passage**
Jesus told Apostles to make disciples of all nations.	Baptism	_____
The Holy Spirit filled Jesus' Apostles with his Gifts so they could continue Jesus' work.	Confirmation	_____
Jesus ate the Passover meal as a Last Supper with his disciples.	Eucharist	_____
Jesus gave Peter the keys to the Kingdom.	Reconciliation	_____
Jesus healed a leper.	Anointing of the Sick	_____
Jesus turned water to wine at a wedding feast.	Matrimony	_____
Jesus asked Peter to tend his sheep.	Holy Orders	_____

Christ Acts in the Church

How is Christ present today when we worship?

God created us to be human, so he knew that we really needed things to touch and smell and taste and count and hear. The Seven Sacraments involve symbols and rituals that we can see, touch, hear, taste, and smell. They help us grasp an invisible God.

We taste the Body of Christ, smell the fragrance of incense, feel the touch of the Sacred Chrism, hear the words spoken and sung, and see the light of a candle's flame and the faces of the assembly gathered to pray. Through our senses, we know the presence of Christ. To receive a Sacrament is to meet Christ.

Because Christ is present, he is acting in the celebration of the Seven Sacraments. When the Church baptizes, Christ baptizes. When the Church witnesses a marriage, Christ is there. When the Church forgives sins, the power of God's forgiveness is right there. When the Church anoints the sick, it is the healing touch of Jesus upon those in need.

Christ's Presence in the Liturgy

Day after day the main place where we meet Christ is in the **assembly**, the baptized members of the community. Next Sunday, look around at the assembled congregation to see the face of Christ. The **priest** gathers our prayers and leads our sacrifice of praise. Next Sunday, when the priest says, "Let us pray," think of your needs.

When the Gospel is read, it is Christ who speaks to his People. Next Sunday, let the Responsorial Psalm and Gospel Acclamation show your belief that Christ is present in his **Word**. Christ is uniquely present in the Eucharist itself, his Body and Blood received in Holy Communion and adored as the Blessed Sacrament. The phrase **Real Presence** is used to describe the Catholic teaching that Jesus is really and truly with us in the Eucharist—Body, Blood, Soul, and Divinity.

Catholic Faith Words

Real Presence a phrase used to describe the Catholic teaching that Jesus is really and truly with us in the Eucharist—Body, Blood, Soul, and Divinity

Looking Back

Jesus was Jewish, and followed the Jewish traditions of prayer and worship. He celebrated great feasts like Passover. The Apostles were also Jewish, and so were many of the first people who believed in Jesus. It's not surprising that the rituals that they would use to remember the presence of the Risen Lord would sound and look like the traditions of their Jewish culture. There are still connections between the Jewish liturgy and our Christian liturgy.

At the Jewish synagogue service, the Torah is read and reflected upon. As the early Christians gathered, it was only natural to read Scripture. Maybe they even read a letter they just received from Peter or Paul! The structure of proclaiming and responding to the Word of God is now part of the Mass called the Liturgy of the Word.

As part of their Jewish background, the Apostles and early Christians would have been accustomed to celebrating the weekly feast of the Sabbath from sundown Friday to sundown Saturday. Christians shifted to celebrating the weekly feast on Sundays— the day of the Resurrection, and thus the Lord's Day—by breaking bread, discussing Scriptures, and honoring the Lord.

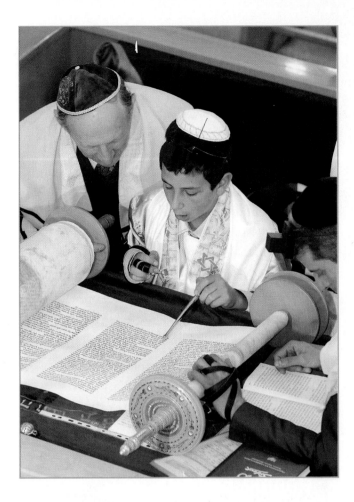

WRITE

To be a Eucharistic person, show gratitude to God and others. Add thanks to your daily prayer. Also express your thankfulness this week in a card, email, or spoken word to persons who have helped you.

IN SUMMARY Catholics Believe

We know that Christ continues to be with us and take care of us in the Seven Sacraments.

- Christ is a Sacrament because he makes God known to us and makes it possible for us to share in God's life. The Church is a Sacrament because in her we come to know God and share in his life through the Seven Sacraments.

- Christ instituted the Sacraments so that we would always know and experience his welcoming, forgiving, healing, and nourishing power.

- Christ is present in the Sacraments, through the assembly gathered, the priest presiding, the Scripture proclaiming, and most especially in the Eucharist, his Body and Blood.

Our Catholic Life

Grace is participation in the life of the Holy Trinity, and helps us to do what God calls us to do. **Actual grace** is the gift God gives us to make the right decisions and think and act according to God's will for you in a particular situation. **Sanctifying grace** allows you to share in God's own life. It is a permanent gift that builds your friendship with God and assures you of eternal life. The grace we receive in the Sacraments is called **sacramental grace**, and each Sacrament provides us with its own particular grace. Sometimes it's hard to recognize grace in our lives, but it is there. Give thanks for the moments of grace God sends you.

> What kind of grace do you most need in your life right now? How will you ask for it?

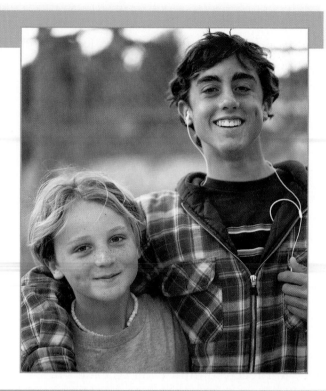

© Our Sunday Visitor

People of Faith

Saint Ludmilla, c. 860–921

Saint Ludmilla was a duchess in Bohemia, part of the Czech Republic today. She and her husband built the first Catholic Church in Prague. Ludmilla helped her grandson Wenceslaus rule Bohemia when he was still a child. Wenceslaus's mother didn't want him to learn about Jesus, so she had Ludmilla killed. However, Wenceslaus never forgot what his grandmother taught him about God and Jesus. As an adult, he spread Christianity throughout Bohemia. Today Saint Ludmilla is venerated as a patron Saint of Bohemia. The Church celebrates her feast day on **September 18.**

For more, go to
aliveinchrist.osv.com

CONSIDER

In the space below, write some ways you can be more mindful of God's presence in your daily life.

at school:

_____

_____

_____

at home:

_____

_____

_____

in your community:

_____

_____

_____

♥ Prayer to Saint Joseph

Leader: Saint Joseph, the foster father of Jesus, you were always present for Jesus and his Mother, Mary. You were always nearby, loving, encouraging, and protecting him from all harm.

Reader 1: When we see images of Saint Joseph, we see in each a loving, protective father. Saint Joseph is also the Patron and Protector of the Universal Church. We can pray for his help and intercession.

Reader 2: A reading from the holy Gospel according to Matthew 1:18–24.

Read Matthew 1:18–24.

The Gospel of the Lord.

All: Praise to you, Lord Jesus Christ. O glorious Saint Joseph, you were chosen by God to be the foster father of Jesus, the most pure spouse of Mary ever Virgin, and the head of the Holy Family. You have been chosen by the Pope as the heavenly patron and protector of the Church founded by Christ. It is with great confidence that we ask for your powerful assistance for the whole Church on Earth. Protect in a special manner, with true fatherly love, the Pope and all bishops and priests in communion with him. Protect all who labor for souls amid the trials and tribulations of this life, and grant that all peoples of the world may follow Christ and the Church he founded.

Reader 3: A reading from the holy Gospel according to Matthew 2:13–15.

Read Matthew 2:13–15.

The Gospel of the Lord.

All: Praise to you, Lord Jesus Christ. Dear Saint Joseph, accept the offering of myself which I now make to you. I dedicate myself to your service, that you may ever be my father, my protector, and my guide in the way of salvation. Obtain for me great purity of heart and a fervent love for the spiritual life. May all my actions, after your example, be directed to the greater glory of God, in union with the divine Heart of Jesus, the Immaculate heart of Mary, and your own paternal heart. Finally, pray for me that I may share in the peace and joy of your holy death.

Reader 4: A reading from the holy Gospel according to Matthew 2:19–23.

Read Matthew 2:19–23.

The Gospel of the Lord.

All: Praise to you, Lord Jesus Christ. Saint Joseph, patron of the universal Church, watch over the Church as carefully as you watched over Jesus. Help protect and guide her, just as you did with Jesus. Saint Joseph, pray for us. Amen.

▶ *Sing or play "Let It Be Done"*

Go to **aliveinchrist.osv.com** for an interactive review.

A **Work with Words** Complete each sentence with the correct term from the Word Bank.

Mediator	Sacraments
counselor	Ascension
salvation	miracles
grace	Pentecost
Baptism	the Gospel

1. Through _____ we freely receive God's help in coming to know and love him.

2. _____ are effective signs of God's grace, instituted by Christ and given to his Church.

3. Jesus is the perfect _____ between God and humanity, because he is fully God and fully man.

4. The Church, a means to _____, is a visible community in the world.

5. On _____, the Holy Spirit descended unto the Apostles and filled them with his Gifts.

B **Check Understanding** Circle the letter of the choice that best completes the sentence.

6. Jesus' whole life is ___ because it is the source of our salvation and new life.
   a. sacramental   c. holy
   b. tradition   d. mysterious

7. The Church is like a ___ because she is a sign of God's love and action in the world.
   a. Spirit   c. Memorial
   b. Rosary   d. Sacrament

8. The term ___ is used to describe the Catholic teaching that Jesus is really and truly with us in the Eucharist—Body, Blood, Soul, and Divinity.
   a. Holy Sign   c. Real Presence
   b. Real Symbol   d. Holy Word

9. The Seven Sacraments use ___ that we can see, touch, hear, taste, and smell.
   a. symbols   c. prayers
   b. rituals   d. a, b, and c

10. Christian liturgy is rooted in the ___ traditions of prayer and worship.
    a. disciples'   c. Gentile
    b. Jewish   d. Church

C **Make Connections** On a separate sheet of paper, write a one-paragraph response to the question: Name the seven "masterworks of God." What role have these celebrations had in your family?

CHAPTER 17

Sacraments of Initiation

💙 Let Us Pray

Leader: We pray in the name of the Father, and of the Son, and of the Holy Spirit. By water and the Spirit, O Lord, we have received the gifts of faith and new life.

"I bow low toward your holy temple;
    I praise your name for your mercy and faithfulness.
For you have exalted over all
    your name and your promise." **Psalm 138:2**

All: God, help us find our place in your Church.

📖 Scripture

"What then shall we say? Shall we persist in sin that grace may abound? Of course not! How can we who died to sin yet live in it? Or are you unaware that we who were baptized into Christ Jesus were baptized into his death? We were indeed buried with him through baptism into death, so that, just as Christ was raised from the dead by the glory of the Father, we too might live in newness of life. … If, then, we have died with Christ, we believe that we shall also live with him." **Romans 6:1–4, 8**

Have you ever thought...

- How is it that because of Baptism we have new life in Christ?

- What helps you feel at home with your family, with your friends, with God?

Getting Started

In this chapter, you will gain a deeper understanding of the purpose and effects of the Sacraments of Baptism and Confirmation and study the parts of the Mass and the effects of the Eucharist.

Catholic Faith Words

- Confirmation
- Gifts of the Holy Spirit
- Eucharist
- transubstantiation

In the web below, list what you know about each of the Sacraments. Include information about the outward signs and ritual actions of each Sacrament and the meaning or effects of the Sacrament.

Sacraments of Initiation

Baptism	Confirmation	Eucharist
_____	_____	_____
_____	_____	_____
_____	_____	_____
_____	_____	_____
_____	_____	_____
_____	_____	_____
_____	_____	_____
_____	_____	_____
_____	_____	_____
_____	_____	_____
_____	_____	_____

We Belong to Christ Illustrate within the frames below some different times when you experienced a strong sense of belonging to the Church or being Catholic.

Baptism

What does Baptism do?

We all want to find a place where we feel at "home." Spiritually, your faith finds home in the Church. It is that place where your soul can find what it has been longing for.

The Church welcomes new members through the Sacraments of Initiation. These Sacraments are about beginnings and belonging. Through them, you are initiated into a relationship with Christ and the Church. Baptism begins your new life in Christ, Confirmation strengthens it, and Eucharist feeds Christ's life within you so that you can follow him. These Sacraments can be received all at once, over a few years, or over a period of time. But no matter when they are celebrated, Baptism is always first.

What Happens

In the Sacrament of Baptism, the person baptized is immersed in water three times—or has water poured over his or her head three times—while the priest or deacon says, "I baptize you in the name of the Father, and of the Son, and of the Holy Spirit. Amen" (Rite of Baptism, no. 60).

Baptism is God's gift to us. Its grace does not require any action on our part. So, Baptism is open to anyone: infant, young child, teen, or adult. In fact, since the earliest times, infants have been baptized in the faith of the Church. In the Baptism of an infant or young child, the parents and godparents agree to bring up the child in the faith.

© Our Sunday Visitor

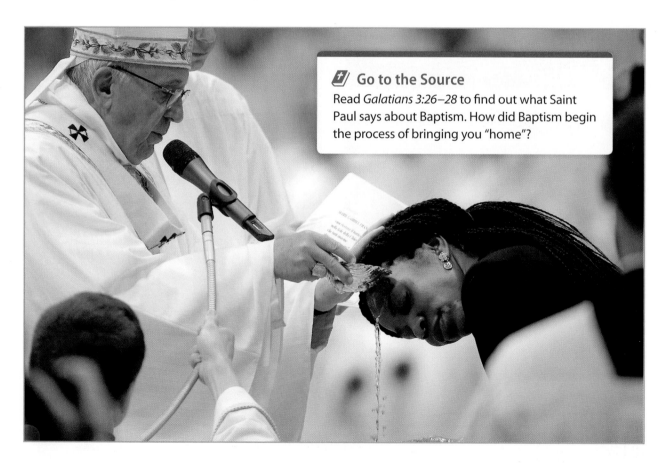

Go to the Source

Read *Galatians 3:26–28* to find out what Saint Paul says about Baptism. How did Baptism begin the process of bringing you "home"?

Rite of Christian Initiation of Adults

In the early years of the Church, there were many adults who chose to become members of the Church. Often they, and their families, would celebrate all three Sacraments of Initiation at one time. Today non-baptized men, women, older children, and those who are baptized from non-Catholic faiths are initiated in a process lasting several months to two years called the Rite of Christian Initiation of Adults (RCIA). They prepare to receive all three Sacraments at the same celebration, usually during the Easter Vigil.

RCIA has several stages, including a time of inquiry in which the person can get to know the Church and see if they want to learn more, then a time for formation and information involving weekly classes. Non-baptized candidates are called catechumens (learners). The catechumens are then called "the elect" to show that they are preparing for the Easter when they will celebrate the Sacraments of Initiation. After that comes mystagogy, a period of fifty days during

which the newly baptized, called neophytes, reflect on the mysteries of the Sacraments, what the celebrations meant to them, and how they can live out their faith.

The Effects of Baptism

- A participation in the Paschal Mystery—dying to sin and rising to new life—and new identity as belonging to Christ: "For all of you who were baptized into Christ have clothed yourselves with Christ" (Galatians 3:27)

- Forgiveness of Original Sin and any personal (actual) sins that may have been committed

- A new relationship with Christ as his sister or brother and a new connection to God the Father as his adopted child

- The gift of the Holy Spirit that incorporates the person into the Body of Christ, the Church

- A share in the mission of Jesus as priest, prophet, and king in God's Kingdom

- A special seal or character that blesses the person to worship. This character is permanent and, because of it, the Sacrament cannot be repeated.

FILL IN THE BLANKS

Fill in the blanks to describe the symbols involved in the Sacrament of Baptism.

- _____ is a sign of cleansing and birth, like the waters God first created.

- Sacred _____, the anointing oil, is a reminder that God has chosen and called each person to be his own.

- The _____ and its light are a sign that Christ is the Light of the World and that all who are baptized are called to be the light of Christ to others.

- The white clothing is a sign of being _____ and being clothed in Christ to imitate him and put on his ways.

Confirmation

What happens during Confirmation?

In Baptism, persons are "christened," meaning they receive Christ, the Anointed One. In **Confirmation**, there is a similar anointing, in which we are strengthened in the grace we received at Baptism, and grow in our relationship with the Anointed One and his Spirit. Blessed and scented oil, called Sacred Chrism, is used in both Sacraments.

At Confirmation, the bishop (or priest) extends his hands over the candidates and prays that the Holy Spirit will come upon them as a Helper and a Guide. Then he anoints each candidate on the forehead, which is done by the laying on of the hands, saying, "[Candidate's name], be sealed with the Gift of the Holy Spirit" (The Rite of Confirmation, no. 27). Like Baptism, Confirmation leaves a spiritual character on the soul. This means that the Sacrament can be received only once.

> **What role does the Spirit play in your journey of faith?**

An Ongoing Journey

Every week, we meet situations that demand more sacrifice, less anger, greater patience, or outreach. The Sacraments give us help along the way.

The Effects of Confirmation

- A deepening and perfection of the life of God in us, which we first received in Baptism

- An outpouring of the Holy Spirit, which increases the Gifts already working in us

- A strengthening of our relationship with God and our unity with Christ

- A perfection of our connection with the Church, a special strengthening by the Holy Spirit to take part in the mission of the Church, to show others by our words and actions that we are Catholics, and to tell others about the Good News of Jesus

The Sacraments are not "things" we deserve or earn. During the celebration of Confirmation, we are sealed in a special way with the **Gifts of the Holy Spirit**. These gifts help us follow the Spirit's guidance and live the Christian life.

Catholic Faith Words

Confirmation the Sacrament of Initiation through which the spiritual life received in Baptism is strengthened and the person is sealed with the Gifts of the Holy Spirit

Gifts of the Holy Spirit seven powerful gifts God gives us to follow guidance of the Holy Spirit and live the Christian life. We are sealed with the Gifts of the Holy Spirit at Confirmation.

CATHOLICS TODAY

In the United States, different people celebrate the Sacrament of Confirmation at different ages. It varies by diocese. Some people are confirmed between the ages of seven and ten; others receive Confirmation when they are twelve or thirteen; others when they are fifteen, sixteen, or seventeen; and still others anytime in between!

The Church teaches us that the person being confirmed should be old enough to reason (which is often considered the age of seven), have been baptized and be free of serious sin, and be prepared to take on greater discipleship.

IDENTIFY

In the space provided, write what you think each Gift of the Holy Spirit describes or means. Then check your ideas against the descriptions on page 375 in the Our Catholic Tradition section of your book.

The Gifts of the Holy Spirit

Wisdom _____

Understanding _____

Right Judgment (Counsel) _____

Courage (Fortitude) _____

Knowledge _____

Reverence (Piety) _____

Wonder and Awe (Fear of the Lord) _____

Select one Gift of the Holy Spirit that you would like to grow in, and briefly explain how it can help you.

_____

_____

Eucharist

What does it mean to eat at the Lord's Table?

Baptism and Confirmation are once-in-a-lifetime Sacraments, but we are offered the benefits of the **Eucharist**, the Sacrament in which the bread and wine become the Body and Blood of Christ, over and over again throughout our lives.

We need food for the journey, nourishment for the soul through listening to the Scripture and through receiving Holy Communion. This is so important that we are welcomed to take part in daily Mass along with our obligation to attend Sunday Mass.

The priest calls for the Holy Spirit to be sent upon the gifts

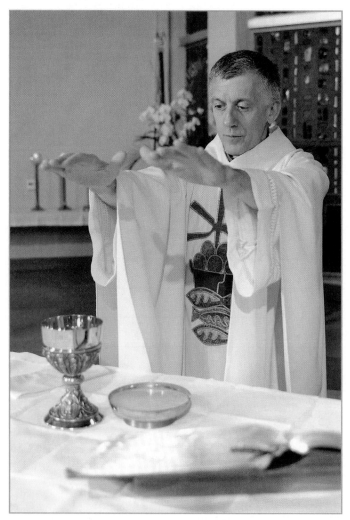

You've probably heard the saying "You are what you eat." That's why it's important to care about a healthful diet. The food you eat today is becoming you in a true physical way. In Holy Communion, we receive the Body and Blood of Christ and become what we eat—the Body of Christ, the Church.

The Parts of the Mass

We begin with the **Introductory Rites**, prayers and songs of thanksgiving to God the Father for all of his gifts, most especially his Son. This part of the Mass gathers us together and prepares us to listen to God's Word.

The first main part of the Mass is the **Liturgy of the Word**. This includes readings from the Scripture, usually from both the Old Testament and New Testament, and always from the Gospels. We also profess the Nicene or Apostles' Creed and offer prayers in the Prayer of the Faithful.

The second main part of the Mass is the **Liturgy of the Eucharist**—the recalling of what Jesus said and did at the Last Supper: "This is my Body, which will be given up for you . . . This is the chalice of my Blood . . ." and the words of the priest and blessing of the Holy Spirit so that the wheat bread and grape wine are consecrated and become the Body and Blood of Christ. To receive

© Our Sunday Visitor

Catholic Faith Words

Eucharist the Sacrament of Initiation during which the bread and wine become the Body and Blood of Christ and all who receive him in Holy Communion are brought closer to him and one another

transubstantiation the process by which, through the power of the Holy Spirit and the words and actions of the priest, the bread and wine are transformed into the Body and Blood of Christ the invitation to the Table of the Lord and reception of Holy Communion, you must be free from serious sin, so it might be necessary to receive the Sacrament of Penance and Reconciliation before Mass.

In the **Concluding Rites**, we are sent out in peace to announce the Gospel by our words and actions.

The most important aspect of the Mass is Jesus' Real Presence in the Eucharist. During the consecration, in the Liturgy of the Eucharist, through the words and actions of the priest and by the power of the Holy Spirit, the bread and wine become the Body and Blood of Christ. This change is called **transubstantiation**. Jesus is truly present under the appearances of bread and wine. This is not just a memorial of what Jesus offered to us. Jesus' sacrifice is made present and we are given the gift of his life.

Jesus taught us that all are welcome at his table—especially those who are neglected,

> ### The Effects of the Eucharist
>
> - Increases our union with the Lord
> - Forgives venial sins and help to avoid serious sin
> - Strengthens our connection with others and supports the unity of all the members of the Church
> - Inspires us to self-sacrifice and commits us to caring for the needs of others

the outcasts, and those in need of healing. The table that Jesus creates is a model for our Church. The connection between Eucharist and justice is real. After we are fed at the Supper of the Lamb, we must go out and feed others with our generosity, talent, service, and resources.

Go to the Source
Divide the following Scripture texts among your classmates. See how Jesus accepted everyone at his table in Luke 15:1–2; Luke 19:1–10; Luke 22:21–23; and Matthew 9:9–13.

CONSIDER

What are some ways that you "feed" people by sharing your time and gifts and satisfying their hunger for love and attention? What are some ways that you could feed people by helping to take care of their physical needs for food, shelter, or clothing?

IN SUMMARY   Catholics Believe

As Christ first welcomed and fed his followers, we are welcomed and belong to the Church through the three Sacraments of Initiation.

- In Baptism, the first Sacrament, we celebrate new life in Christ through the forgiveness of sins and incorporation into the Church.

- In Confirmation, the spiritual life received in Baptism is strengthened and we are sealed with the Gift of the Holy Spirit so that we can live out our journey of faith.

- In the Eucharist, the Sacrament that we celebrate regularly, we are fed with the Body and Blood of Christ and are brought closer to Christ and one another.

📶 Go to **aliveinchrist.osv.com** for an interactive review.

A Work with Words **Circle the letter of the choice that best completes the sentence.**

1. In ___, a person experiences a rising to new life and new identity as belonging to Christ, through the forgiveness of sins and incorporation into the Church.
   a. Baptism
   c. Confirmation
   b. Eucharist
   d. Church

2. We receive the Body and Blood of Christ during the Sacrament of ___.
   a. Baptism
   c. Confirmation
   b. Eucharist
   d. Initiation

3. ___ is the process by which, through the power of the Holy Spirit and the words and actions of the priest, the bread and wine are transformed into the Body and Blood of Christ.
   a. Confirmation
   c. Transubstantiation
   b. Salvation
   d. Transfiguration

4. One of the effects of the Sacrament of ___ is that we are sealed with the Gifts of the Holy Spirit, which increases the Gifts already working in us.
   a. Baptism
   c. Confirmation
   b. Eucharist
   d. Pentecost

B Check Understanding **Complete each sentence with the correct terms from the Word Bank.**

Initiation	Baptism
venial sins	spiritual character
Invitation	Last Supper
Sacred Chrism	Candle
mystagogy	

5. The Church welcomes new members through the celebration of the Sacraments of

   _____.

6. In Baptism, the _____ is a reminder that God has chosen and called each one to be his own.

7. The Rite of Christian Initiation of Adults ends with _____, a period of fifty days during which the newly baptized reflect on the mysteries of the Sacraments.

8. As in Baptism, a person who celebrates the Sacrament of Confirmation receives a

   _____ on one's soul.

9. During the Liturgy of the Eucharist, we remember what Jesus said and did at the

   _____.

10. The Eucharist forgives

    _____ and helps us avoid serious sin.

C Make Connections **On a separate sheet of paper, write a one-paragraph response to the question: Which part of the Celebration of the Eucharist is most meaningful for you? Explain your answer.**

© Our Sunday Visitor

Sacraments of Healing

♡ Let Us Pray

Leader: God, you reach out to us in loving forgiveness. Your love heals all of our hurts. Be with us as we turn to you for healing and forgiveness.

"Look upon my affliction and suffering;
take away all my sins." **Psalm 25:18**

All: God, please heal us and help us to forgive.

📖 Scripture

"So whoever is in Christ is a new creation: the old things have passed away; behold, new things have come. And all this is from God, who has reconciled us to himself through Christ and given us the ministry of reconciliation, namely, God was reconciling the world to himself in Christ, not counting their trespasses against them and entrusting to us the message of reconciliation. So we are ambassadors for Christ, as if God were appealing through us. We implore you on behalf of Christ, be reconciled to God. For our sake he made him to be sin who did not know sin, so that we might become the righteousness of God in him."

2 Corinthians 5:17–21

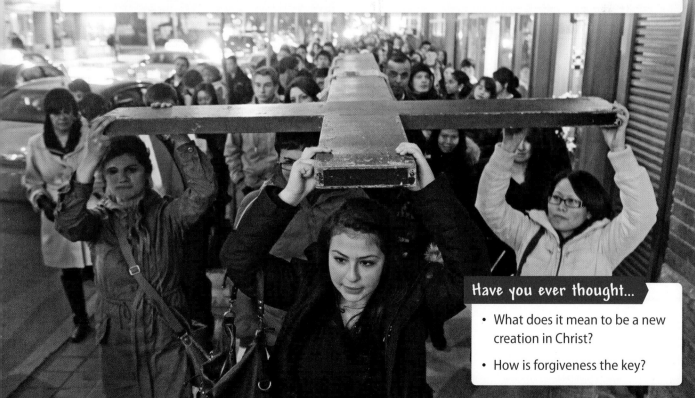

Have you ever thought...

- What does it mean to be a new creation in Christ?

- How is forgiveness the key?

Getting Started

In this chapter, you will discover the relationship between healing and forgiveness, understand that we can count on God's forgiveness and healing, and learn the form and effects of the Sacrament of Penance and Reconciliation.

In the web below, list what you know about these two Sacraments. Include information about the outward signs and ritual actions of each Sacrament and the meaning or effects of the Sacrament.

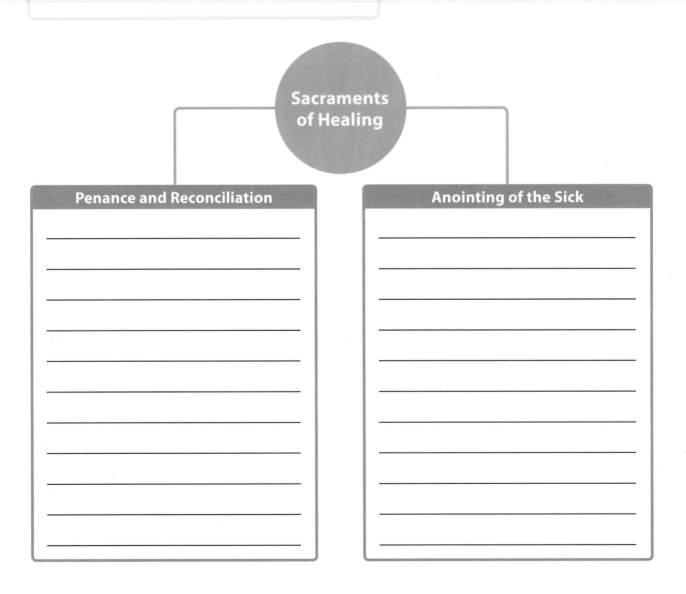

Sacraments of Healing

Penance and Reconciliation

_____

_____

_____

_____

_____

_____

_____

_____

_____

Anointing of the Sick

_____

_____

_____

_____

_____

_____

_____

_____

_____

Forgiveness is Key We don't have to travel far and wide to be ambassadors for Christ (see 2 Corinthians 5:20). We can practice forgiveness and reconciliation every day, where we are. What do you believe about forgiveness? Design a "forgiveness key" that symbolizes what you believe about forgiveness, and that you can symbolically carry with you as an ambassador for Christ.

What "doors" in your life can be opened by this key?

_____

_____

_____

_____

_____

_____

_____

_____

_____

_____

A Merciful God

Why can we count on God's forgiveness and healing?

At some point or another, each of us realizes that we've done something we regret, or that we have been blaming a friend or parent for something that really isn't his or her fault. We might be confused and worried about someone who is in pain, needing help to get through a really difficult time, or facing an illness. At times like these, we need to give or receive compassion, hope, and possibly forgiveness. And God can give us all of these. Jesus shows us that God's compassion does not end.

Scripture

"Jesus went around to all the towns and villages, teaching in their synagogues, proclaiming the gospel of the kingdom, and curing every disease and illness. At the sight of the crowds, his heart was moved with pity for them because they were troubled and abandoned, like sheep without a shepherd." **Matthew 9:35–36**

The Gospels are filled with accounts of Jesus healing those who were sick, and forgiving the sins of those who truly believed. Whether they were emotional, spiritual, or physical healings, these life-changing events had a tremendous impact. Most people believed, changed their lifestyles, and went out to tell others about Jesus and his message.

Always There

God is always there to heal us spiritually (when we feel separated from God), emotionally (when we're in psychological pain), and physically (when we are sick or injured). Because Jesus forgave sinners and healed the sick, we know that's just the way God is—forgiving and eager to heal. The Church celebrates Jesus' forgiveness and healing in two Sacraments of Healing: the Sacrament of Reconciliation and the Sacrament of the Anointing of the Sick.

> **How could your day be different if you remembered God's compassion for you and his desire to heal and forgive?**

Holding Ourselves Up to the Light

Did you ever put on a "clean" T-shirt only to discover spots in the light? When we hold ourselves up to the light of Christ, we all have "spots": bad attitudes, grudges, prejudices, emotional wounds, bad memories, and sins. With God's help we recognize and admit our need for and desire to change. We are open to conversion.

Conversion can mean many things:

- a return to God, sorrow for sin, trust in God's mercy, commitment to do better in the future, rooting out bad habits, and more.
- making ourselves more and more like Christ.
- ongoing, always possible, always needed.
- goes together with repentance.

Repentance, also called **contrition**, is being truly sorry for disobeying God and committing to try not to sin again. If contrition comes out of love for God above all things, it is called "perfect"; if someone is sorry for sins because they feel guilty or are afraid of the punishment, it is called "imperfect contrition." Both are promptings of the Holy Spirit in us, moving us to seek forgiveness. We sometimes stray from the path by venial sin, which weakens our relationship with God.

Catholic Faith Words

contrition true sorrow for disobeying God and the commitment to try to avoid sin in the future

Penance and Reconciliation the Sacrament of Healing that celebrates God's mercy and forgiveness and a sinner's reconciliation with God and the Church through absolution from a priest

Some people may walk away from God (through a grave, or mortal sin). The Sacrament of **Penance and Reconciliation**— also called the Sacrament of conversion, confession, or penance—is the Sacrament of forgiveness for sins committed after Baptism. Required for the forgiveness of mortal sin and recommended for the forgiveness of venial sin, it is a sure way to get back on the path of conversion.

DESCRIBE

In what ways have you been (or could be) open to conversion? Describe one or two conversions you have been through that improved the way you walk with God. Try finishing this phrase:

I used to (think/feel/believe/try to)

_____

_____

_____

_____

but now I

_____

_____

_____

and it has helped my relationship with God because

_____

_____

_____

_____

Reconciliation

What are the rites and effects of this Sacrament?

Today the Church celebrates the Sacrament of Penance and Reconciliation in three ways, with one form for the Rite for Reconciliation of Individual Penitents, and two for Several Penitents.

No matter which Rite (see page 371 in the Our Catholic Tradition section of your book) is used in the celebration of the Sacrament of Penance and Reconciliation, it always contains four important elements: contrition, confession, **penance**, and **absolution**.

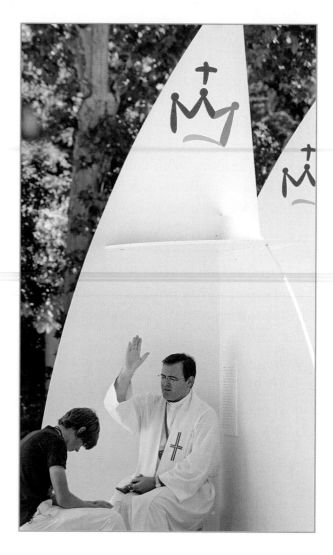

© Our Sunday Visitor

Catholic Faith Words

penance the name for the prayer, offering, or good work the priest gives you in the Sacrament of Reconciliation

absolution words spoken by the priest during the Sacrament of Penance and Reconciliation to grant forgiveness of sins in God's name

The Sacrament of Penance and Reconciliation

Contrition •	• An action or prayer given by the priest as a way to repair the harm caused by sin and to become a stronger disciple of Christ.
Confession •	• Involves an examination of conscience, realization of sin, and true sorrow along with a desire to try to do better in the future.
Penance •	• The words spoken by the priest during the Sacrament to grant forgiveness of sins in God's name.
Absolution •	• An essential element of the Sacrament of Penance and Reconciliation, this is telling one's sins to the priest.

★ Match the part of the Sacrament of Penance and Reconciliation with its effect.

Whether the Sacrament takes place with an individual meeting with the priest for the entire celebration, or with a group of penitents gathering together for prayers and reflection, with individual confession and absolution, there is a similar structure to the celebration.

- gathering
- reading Scripture
- expressing contrition
- confessing sin individually and privately to a priest who can forgive sins in Christ's name by the authority of the Church. Priests cannot tell anyone what you have told them; this is called the Sacramental Seal of Confession.
- receiving a penance and having sins absolved by a priest
- praising God

You might be thinking you don't want to tell someone all the things you've done. But you need to remember that you are actually talking to Christ when you talk to the priest. And there are so many spiritual benefits from receiving the Sacrament: reconciliation with God and the Church, freedom from eternal separation from God, a peaceful conscience, spiritual help and guidance, and strength to live as a disciple of Christ.

Let Go

Sometimes we hold a grudge as bitter revenge for our hurt feelings even if the person who hurt us is unaware. The same might be true of prejudices, bad memories, emotional wounds, and psychological scars. We become like Saint Peter, who wondered how many times he absolutely had to forgive. Or we're like the Unforgiving Servant who was excused a huge debt, but wouldn't let go of a small debt someone owed him. (See Matthew 18:21–35.)

Go to the Source

Read the Parable of the Unforgiving Servant found in Matthew 18:21–35. Do you feel more like Peter, the Unforgiving Servant, or the person who owes? What is your favorite line in the parable? Why?

Consider these ways to become freed from emotional pain.

- When angry or vengeful thoughts pop into your mind, redirect your thoughts and adrenaline through activity or prayer.
- Talk with your parents or a mentor, a trusted friend, or an older sibling.
- Talk to your parents and ask if they think you should talk to a counselor if other things aren't working.

CREATE

Turn to page 373 to review the Ten Commandments. Using the Commandments as a guide, create an examination of conscience. On the lines below, write a reflection question that corresponds to two different Commandments.

_____

_____

Anointing of the Sick

What are the rituals and effects of this Sacrament?

In the District of the Decapolis, people brought a man with a hearing loss and a speech impediment to Jesus. At Bethsaida people brought a man who was blind. When the people of Gennesaret saw Jesus, they scurried about to bring the sick on mats. Wherever Jesus went, people counted on his power to heal. Fortunately, Jesus left his power to heal in his Church.

Healing the sick was so much a part of the life of Jesus that the first thing the seventy-two disciples were told to do was "Cure the sick" in each town, "and say to them, 'The kingdom of God is at hand for you'" (**Luke 10:9**). They had the simple faith to follow his example.

The early Church continued the practice of curing the sick. The letter of James tells us about praying over sick people and anointing them. We learn that the faith of the community is essential for healing to take place.

✠ Scripture

"Is anyone among you suffering? He should pray. Is anyone is good spirits? He should sing praise. Is anyone among you sick? He should summon the presbyters of the church and they should pray over him and anoint [him] with oil in the name of the Lord, and the prayer of faith will save the sick person, and the Lord will raise him up. If he has committed any sins, he will be forgiven."
James 5:13–15

The Church does the same today in the **Anointing of the Sick**. When someone falls seriously ill or the illness worsens, or when someone is in danger of death, they are invited to seek the prayers and anointing of the Church. Only priests can administer the Sacrament, using oil consecrated by the bishop during Holy Week. The ritual consists of laying on of hands and anointing the forehead and hands while praying for the grace of the Sacrament to strengthen the person to be able to handle the difficulties of serious illness or old age.

Why It's Important

What do you think of when you hear words like courage, health, peace, grace, and suffering? Probably a whole range of things. These words can be used to describe the effects of the Anointing of the Sick.

This Sacrament has a tremendous impact on those who receive it, and that's why the Church wants to make sure that everyone knows that this Sacrament is for anyone who is seriously sick, no matter the age or reason.

As in all the Sacraments, the Anointing of the Sick gives a special grace to the person who receives it. In this Sacrament, the person who is sick is united to Christ's suffering and receives spiritual healing. That's pretty amazing when you think about it. The Son of God actually suffered, and so God understands our suffering. And, because new life comes from Jesus' suffering, people are connected to his new life in this Sacrament.

Catholic Faith Words

Anointing of the Sick one of the Sacraments of Healing for people who are seriously ill or in danger of dying. In the Sacrament, the person's forehead and hands are anointed with the blessed oil of the sick.

The Sacrament gives courage, peace, and spiritual healing to endure suffering or old age, and sometimes health is restored. For those who are near death, the Sacrament helps prepare them and their sins are forgiven if they are unable to receive Penance.

CONSIDER

We sometimes want to help someone who is sick, but don't know how to do it. One way is to simply say, "I will keep you in my prayers, okay?" or "I'll say a prayer for you." Think of some other ways you can reach out to those who are sick.

IN SUMMARY   Catholics Believe

We know that God heals us spiritually, emotionally, and sometimes physically in the Sacraments of Healing.

- Jesus' words and actions show us that God is compassionate, always willing to forgive and care for those who are willing to turn to him and believe.

- In the Sacrament of Penance and Reconciliation, those who are truly sorry for their sins receive God's forgiveness and are reconciled with him and the Church.

- In the Sacrament of the Anointing of the Sick, those who are seriously ill or are suffering from old age receive God's grace to be strong, courageous, and hopeful in their trials.

Our Catholic Life

Giving and receiving **forgiveness** is an important way we can show the work and grace of God in our lives. Remember how you have felt when you've been forgiven for something or chosen to forgive someone else for hurting you. When you are in emotional or physical pain, or need to be forgiven, you can always turn to God in prayer. If you need to forgive someone, ask God to help you do that, too. It is one of the Precepts of the Church to receive the Sacrament of Penance and Reconciliation at least once a year to have your personal sins forgiven and your relationships with God and the Church healed. Parishes often have Reconciliation services during the seasons of Advent and Lent.

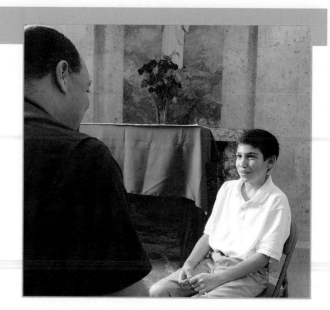

> How would you describe Reconciliation to someone who is nervous about confessing their sins?

People of Faith

Blessed Carlos Manuel Cecilio Rodriguez Santiago, 1918–1963

As a child in Puerto Rico, Carlos Santiago began experiencing symptoms of an illness from which he would suffer for the rest of his life. However, it never undermined his commitment to Christ and his Church. Carlos used his modest salary as a translator to publish two Christian magazines. He also worked at a university, where he evangelized students and teachers. He encouraged liturgical renewal, and many of his reforms were adopted by the Church at the Second Vatican Council in the 1960s. The Church celebrates his feast day on **July 13**.

📶 For more, go to
aliveinchrist.osv.com

IDENTIFY

You can keep in mind the benefits of forgiveness by turning back to your Bible when you are struggling. Use your Bible to match the beginnings of these scriptural quotes to the correct endings.

1. Forgiving one another . . . _____

2. I have brushed away your offenses like a cloud . . . _____

3. You are a forgiving God, gracious and merciful . . . _____

   A. your sins like a mist. (Isaiah 44:22)
   B. slow to anger and rich in mercy. (Nehemiah 9:17)
   C. as God has forgiven you in Christ. (Ephesians 4:32)

♥ Psalm of Lament

Leader: Be with us, O God,
As we sit here in quiet,
as we look deep inside at the ways
we have turned away from you.

Side 1: The Lord is my light and my salvation;
whom should I fear?

The Lord is the stronghold of my life:
of whom should I be afraid?

Side 2: One thing I asked of the Lord,
that will I seek after:
to live in the house of the Lord
all the days of my life,
to behold the beauty of the Lord,
and to inquire in his Temple.

Side 1: For he will hide me in his shelter
in the day of trouble;

he will conceal me under the cover of his tent;
he will set me high on a rock.

Side 2: Hear, O Lord, when I cry aloud,
Be gracious to me and answer me!
"Come," my heart says, "seek his face!"
Your face, Lord, do I seek.
Do not hide your face from me.
You are my salvation; do not cast me off!
Do not forsake me, God my savior!
Based on Psalm 27:1, 4, 5, 7, 9

Leader: O God of all goodness,
Your love heals all.

Come now and be with us, as we turn
toward you.

Help us to be patient when we stumble
and fall,
help us to be forgiving of ourselves and
each other.

Strengthen our determination to be more
and more like Jesus.

All: Amen.

▶ *Sing or play "The Lord Is My Light and My Salvation"*

Go to **aliveinchrist.osv.com** for an interactive review.

A **Work with Words** Complete each sentence with the correct term from the Word Bank.

Baptism	contrition
Penance and Reconciliation	forgiveness
	conversion
Anointing of the Sick	Eucharist
suffering	

1. The Sacrament of _____ consists of laying on of hands and anointing a person's forehead and hands with oil while praying for the grace of the Sacrament to strengthen the person.

2. _____ is being truly sorry for disobeying God and committing oneself to avoid sin in the future.

3. The Sacrament of _____ is the Sacrament of forgiveness for sins committed after Baptism. It celebrates God's mercy and forgiveness and reconciles a sinner with God and the Church.

4. In the Sacrament of Anointing of the Sick, the sick person is united to Christ's _____.

5. _____ can mean many things: a return to God, sorrow for sin, trust in God's mercy, commitment to do better in the future, and more.

B **Check Understanding** Indicate whether the following statements are true or false. Then rewrite false statements to make them true.

6. Perfect conversion comes out of love for God above all things. **True/False**

   _____

   _____

7. The Sacrament of Penance and Reconciliation is required for forgiveness of mortal sin committed after Baptism and recommended for forgiveness of venial sin. **True/False**

   _____

   _____

8. The Sacrament of Penance and Reconciliation always includes contrition, confession, anointing, and absolution. **True/False**

   _____

   _____

9. Priests in confession cannot tell anyone what you have told them; this is called the Sacramental Seal of Confession. **True/False**

   _____

   _____

10. Only priests can give the Sacrament of Reconciliation using the oil consecrated by the bishop during Holy Week. **True/False**

   _____

   _____

C **Make Connections** On a separate sheet of paper, write a one-paragraph response to the question: Write about a time when someone forgave you or a time when you forgave someone. What was the experience of forgiveness like, and how did it affect your relationship with that person?

A Work with Words **Use the clues below to complete the crossword puzzle.**

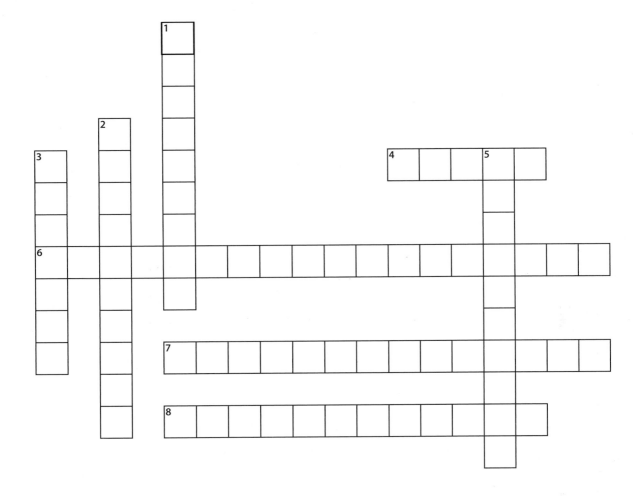

Across

4. God's free, loving gift of his own life and help to do what he calls us to do

6. the process by which, through the power of the Holy Spirit and the words and actions of the priest, the bread and wine become the Body and Blood of Christ

7. the Sacrament of Penance and ____ celebrates God's mercy and forgiveness

8. One of the Sacraments of Initiation

Down

1. the Sacrament during which the bread and wine become the Body and Blood of Christ

2. Seven effective signs of God's grace instituted by Christ and given to his Church

3. Sacrament through which a person experiences new life in Christ and forgiveness of sins and incorporation into the Church

5. Being truly sorry for disobeying God and committing to try to avoid sin in the future

B **Check Understanding** Circle the letter of the choice that best completes the sentence.

9. Jesus is the perfect ____ between God and man, because he is fully God and fully man.

   a. Mediator **b.** Symbol **c.** Division **d.** Conversion

10. The Church, a means to ____, is a visible community in the world.

   a. salvation **b.** grace **c.** divinity **d.** power

11. The Sacrament of Reconciliation reflects Jesus' giving ____ the power to forgive sins.

   a. us **b.** the Church **c.** John **d.** one person

12. All Seven Sacraments involve ____ and ____ that we can see, touch, hear, taste, and smell.

   a. symbols, rituals **b.** oil, blessings **c.** attitudes, gifts **d.** signs, words

13. The Church welcomes new members through the Sacraments of ____

   a. Contrition **b.** Initiation **c.** Conviction **d.** Invitation

14. In Baptism, the ____ is a reminder that God has chosen and called each one to be his own.

   a. water **b.** candle **c.** Sacred Chrism **d.** prayer

15. Like Baptism, Confirmation imparts a(n) ____ character on one's soul.

   a. acceptable **b.** invisible **c.** conversion **d.** spiritual

16. ____ can mean many things: a return to God, sorrow for sin, trust in God's mercy, a commitment to do better in the future, and more.

   a. Contrition **b.** Sacraments **c.** Conversion **d.** Reconciliation

17. The Sacrament of Anointing of ____ consists of the priest's laying on of hands and putting oil on the forehead and hands.

   a. the Sick **b.** Reconciliation **c.** the Dying **d.** Baptism

18. The Sacrament of Penance and Reconciliation always includes contrition, ____, penance, and absolution.

   a. conversion **b.** confession **c.** penance **d.** consideration

19. In Confirmation, a person is sealed with the ____ of the Holy Spirit.

   a. Sacraments **b.** Gifts **c.** Chrism **d.** Confession

20. ____ refers to the words spoken by the priest during the Sacrament of Penance and Reconciliation to grant forgiveness of sins in God's name.

   a. Absolution **b.** Penance **c.** Confession **d.** Contrition

Make Connections   Write a short answer to these questions.

21. How do you experience God through the customs and practices of the Church? Give a specific example.

_____

_____

_____

_____

22. What does it mean to live out the Eucharist? How are you living out the Eucharist in your family, at school, and in the world?

_____

_____

_____

_____

23. What are the benefits of the Sacrament of Penance and Reconciliation?

_____

_____

_____

_____

24. Choose one Sacrament and describe how Jesus instituted it.

_____

_____

_____

_____

25. How does the Sacrament of Confirmation strengthen our connection with the Church?

_____

_____

_____

_____

KINGDOM OF GOD

How does listening for and responding to God's invitation help you to be happy in this world and the next?

CHURCH HISTORY TIMELINE

528	Benedict begins monastery at Monte Cassino
910	Monastery at Cluny founded
1205	Saint Francis of Assisi establishes what becomes the Franciscan Order
2013	Jorge Bergoglio elected as Pope Francis

Go to page 348 for more

© Our Sunday Visitor

Our Catholic Tradition

- We share a call to know, love, and serve the Lord, and share our time, talent, and treasure. God's Word, the Church, family, and prayer help us discern and respond to our vocation. (CCC, 2030)

- God's Kingdom is fully present in Heaven but not complete on Earth. We work toward the Kingdom through prayer, sharing the Good News, action, and advocacy for those in need. (CCC, 2820)

- By his Death and Resurrection, Jesus makes it possible for believers to have eternal life. We will be judged at the time of our death based on how we have accepted and acted on God's grace in our lives. (CCC, 934, 1019)

Our Catholic Life

- We are called to faith. Each of us must live our particular vocation, whether married, single, ordained, or consecrated. (CCC, 871–873)

- We will be judged at our death based upon the ways we have accepted and acted on God's grace in our lives. God desires all of us to make the right choices in life, so we can be with him forever in the happiness of Heaven. (CCC, 1051)

- The Works of Mercy are ways to respond to Jesus when we see him in those who are poor or in need. (CCC, 2447)

CHAPTER 19

Called by God

❤ Let Us Pray

Leader: Lord, you call us by name. Help us to know your voice when you call; help us to say "Yes, Lord."

"Know that the LORD works wonders for his faithful one; the LORD hears when I call out to him." **Psalm 4:4**

All: O God, help us know your will for our lives. Help us hear you when you call.

✝ Scripture

The LORD called to Samuel, who answered, "Here I am." He ran to Eli and said, "Here I am. You called me." "I did not call you." Eli answered. "Go back to sleep." So he went back to sleep.

Samuel did not yet recognize the LORD, since the word of the LORD had not yet been revealed to him. The LORD called Samuel again ... Then Eli understood that the LORD was calling the youth. So he said to Samuel, "Go to sleep, and if you are called, reply, 'Speak, LORD, for your servant is listening.'"

When Samuel went to sleep in his place, the LORD came and stood there, calling out as before: Samuel, Samuel! Samuel answered, "Speak, for your servant is listening." **1 Samuel 3:4–10**

Have you ever thought...

- What does it mean to be called by God?

- How can your gifts serve God and make a difference for others?

Getting Started

In this chapter, you will learn about the role of the family in faith and the meaning of vocation. You will also explore how God calls each of us to use the gifts he has given us.

In the chart below, describe what each term means to you and how it is important in our lives as individuals, families, school communities, and the Church.

In Your Own Words		
Vocation	**Discernment**	**Service**

Do You Hear God's Call? Think of a time when someone who cared about
you encouraged you to be a better friend, brother or sister, son or daughter.
God's voice comes to us in many ways. Write the names of the people who have
been God's voice in your life.

_____

_____

_____

_____

_____

_____

Choose one of the people you listed above and describe how he or she helped
you hear and respond to God's voice in your life.

_____

_____

_____

_____

_____

_____

_____

_____

_____

_____

_____

_____

Jesus in the Temple, among the teachers

The Importance of Family

What role does the family have in faith?

Each of us has potential gifts and talents. Some of us are artistic, some are athletic, some are thinkers, and some are speakers. And many have more than one of these gifts. We might discover our talents early in life, or we might stumble across them by accident. Our families often point out gifts and talents they see in us, and our teachers, coaches, and friends can help us figure them out, too. When we use our talents to work together, we can bring about good in the world.

Despite our different talents, we all share the same calling to know and love God. We are first called to this mission in our Baptism, and our parents and guardians play a pivotal role in our responding to that call.

A mother found herself praying one day. She and her husband had lost track of their son, who was around twelve years old. The parents' names were Mary and Joseph, and they finally found their son, Jesus, in the Temple, teaching the teachers. They had looked for him for three days, probably worrying and praying all the while. But, even though the Bible tells us they were upset with Jesus, they were also amazed by him (see Luke 2:51).

> ### ⊞ Go to the Source
> Read *Luke 2:41–52*. Imagine that you were a friend of Jesus when he was growing up. What might you have seen him doing in daily life? What do you think it would be like to have Jesus as a friend or classmate today?

The Gospel according to Luke also tells us that Mary "kept all these things in her heart" (**Luke 2:51**). She and Joseph recognized Jesus' great gifts, nurtured him with love, prayed with him, and helped him fulfill God's will.

Prayer begins in our family. Parents and guardians put roofs over our heads, clothes on our backs, and food on our plates, and provide for our spiritual needs. If you become a parent, you will be responsible for helping your children grow in faith.

> **What different roles do the people in your family have?**

Faith Begins at Home

Before you were baptized, your parents and godparents were given an important task. They were told: "You must make it your constant care to bring him/her up in the practice of the faith" (Rite of Baptism).

Constant means all the time; every day. This kind of care includes things like teaching you to pray, telling you to "turn the other cheek" instead of getting even, or getting you to Mass on Sunday.

The home is the first place where children learn about God and the Catholic faith. It is here that they should first appreciate what a community of love is. They should experience solid Catholic virtues and values. In that sense, a family is a unique dimension of the Church. A Catholic home and family is a **domestic Church**—a holy community of grace and prayer where children first learn about God through the love, teaching, and good examples of parents and family. For example, when such a family gathers around a table for a meal or in the car on the way to school, they can thank God for the gifts they received that day.

No family is perfect. All families face challenges and have growing pains. Sometimes a home seems more like a domestic Church than at other times. The important thing for families to do, even in hard times, is to keep trying and to ask God for help.

Witnesses to Christ

Lay people are called to be witnesses to Christ at all times and places, as parents or single persons, at work, in home, and in the community. **Laity** is the name for all the baptized members of the Church who share in Jesus' mission but are not ordained. Lay people witness to Jesus' message in their families, workplaces, and civic communities.

We are witnesses when our words and actions reflect the teachings of Jesus and the Church. At home, in school, on the bus, or at work we can show others what it means to follow Christ. And we don't do this alone. God gives us the love and strength to make it happen.

Catholic Faith Words

domestic Church a name for the Catholic family, because it is the community of Christians in the home. God made the family to be the first place we learn about loving others and following Christ.

laity all baptized members of the Church who share in Jesus' mission and witness to him and his message but are not priests or consecrated sisters or brothers; sometimes called lay people

CONSIDER

Think about how you can add prayer to your daily routine. Be creative. Keep it simple. Think about how you can pray at different times and in different places: before bed, at breakfast, after a ball game or practice. Get ideas from the people in your family on other ways to build your domestic Church.

_____

_____

_____

_____

A Common Mission

What does it mean to have a vocation?

In Baptism and Confirmation, we are called to be holy in every aspect of our lives—when we're alone, with our family and friends, and as part of our Church. At Baptism, we are anointed with consecrated, sweet-smelling oil called Sacred Chrism as the priest or deacon tells us that Christ unites us to his People and his Body, and we share in Christ's ministry as Priest, Prophet, and King.

Living It Out

You can't apply for a job as a king. It's not as simple as our deciding alone to become an ordained priest, or a religious sister or brother. Those vocations begin with a call from God and require years of prayer and study. **Vocation** is the purpose for which God made us, and the particular way to answer and live out that call to love and serve God and others.

We all have a vocation as baptized members of the Church. Some have a vocation to priesthood or religious life. Others live out their vocation as part of a married couple or through single life. God may give married Catholics the gift of children, while sisters and brothers in religious communities dedicate their lives to the faith in many different ministries and lifestyles. Whatever path you follow is a sacred one when you take Christ's love with you and share it with others.

> **Who do you turn to for help when you are making a big decision? Why?**

What About You?

Do you get tired of being asked, "What do you want to be when you grow up?" It's normal for the answer to change many times as you get older. Maybe you wanted to be a star athlete, but didn't have the physical skills. Dreams and plans change for many reasons.

The process by which you reflect, discuss, and pray about how God might be calling you to a particular vocation is called **discernment**. Think about what you enjoy doing, and what you are good at. Talk with your parents, family, friends, Church leaders, and others who know you best. They should respect and encourage your choices of a vocation. This is more likely if they understand what you are thinking.

Pray with them, like Jesus surely did with his parents. Parents can encourage their children to see that they are called to follow Jesus, whatever they do.

Lay People Share in Jesus' Mission

○ **Priest**	Like Jesus, we offer our lives to God and bring his love to the world. We pray for those in need, we offer what we do at school and at home as a gift to God, and we participate in the Mass.
○ **Prophet**	Like Jesus and the Apostles, as prophets we speak God's powerful truth to people by the way we act and the things we say. We show them what it means to follow Christ.
○ **King**	Christ is King, and all of the baptized are part of the Body of Christ. We are co-heirs, with Christ, to the Kingdom of God.
What I Did This Week	_____ _____ _____ _____

> * Place a check mark by one way you have shared in Jesus' mission this week. In the space provided, explain what happened.

Catholic Faith Words

vocation the purpose for which God made us and the particular way to answer and live out his call, whether as a lay person (married or single), a member of a religious community, or a member of the ordained ministry

discernment the process by which a person reflects, discusses, and prays about how God might be calling him or her to live out a particular vocation

LIST

List some things you enjoy doing and those things you take seriously. How can you use these talents to make a difference in the lives of people around you?

Things I Enjoy Doing

1. _____

2. _____

Things I Take Seriously

1. _____

2. _____

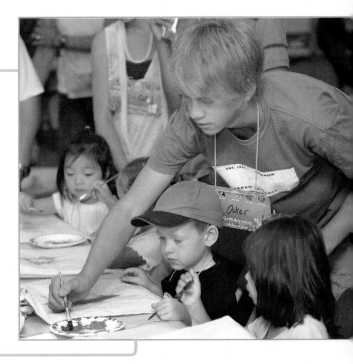

Listening for God's Call

What gifts does the Church call on you to share?

We can be inspired by the words and witness of priests, religious women and men, lay leaders, and good Catholic parents. There are many needs in our Church, and we're called to listen and respond.

Sometimes we respond with our treasure, like when disaster strikes a poor country. The collection basket is passed, and we give what we can.

As we grow older, and our gifts develop, we also share our talent and time. We might be altar servers, work at a soup kitchen, or help at Vacation Bible School. We might read at Mass, teach a class, or make an even bigger commitment to participate in parish life.

When a man becomes a parish priest, he will promise to respect and obey his bishop, live a simple lifestyle, and be celibate. Celibacy means to not get married and to not have sexual relations. These promises require great sacrifices, but they're made out of love for God and the Church community.

Sacred Vows

Other people may choose to serve God by entering **consecrated religious life.** This includes members of religious orders, who are known as brothers or sisters, as well as priests in religious orders. The men and women called to live a consecrated life live in a community and take vows of poverty, chastity, and obedience.

> ### Catholic Faith Words
>
> **consecrated religious life** a state of life lived by religious sisters, brothers, and priests in community and characterized by the vows of poverty, chastity, and obedience

A religious brother works in the library of San Salvador de Leyre monastery in Navarra, Spain

The Vows

In **poverty,** a consecrated person owns nothing in his or her own name. His or her few possessions are given to him or her and often shared with others. This helps the person to better understand and serve those who are poor.

Obedience shows that the common good is more important than our personal desires and helps a person to more fully serve the Church.

For men and women in consecrated life, **chastity** means living a celibate life. It shows that their love for God is the most important thing.

Although these vows, also called evangelical counsels, are required for people in consecrated religious life, Christ calls all of his disciples to live by them. Everyone should strive to live simply, love God above all things, and care deeply for others. A married couple needs to treat their relationship as a sacred partnership and mutual vocation. Through their communion, they are meant to grow closer together and nearer to the Lord.

> **In what ways do you feel called to serve the Church community and all God's people?**

REPORT

Brainstorm a list of all the different ministries and vocations that keep your parish running. Go beyond the immediately familiar groups or people and think about others working behind the scenes as well. Share a brief report on these ministries or vocations with your class or ask one person in your parish if he or she will speak to the class about his or her vocation.

IN SUMMARY Catholics Believe

We share a common call to know, love, and serve the Lord. The Church helps us respond to our unique call.

- We are called to relationship. We discern our vocation with the help of God's Word, family, the Church, and prayer.

- We are called to work. The Church asks us to share our time, talent, and treasure.

- We are called to faith. Each of us must live our particular vocation, whether married, single, ordained, or consecrated.

Our Catholic Life

Jesus and the Jewish people knew that being active in their religion, community, and local government was essential to their faith. With Jesus as their model, many saintly men and women of the Church started out and remained members of the **laity**. We can learn from their example by sharing in the work of the laity in our parishes and schools. As laity, we speak up for what is right and teach others to share in the mission of Christ through our words and actions. Baptized lay people participate in Christ's mission when we speak the truth, work for what is right and just, and help those in need, especially in our works of service.

> How do you continue Christ's mission on Earth? What makes your work easy or hard?

People of Faith

Saint Anthony of Padua, 1195–1231

Fernando Martins de Bulhões was an Augustinian priest, and later a Franciscan friar, taking the name Anthony. One day, when no one was prepared to give a sermon at the hospital where he worked, Anthony was asked to preach what the Spirit told him to say. His homily impressed Saint Francis so much that he had Anthony train young men to become Franciscan priests. Pope Gregory IX called him "a jewel case of the Bible." He was named a Doctor of the Church in 1946 and today is especially remembered as the patron Saint of finding lost objects. The Church celebrates his feast day on **June 13**.

For more, go to
aliveinchrist.osv.com

IDENTIFY

You're called to many things. Take some time to evaluate how you're responding by thinking about and answering the questions below.

How are you responding to the call of faith at this time in your life?

_____

_____

_____

How are you responding to your call in the subjects you are studying, the skills you are developing, and your after-school commitments?

_____

_____

_____

_____

Vocation Prayer

Reader 1: God, our Father and Creator, you have called each one of us to a vocation. Every vocation is a holy calling. Every vocation asks us to love and serve you and others. The Church, the Holy Spirit, and our families will guide us in finding the vocation you have planned for us. Help us to be patient and generous. Help us also to find the best way to use our gifts.

Reader 2: O God, you have given to the Church the gift of priesthood and religious vocations. Those whom you call to these vocations serve your Church and the People of God with a special and constant devotion. For all those called to the priesthood and to religious vocations:

All: We ask your abundant blessings, O God.

Reader 3: God and Father, you are the heavenly Father of all, the Creator of family. You have called many to the holy vocation of marriage and parenthood. The family, we know, is the domestic Church, the first community to share the faith with children. For all those whom you will call to marriage and to lives as mothers and fathers:

All: We ask your abundant blessings, O God.

Reader 4: God, some of your sons and daughters are also called to be holy in the committed single life. Dedicated single people can serve you, the Church, and the community. For all those called to live holy and fruitful lives as single men and women:

All: We ask your abundant blessings, O God.

Reader 1: Jesus, Son of God, and our Savior, you called Saint Ignatius of Loyola in a new way when he was wounded and disillusioned as a soldier. Together, we pray his prayer, a Prayer for a Generous Spirit, knowing that you will also call us to serve God in different life vocations and in different jobs and professions.

All: Lord, teach me to be generous.
Teach me to serve you as you deserve;
to give and not to count the cost,
to fight and not to heed the wounds,
to toil and not to seek for rest,
to labor and not ask for reward,
save that of knowing that I do your will.

All: Amen.

▶ *Sing or play "Find Us Ready"*

Go to **aliveinchrist.osv.com** for an interactive review.

A **Work with Words** Complete each sentence with the correct term from the Word Bank.

Sacred Chrism	domestic School
laity	domestic Church
witness	vocation
family	community

1. A member of the _____ is a baptized member of the Church who shares in Jesus' mission and witnesses to him, especially in his or her families, workplaces, and the civic community.

2. The purpose for which God made us and the particular way to answer his call is a _____.

3. The _____ is the first place to learn about the good within people and discover Christ's love.

4. A home and family can be a _____—the community of the home where children learn about God through the love, teaching, and example of parents and other family members.

5. Those who live in consecrated religious life live in _____.

B **Check Understanding** Indicate whether the following statements are true or false. Then rewrite false statements to make them true.

6. Parents and godparents promise to make it their "constant care to bring him (her) up in the practice of the faith" before a child is confirmed. **True/False**

_____

_____

7. Men and women called to live a consecrated religious life take vows of poverty, modesty, and obedience. **True/False**

_____

_____

8. Lay people share in Jesus' priesthood by praying and offering what we do as a gift to God. **True/False**

_____

_____

9. In Baptism and Confirmation, we are called to be holy in all parts of our lives. **True/False**

_____

_____

10. When you use discernment, you pray silently and wait for God's sign. **True/False**

_____

_____

C **Make Connections** On a separate sheet of paper, write a one-paragraph response to the question: What vocation do you think you will be called to, and how will your gifts from God help you follow that path?

CHAPTER 20

Act with Justice

♥ Let Us Pray

Leader: Jesus, give us the wisdom to learn about our faith and the courage to live our faith. Help us bring your message of hope to the world.

> "Justice and judgment are the foundation of your throne; mercy and faithfulness march before you." **Psalm 89:15**

All: Jesus, guide us to hear your voice and to act with justice.

📖 Scripture

The LORD rules forever,
  has set up his throne for judgment.

It is he who judges the world with justice,
  who judges the peoples with fairness.

The LORD is a stronghold for the oppressed,
  a stronghold in times of trouble.

Those who know your name trust in you; you
  never forsake those who seek you, LORD. …

To you the helpless can entrust their cause; you
  are the defender of orphans. …

You win justice for the orphaned and oppressed;
  no one on earth will cause terror again.
  Psalm 9:8–11, 10:14, 18

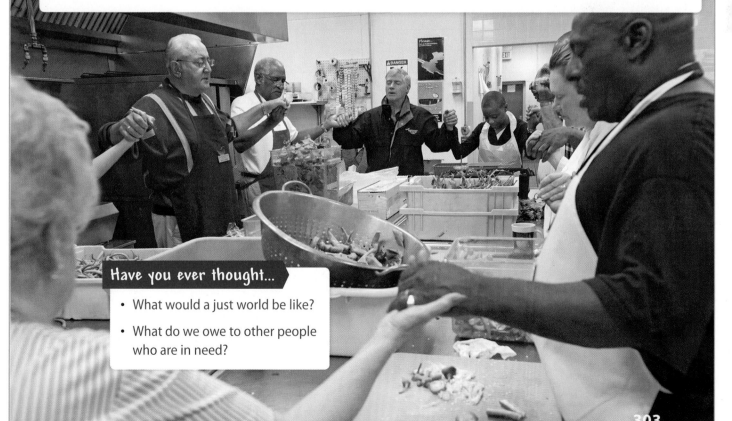

Have you ever thought...

- What would a just world be like?
- What do we owe to other people who are in need?

Getting Started

In this chapter, you will learn about what it means to live in the Kingdom of God. You will also learn ways that you can serve and attitudes you need in order to be part of God's Kingdom.

Catholic Faith Words

- justice
- peace
- solidarity

Fill in the chart with words or phrases that describe justice. Use the letter at the beginning of the line as the first letter of your words, terms or phrases. One has been done for you.

What Is Justice?	
J	
U	
S	
T	
I	
C	ompassion: show kindness and care for others.
E	

© Our Sunday Visitor

Fair or Just? Recall a situation in which you or someone you know was treated unfairly. Record the story in the space below. Then tell why you think it was unfair.

_____

_____

_____

_____

_____

_____

_____

_____

_____

_____

Record three situations or issues in the world that you know have changed because people have cried out for justice.

1. _____

2. _____

3. _____

Explain what you think the differences are between what is fair and what is just.

_____

_____

_____

_____

_____

_____

_____

_____

_____

_____

_____

> **Go to the Source**
>
> Read *Luke 4:14–22* to discover where Jesus announced his mission and how those who heard him responded.

All Are Invited

What does Jesus offer us?

We all deserve to be treated fairly and to be given the same respect. Jesus told us to "do to others whatever you would have them do to you" (**Matthew 7:12**). His words and actions remind us that we are equal in God's eyes. We need to show the world by our actions that all people are equal, deserving of what is their due, and worthy of fair treatment.

We all also have the responsibility to make sure that groups of people, society, and its organizations promote human dignity and don't undermine it. Sometimes we have to work to change the way things are so that people can get what they deserve and need. This is the **justice** Jesus taught us: giving God and others what is due to them as children of God made in his image, and possessing equal human dignity.

On a Mission

It is the Father's will that Jesus bring the Kingdom of Heaven to life right here on Earth. "The kingdom of God is at hand," Jesus said as he began his ministry. "Repent, and believe in the gospel" (**Mark 1:15**).

But what is God's Kingdom? It's not a physical location, or a fairy tale. The Kingdom of God, sometimes called the Kingdom of Heaven, or the Reign of God, is God's rule of peace, justice, and love that exists in Heaven, but has not yet come in its fullness on Earth. Jesus invited everyone to the Kingdom. All that's required is that people choose to believe, to

Catholic Faith Words

justice the constant and firm desire to give God and other people what is their due as children of God made in his image and possessing equal human dignity have faith, and to make a change in their lives and the way they look at the world and others.

Jesus came to teach us about the Kingdom of God. At the beginning of his ministry, he made it clear that he had fulfilled the words of the prophet Isaiah: that he had come to bring the Good News to the poor, to proclaim liberty to captives, recovery of sight to the blind, and to free the oppressed. (See Luke 4:14–22.)

> **In what ways did Jesus do the things he said he had come to do?**

Making It Real

Jesus reached out to people whom most leaders in his time would have pushed away: women, children, lepers, and especially those who were poor and in need. He challenged society and those in authority to act justly themselves, and to change the attitudes and structures that kept people from having what they needed to live.

An important attitude of the Kingdom is that we prefer God to all else. We put God first in our lives, and working for the Kingdom seems second nature. Through his parables and other teachings, Jesus tells us that words are not enough to enter the Kingdom. Our actions need to show that we believe and are working toward what is just, peaceful, and loving. The Kingdom and justice are so closely tied that you can't have one without the other. That's something Jesus showed us.

Underline the things Jesus came to do, and what our actions need to be in order to live for the Kingdom.

Think of someone in your community who has made it his or her life's work to help others. How does this person's work help solve poverty, end hunger, or fight injustice? How does he or she put God first in life? List two things you could do to help this person.

I could help

_____

by:

_____

_____

_____

_____

_____

_____

_____

_____

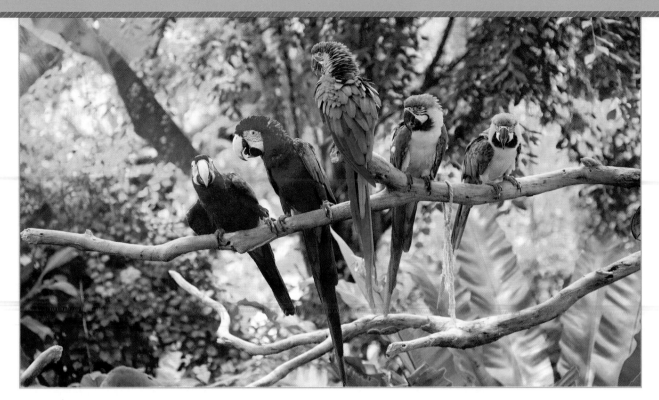

Red and blue and yellow macaws rest on a branch in a rainforest

Not Yet Complete

How can we work with God as he builds his Kingdom?

If Jesus came to proclaim and witness to God's Kingdom, why isn't the world a place of perfect **peace**, love, and justice? Why does so much injustice still exist? It's because the Kingdom is here, but it's not yet complete. Jesus gave us the Church to continue his mission and work. At the Second Coming, when Christ comes again in his glory at the end of time to judge the living and the dead, then the Kingdom will be complete and all creation will be fulfilled.

The Kingdom Grows

The amazing thing about the Kingdom of God is that it's meant to grow and expand. Jesus once told this parable to help his followers understand the Kingdom.

Scripture

"The kingdom of heaven is like a mustard seed that a person took and sowed in a field. It is the smallest of all the seeds, yet when full-grown it is the largest of plants. It becomes a large bush, and the 'birds of the sky come and dwell in its branches.'"

Matthew 13:31–32

But how does the Kingdom grow? It grows by God's presence and work and the ways we work with him to spread the Gospel message. What an amazing idea: Jesus sends us on a mission to bring his life and love to others, just like he sent the first disciples.

> **How do you think the Kingdom has grown since Jesus' time?**

> **How can you continue to be a sign of God's Kingdom?**

Catholic Faith Words

peace a state of calm and harmony when things are in their proper order and people settle problems with kindness and justice

So What Should We Do?

We need to say and do things that reflect God's love, peace, and justice. We can start with our family and friends. How do we respond to their needs? Are we trustworthy? Do we tell them the truth even when it might be difficult? Do we consider how our choices will affect them? When we make the wrong decisions, we affect others, perhaps even taking away from their dignity. We can avoid saying hurtful things during tense conversations as a way to prevent conflicts.

There's a lot we can do in our immediate circle, but then we need to take it a step further. We realize that social justice comes about by people working together.

Our parishes make choices to do good, to participate in activities that treat people fairly, and to take a stand for what is right regarding local, national, and global issues. The Church has many nonprofit agencies and organizations that look out for others and seek to change what harms others and keeps them from following Jesus. In all of these activities, the Church trusts that the Holy Spirit leads us where we need to be.

CATHOLICS TODAY

We can cooperate with God as he builds his Kingdom, including praying for it to come. We do this when we pray the Lord's Prayer: "Thy kingdom come, thy will be done on earth as it is in heaven." This prayer is made up of praise, hope, petition, and a desire for goodness.

- We begin by giving glory to God, our Father. We praise the goodness of his name. We ask the Father to build up his Kingdom and that he join our will to his to fulfill his plan of salvation for all.

- We follow this by asking God for what we need to help make his Kingdom spread. We need "daily bread"—not just food to eat, but also the love and joy that keep us going. We ask God not only to forgive our sins, but also to help us forgive those who have hurt us.

The Lord's Prayer is often called the perfect prayer because it captures the message of the Gospels. Praying to our Father should make our hearts more trusting and humble, and at the same time inspire a desire to be more like God. For the full text of the Lord's Prayer, see page 383 in the Our Catholic Tradition section of your book.

DESIGN

Work in small groups to design a collage of signs of the Kingdom in your local community. Use photos cut from magazines or newspapers, or create your own drawings. Write captions to describe how the images are signs of God's love, peace, and justice.

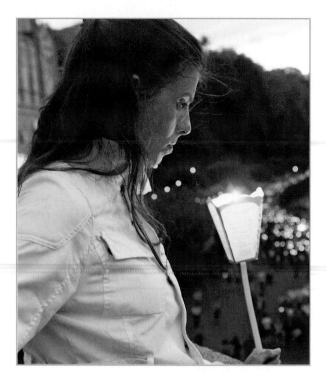

Living for the Kingdom

What attitudes reflect God's Kingdom?

You can't fight City Hall. . . Whoever gets the most toys, wins. . . Bigger is better. . . If you can't beat 'em, join 'em.

We hear messages like these a lot, whether it's on social media sites or in real life. Sometimes the lines blur, and our lives become too much like a video game or a reality show. Often, competing and consuming become more important than cooperating. In the struggle for money, popularity, and power, many good people get chewed up and spit out. Maybe you've heard this message: *Nice guys finish last.* Is that what happened to Jesus?

We know better than that. Through his Death on the Cross and his Resurrection, Jesus accomplished the coming of his Kingdom. Some people might see a crucifix and think that Jesus failed. We know that Jesus won the ultimate battle when he defeated death itself by rising to new life.

Go to the Source

Read *Luke 18:18–30.* Jesus teaches that we must detach ourselves from our riches if we want to enter the Kingdom of God. Discuss what your riches are, how difficult or easy it is to give them up, and where you might start simplifying your lifestyle.

Our Brothers' and Sisters' Keepers

Our Church teaches that government and business leaders must respect people's fundamental rights and also the conditions that let them use their rights. Everyone has a right to life and to the necessities of life such as food, clothing, shelter, medicine, and education. People have the right to vote, speak freely, own property, and run their own businesses. If governments or businesses don't let people have these rights, the Church speaks out. Ultimately, "We must obey God rather than men" (**Acts 5:29**).

Solidarity is a word our Church uses to describe unity with all of our brothers and sisters throughout the world. In solidarity, we practice the sharing of spiritual and material goods. It encourages us to be generous and to live simply, so that others might be blessed with our generosity. Solidarity is a Christian principle that motivates us to share our spiritual gifts, even more so than our material ones.

Objects and people, even the ones you love or who love you the most, are no substitute for God. Life is freer and simpler when you

Catholic Faith Words

solidarity a Christian principle that motivates believers to share their spiritual gifts as well as their material ones

The Catholic Church calls for acts of justice around the world. A brave example of this happened in the 1980s when Pope Saint John Paul II showed his support for a workers' movement called "Solidarity" in his native Poland. He encouraged workers to rise up for their rights. This led to new freedom in Poland and eventually contributed to the end of oppressive governments throughout Eastern Europe, including Russia. Even today, Pope Francis continues this mission of the Church by speaking out against injustice.

Pope John Paul II with President Lech Walesa, leader of the Polish Solidarity movement

make God's love your true goal. Believing in God makes it possible for you to put him, not things or accomplishments, first in your life.

In the Beatitudes found in the Gospel according to Matthew, Jesus teaches us: "Blessed are the poor in spirit, for theirs is the kingdom of heaven" (**Matthew 5:3**). Poor in spirit doesn't mean not having money. Even rich people can be poor in spirit. It means that we humans cannot make money or riches into a god, but we need to depend on the one true God for strength and guidance.

The Tenth Commandment teaches us:

- to be glad for others' good fortune and not envious of them
- not to be jealous of the things others have
- not to be greedy or overly concerned about power or being in charge (See Exodus 20:17.)

It's sometimes difficult not to want what others have. But we can keep things in perspective. Prayer, goodwill toward others, and trusting in God's care of us help us resist envy.

IN SUMMARY Catholics Believe

Jesus made justice a priority. It was central to his teaching on God's Kingdom for which we all long.

- Jesus welcomes all people to God's Kingdom of love, peace, and justice. As his followers, we have to show others we are called to give God and others their due, respecting the dignity of all, and work to end hunger, poverty, and injustice.

- God's Kingdom is present but not yet complete. We prepare for and work toward the Kingdom through worship and prayer, sharing Jesus' Good News, just action, and advocacy for those in need.

- We need to rely on God, trust in his care, and have the right attitude toward money and things. Doing so helps us concentrate on what's important and work for the rights of others.

Our Catholic Life

With all the ways we have to share our reactions to what people are doing and thinking, as well as our opinions on local and worldwide events, with people around the world on **social media** sites, it can be hard to know when to hold back on those reactions or even sometimes exactly what to say. The Catholic Church has an important role in sharing her messages and views on events in a way that makes clear she is Christ's Church, and that her members are able to act as good examples, both online and off. Pope Francis shares the Church's message regularly online, and offers a role model for how to communicate it. The next time you post a status, think about the message you are sending. Does it reflect well on you as a member of the Church?

> **What is one thing you could share online this week about the Catholic Church?**

People of Faith

Pope Leo XIII, 1878–1903

Gioacchino Vincenzo Raffaele Luigi Pecci witnessed political and social upheavals and helped define the role of the modern Church. His papacy, as Leo XIII, helped the Church survive a stormy period in history. Following the example of Jesus in his pursuit of justice and peace, Leo helped settle troubles between nations and within nations, including helping end the persecution of Catholics in Germany. By the time of Leo's death, he was already regarded as one of the greatest Popes of all time.

For more, go to
aliveinchrist.osv.com

IDENTIFY

Think about an issue that concerns you. Write your response to these decision-making steps.

See an issue that gets me thinking

_____

Judge what I've learned from the news

_____

What Jesus and the Church say

_____

Act on things I can do

_____

_____

_____

♥ A Prayer of Petition

Leader: Lord Jesus, we know that you came to establish the Kingdom of God here on Earth. You wanted God's rule of peace and justice to take root among us. You wanted everyone to welcome and live in this Kingdom, which you also called the Kingdom of Heaven. You came to bring Good News to the poor, proclaim liberty to the captives, and to heal people. You have called us, and all of your followers, to continue your Kingdom work. But, as Saint Teresa of Calcutta said in her prayer, this Kingdom work is hard. It is often rejected or unappreciated. Give us the strength—as you gave Saint Teresa—to "do it anyway." Let's pray Saint Teresa's prayer:

Side 1: People are often unreasonable, irrational, and self-centered. Forgive them anyway.

Side 2: If you are kind, people may accuse you of selfish, ulterior motives. Be kind anyway.

Side 1: If you are successful, you will win some unfaithful friends and some genuine enemies. Succeed anyway.

Side 2: If you are honest and sincere, people may deceive you. Be honest and sincere anyway.

Side 1: What you spend years creating, others could destroy overnight. Create anyway.

Side 2: If you find serenity and happiness, some may be jealous. Be happy anyway.

Side 1: The good you do today will often be forgotten. Do good anyway.

Side 2: Give the best you have, and it will never be enough. Give your best anyway.

Leader: "In the final analysis it is between you and God" said Mother Teresa as she was known in her lifetime. "It was never between you and them anyway." We know, Jesus, that your Kingdom is not fully established among us. As young Catholics, we too have the responsibility to work for justice. When each of us tries to live, speak, and share with charity and respect, we help people see God's Kingdom in our midst.

Take turns praying for the works of justice that each of you can do, for example: "Lord, give me the courage to confront those who bully and speak up for those who are victims of bullying."

All: Lord, even if this is hard, help us to do it anyway. Amen.

▶ *Sing or play "We Will Follow"*

Go to **aliveinchrist.osv.com** for an interactive review.

A Work with Words Circle the letter of the choice that best completes the sentence.

1. ___ gives God and other people what is due to them as children of God made in his image and possessing equal human dignity.

   a. Tolerance   c. Patience

   b. Justice   d. Kindness

2. Solidarity is a Christian ___ that motivates believers to share their spiritual gifts as well as their material ones.

   a. prayer   c. principle

   b. tradition   d. law

3. To ___ means to be sorry for our sins and change our ways.

   a. anoint   c. repent

   b. pray   d. rehabilitate

4. The Kingdom of God is God's rule of love, ___, and justice in our hearts, lives, and the world. This Kingdom exists in Heaven, but has not yet come in its fullness on Earth.

   a. peace   c. holiness

   b. repentance   d. mission

B Check Understanding Complete each sentence with the correct term from the Word Bank.

Rosary	Kingdom
sin	Lord's Prayer
salvation	envious
justice	mustard seed

5. The Tenth Commandment teaches us not to be _____ of what others have and accomplish.

6. Hunger, poverty, and injustice all come from _____.

7. When Christ comes again, the _____ of God will be complete.

8. In a parable, Jesus tells us that the Kingdom of Heaven is like a _____.

9. Jesus showed us that you cannot have the Kingdom without _____.

10. The _____ is often called the perfect prayer because it sums up the message of the Gospels.

C Make Connections On a separate sheet of paper, write a one-paragraph response to the question: How does the Lord's Prayer connect with your life? Write the prayer one line at a time. Below each line, write what it means for you right now.

© Our Sunday Visitor

Our Reason for Hope

♥ Let Us Pray

Leader: Jesus, by your Death and Resurrection you transformed death into new life. Give us the hope that comes with the Resurrection and the grace to live life as you taught.

"But I trust in your mercy.
    Grant my heart joy in your salvation,
I will sing to the LORD,
    for he has dealt bountifully with me!" **Psalm 13:6**

All: O God, teach us to watch and pray. Teach us to trust in your goodness, and in your plan for us to be with you forever.

📖 Scripture

"We know that all creation is groaning in labor pains even until now; and not only that, but we ourselves, who have the firstfruits of the Spirit, we also groan within ourselves as we wait for adoption, the redemption of our bodies. For in hope we were saved. Now hope that sees for itself is not hope. For who hopes for what one sees? But if we hope for what we do not see, we wait with endurance …. We know that all things work for good for those who love God, who are called according to his purpose."
Romans 8:22–25, 28

Have you ever thought...

- What does it mean to wait with hope?
- What does it take to get to Heaven?

Getting Started

In this chapter, you will learn about Jesus' promises of eternal life and the meaning of the Second Coming. You will also study the Church's teachings about life after death, and how her members act through the Works of Mercy to show God's Kingdom to the world.

Catholic Faith Words

- Heaven
- Hell
- Particular Judgment
- Purgatory
- Last Judgment
- Works of Mercy

In the web below, record what you know about Heaven, Hell, and Purgatory. Share your ideas with the class. You may add to the web as you study the chapter.

The Last Things

Heaven

_____

_____

_____

_____

Hell

_____

_____

_____

_____

Purgatory

_____

_____

_____

_____

© Our Sunday Visitor

The Person You Want to Be On a gravestone, we often see the years a person was born and died, with a hyphen in between (July 25, 1945–October 30, 1995). Someone once said, "Life is all about what you do in the hyphen." When you think about your life and that it had a beginning and will have an end, what do you hope to do with your hyphen? What kind of person do you want to be?

_____

_____

_____

_____

_____

_____

_____

_____

_____

_____

_____

_____

_____

_____

_____

_____

_____

_____

_____

_____

Jesus Gives Us Hope

What does Jesus promise about eternal life?

We always worry about death when someone is seriously ill. But it's also natural to wonder about what will come after. We might think about how things will be different when someone we love is no longer with us. Our concern for a relative or friend who is very sick might send us running to be with that person and help however we could.

Martha told Jesus that she believed he is the Messiah. Because of her belief, and because Jesus wants people to believe in him and give glory to his Father who sent him, Jesus called Lazarus out of the tomb. Lazarus did not rise under his own power, but under the power of God. Jesus showed that he had power over humanity's greatest fear, death.

> **What kind of life is Jesus offering us?**

Scripture

One day while traveling with his disciples, Jesus heard that his friend Lazarus was ill. Then Lazarus died. When Jesus arrived at their home, Lazarus's sister Martha said, "Lord, if you had been here, my brother would not have died. But even now I know that whatever you ask of God, God will give you."

Jesus told her:

"I am the resurrection and the life; whoever believes in me, even if he dies, will live, and everyone who lives and believes in me will never die. Do you believe this?"

She said to him, "Yes, Lord, I have come to believe that you are the Messiah, the Son of God." **Based on John 11:1–44**

Go to the Source

Read *John 11:1–44* and think about Jesus' love for his friends.

The Raising of Lazarus, **Maurice Denis**

Christian Hope

Lazarus and his sisters were great friends with Jesus. Because of this, Jesus came for Lazarus. Because of Martha's belief, he raised Lazarus. Because of their hope and belief, Jesus gave them even more reason to hope.

Lazarus's return to earthly life is very different from Jesus' Resurrection. Jesus rose to new life, a glorified life in which he returned to the Father. Jesus' Resurrection gives those who believe hope.

As you know, hope is one of the three Theological Virtues. The other two are faith and charity (love). The Theological Virtues are gifts from God that help you live your life in ways that strengthen your relationship with the Holy Trinity.

Christian hope puts things into this perspective: that happiness comes from life with God. It helps you put your trust in Jesus' promises and the strength of the Holy Spirit. This hope keeps you motivated and going even during difficult times. It helps you put the right emphasis on the things that really matter, the things that relate to loving God and others.

Saint Paul wrote to the Colossians that Jesus is "the beginning, the firstborn from the dead" (**Colossians 1:18**). There will be more to come. Because of Jesus' Resurrection to new life, we, too, hope to rise again.

Saint Paul wrote to the Romans that if the Spirit of God is in us, it will give life to our bodies, even though they are dead. (See Romans 8:11.) Our Baptism joins us with Christ; we die with him to sin, and we live a full and new life in God.

A tapestry in the Cathedral of Los Angeles depicts Saints and holy people such as Bridget of Sweden, Justin de Jacobis, Boniface, Martin de Porres, John Vianney, and the children of Fátima.

BRAINSTORM

In groups of three, brainstorm reason(s) why the Saints help give us hope in eternal life. Also talk about what makes it hard to have such hope.

_____

_____

_____

_____

_____

_____

_____

_____

_____

Life after Death

How will we be judged by God?

No one can be sure what **Heaven** will be like, but Sacred Tradition tells us that Heaven is the state, or experience, of being happy with God forever for all who die in his friendship. The souls of the just experience the full joy of living in God's presence forevermore.

Jesus warns us about judgment at our death in a parable he tells about a rich man who ignored a beggar. They both eventually die, but the beggar is carried away by angels, while the rich man winds up in the netherworld, which we know as Hell. There he suffers in flames.

Jesus also describes a great chasm—a gap that would probably make the Grand Canyon look like a gopher hole—between the rich man and Heaven. (See Luke 16:19–31.) **Hell** is the state, or experience, of eternal separation from God because of a choice to turn away from him and not seek forgiveness. God is the source of our life and happiness. Imagine being apart from him forever, without life or happiness.

> **If you knew your life would end tomorrow, what would you do?**

How Late Is Too Late?

When we die, we'll be out of time to accept or to reject the love and grace Jesus offers us. We can take it or leave it today, but at the moment we die, our destiny for eternity will be based on whether we have accepted God's love. After a person's death, God decides where that person will spend eternity according to his or her faith and works. Each person's soul is rewarded with the blessings of Heaven, given a time of purification called Purgatory, or condemned to eternal separation from God in Hell. We call this individual judgment the **Particular Judgment**.

God's willingness to accept our repentance, forgive us, and bring us to eternal happiness is available to us as long as we live. Jesus proves this on the Cross.

Scripture

One of the criminals crucified with Jesus admits that he has sinned and asks, "Jesus, remember me when you come into your kingdom." Jesus tells him ". . . today you will be with me in Paradise." **Luke 23:42–43**

Catholic Faith Words

Heaven the state, or experience, of the full joy of living eternally in God's presence

Hell the state, or experience, of eternal separation from God because of a choice to turn away from him and not seek forgiveness

Particular Judgment the individual judgment by God at the time of a person's death; when God decides, after a person's death, where that person will spend eternity according to his or her faith and works

Purgatory a state of final cleansing after death and before entering into Heaven that removes any remaining personal obstacles to eternal union with God. Purgatory frees the person from temporal punishment (being deprived of the entrance into Heaven for a time) due to sin.

But we can never know for sure when we will die. And think about this: Isn't it much more satisfying to go through life with the inner peace that comes with knowing that you are living as God asks?

God's way is not just about happiness later in Heaven; living in his love and guidance is the surest way to peace and joy in this lifetime, too.

So what is **Purgatory**? We receive God's grace through Baptism and accept his loving friendship. If we accept God's grace and have repented of our sins, die in God's friendship, and are perfectly purified, we are welcomed into Heaven. However, if we have remained in God's friendship but are in need of satisfaction for temporal punishment for sins already forgiven, we will enter a condition called Purgatory. Purgatory is not a place, but a state of purification between death and Heaven that removes any remaining personal obstacles to eternal union with God. This cleansing needs to happen before we experience the joy of eternal happiness with God.

Purgatory purifies us, but it's very different from the punishment of Hell. Our prayers for the dead help provide the grace that the souls in Purgatory need to be welcomed into God's heavenly Kingdom.

IDENTIFY AND LIST

Think about some actions and behaviors that would be disobeying or turning away from God. Then list three positive behaviors or actions that can counter these and help you strengthen your relationship with God.

1. _____

2. _____

3. _____

The Second Coming

How can we be with Jesus on the last day?

Someday, at God's word, our world will end. Nobody knows for sure when or why, or exactly what it will look or be like. We just know that life as we know it will end and creation will be transformed. And as we pray in the Nicene Creed at Mass, Jesus "will come again in glory to judge the living and the dead."

Who Will Inherit the Kingdom?

Jesus described pretty simply what will happen when he comes again.

> ### 📖 Go to the Source
>
> Read *Matthew 25:31–46* to find out how Jesus, the King of Glory, will judge all people at the end of time.

The Resurrection of Jesus, from the Church of St. Ann, in Emmaus, Pennsylvania

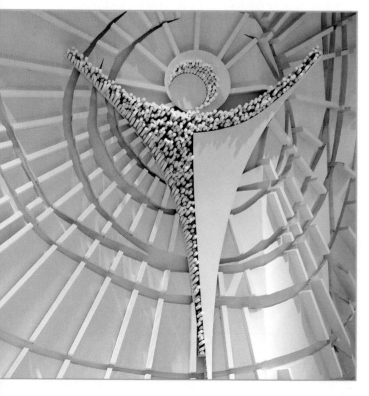

At the Second Coming, the **Last Judgment** will take place, during which all the living and dead will be judged. The Last Judgment is God's final triumph over evil that will occur at the end of time when Christ returns and judges all the living and the dead. Then, all will fully see and understand God's plan for creation.

Those who have died will appear in their own bodies before Christ. In the description of this judgment in the Gospel according to Matthew, the glorified Christ will sit on a throne, putting the righteous people on his right side and the others on his left.

The faithful people will have life forever in Heaven with God because they had a relationship with Jesus and showed this by living good lives and reaching out to people in need. This includes feeding someone who was hungry, welcoming a stranger, or taking care of a sick person. At the end of the world, Jesus will reveal the secrets of our hearts and judge each of us in light of our works and the degree that we accepted his grace or refused it and sinned. Jesus knows what each one of us does, just as he knows when we turn to him or turn away from him in our lives.

The Kingdom that Jesus talked so much about will come into fullness at the Last Judgment. As Christ has risen, so will we. Our bodies will be transformed by reuniting

> ### Catholic Faith Words
>
> **Last Judgment** God's final triumph over evil that will occur at the end of time when Christ returns and judges all the living and the dead. Then, all will fully see and understand God's plan for creation.
>
> **Works of Mercy** actions that show care for the physical and spiritual needs of others

with our souls. The righteous will be with Jesus forever and the world will be transformed.

> **What do you think about being judged?**
> **What can you do to prepare yourself?**

The Works of Mercy

The **Works of Mercy** are ways to respond to Jesus when we see him in the poor and needy. The Corporal Works of Mercy are actions that provide for people's physical needs, and the Spiritual Works of Mercy are actions that address the needs of the heart, mind, and soul.

Often several Works of Mercy are done together. For instance, if a friend's grandmother dies, you're more likely to comfort your friend and pray for her grandma, while somebody else will deliver flowers and other people will assist with the funeral. Jesus is pleased with whatever we do for people in need.

 Fill in the right column of the chart with ideas on how you can perform the Works of Mercy listed in the left column. Some have been done for you.

The Works of Mercy	
Corporal	**One Thing You Can Do**
Feed the hungry.	Donate to a food drive.
Give drink to the thirsty.	
Clothe the naked.	Donate your old clothing.
Shelter the homeless.	
Visit the sick.	
Visit those in prison.	Support parish outreach.
Bury the dead.	
Spiritual	**One Thing You Can Do**
Counsel the doubtful.	
Instruct the ignorant.	Help teach kids at church.
Admonish the sinner.	
Comfort the sorrowful.	Help a friend who's sad.
Bear wrongs patiently.	
Pray for the living and the dead.	Pray for a loved one.

IN SUMMARY Catholics Believe

By his Death and Resurrection, Jesus makes it possible for believers to have eternal life—life with God forever.

- Christian hope is based upon putting our trust in God and having hope that we will rise one day as Jesus did.

- We will be judged at our death based upon the ways we have accepted and acted on

God's grace in our lives. God desires all of us to make the right choices in life, so we can be with him forever in the happiness of Heaven.

- Jesus will come at the end of time to judge the living and the dead, and the Kingdom of God will be complete and full in its glory.

Our Catholic Life

Two special days celebrated during the liturgical year are All Saints Day, which occurs on November 1, and **All Souls Day**, which is celebrated on November 2. All Saints Day is a Holy Day of Obligation for Catholics in the United States, but All Souls Day is important, too. On All Souls Day, the Catholic Church prays for those who have died in friendship with God but are undergoing final purfication before enjoying eternal happiness with him in Heaven. During All Souls Day celebrations, Catholics attend Mass, sometimes visit gravesites, and sometimes participate in processions through towns and cities. While Catholics are always encouraged to pray for the dead as well as the living, All Souls Day is a special occasion in which to do so.

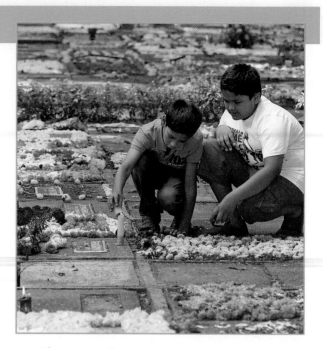

> What special prayers can you use to remember those you know who have died?

People of Faith

Saint Francis de Sales, 1567–1622

Saint Francis de Sales was born into a noble French family and was extremely well educated. He devoted his life to teaching other people about God's love. His way of teaching is sometimes called the Way of Divine Love. In 1877 Blessed Pope Pius IX named him a Doctor of the Church. In one of his most famous books, *Introduction to the Devout Life,* he explains how an ordinary person can lead a holy life. People still follow his advice today. The Church celebrates his feast day on **January 24**.

For more, go to
aliveinchrist.osv.com

CONSIDER

You can take the meaning of Christian hope to heart to change your outlook on troubling issues. Consider what it really means to trust in God, and apply it to your relationships. Using what you have learned this year, you can offer hope-filled advice to friends and family. On the lines below, name something you can do to become a more hope-filled person.

_____

_____

_____

_____

_____

_____

_____

_____

♥ Praying Psalm 23

Leader: Psalm 23 reminds us that we have good reason to be hopeful.

Side 1: The LORD is my shepherd; there is nothing I lack.

Side 2: God, I know that you love me and know what I need. I don't need an endless pile of things and piles of spending money. My needs are deeper. Help me to understand and accept the way you are leading me through my parents, teachers, and the Church. Help me to trust.

Side 1: to still waters he leads me; he restores my soul.

He guides me along right paths for the sake of his name.

Side 2: Jesus, my Good Shepherd, you know how stressed I get sometimes. You are calling me to find my peace in the things that really matter. Help me to follow your lead, and to grow in virtue, especially love.

Side 1: Even though I walk through the valley of the shadow of death,

I will fear no evil, for you are with me; your rod and your staff comfort me.

Side 2: Lord and Savior, I know that even though I'm young, I will someday face the end of my life. Even before that day, I will face many frightening situations. I draw comfort in knowing you are always nearby, even when nobody else is.

Side 1: You set a table before me in front of my enemies;

You anoint my head with oil; my cup overflows.

Side 2: Jesus, you know that there are many things that try to block the person I'm trying to be. Some of my "enemies" are my own faults and weaknesses. No worries. You will feed and provide for me even in the face of those things. You will treat me as if I were royalty, anointing my head with oil.

Side 1: Indeed, goodness and mercy will pursue me all the days of my life;

I will dwell in the house of the LORD for endless days.

Side 2: God, although I often forget, I know I can place my trust and hope in you. I know that you will love and protect forever. What more could anyone want from a shepherd? Lead me, Lord.

Leader: Let's sing together.

▶ *Sing or play "My Sheep"*

Go to **aliveinchrist.osv.com** for an interactive review.

A Work with Words Circle the letter of the choice that best completes the sentence.

1. Faith, hope, and charity are ____.
   a. Moral Virtues
   b. Canon Laws
   c. Theological Virtues
   d. Sacraments

2. In Jesus' parable of the rich man and the beggar, the rich man is sent to ____.
   a. the netherworld
   b. Purgatory
   c. Heaven
   d. both a and c

3. ____ Judgment is the individual judgment by God at the time of a person's death when God decides where that person will spend eternity.
   a. Divine
   b. Particular
   c. Eternal
   d. Honest

4. Purgatory is a process of being ____ before entering Heaven.
   a. purified
   b. judged
   c. condemned
   d. rewarded

5. In the Gospel according to John, when Jesus goes to raise Lazarus from the dead, Jesus says he is the ____ and the ____.
   a. source, life
   b. Resurrection, life
   c. hope, peace
   d. mercy, grace

B Check Understanding Indicate whether the following statements are true or false. Then rewrite false statements to make them true.

6. Sacred Tradition defines Heaven as the state, or experience, of the full joy of living eternally in God's presence. **True/False**

   _____

   _____

7. Hell is defined as a state where people are separaed from God for a short time. **True/False**

   _____

   _____

8. Prayers for the dead help provide the grace needed by souls in Hell in order to be welcomed into Heaven. **True/False**

   _____

   _____

9. At the Second Coming of Jesus, the Last Judgment will take place. **True/False**

   _____

   _____

10. At the Last Judgment, those who have died in God's good graces will become spirits. **True/False**

   _____

   _____

C Make Connections On a separate sheet of paper, write a one-paragraph response to the question: Think about the Corporal and Spiritual Works of Mercy. What would happen in your life and in the lives of others if you responded to people's needs with God's love? Give a specific example.

A Work with Words **Match the terms on the left with the correct definitions or descriptions on the right.**

___ **1.** laity

___ **2.** domestic Church

___ **3.** vocation

___ **4.** justice

___ **5.** repent

___ **6.** Kingdom of God

___ **7.** solidarity

___ **8.** Theological Virtues

___ **9.** Particular Judgment

___ **10.** Purgatory

___ **11.** evangelical counsels

a. the constant and firm desire to give God and other people what is due to them

b. unity of all people around the world

c. God's rule of love, peace, and justice that exists in Heaven but has not yet come in its fullness on Earth

d. the family as a community of grace and prayer

e. faith, hope, and charity

f. time when souls are rewarded with Heaven, given a time of purification called Purgatory, or condemned to Hell

g. baptized members of the Church who share in Jesus' mission and witness to him, especially in their families, workplaces, and civic communities

h. the state of being cleansed, or purified, before being able to enter Heaven

i. the purpose for which God made us and the particular way to answer his call

j. to be sorry for sin and change behavior

k. poverty, obedience, and chastity

B **Check Understanding**   Indicate whether the following statements are true or false. Then rewrite false statements to make them true.

12. The family is the first place to learn about the good within people and discover Christ's love. **True/False**

_____

_____

13. Lay people share in Jesus' priesthood by teaching in parables as he did. **True/False**

_____

_____

14. When you use discernment, you weigh your choices and pray for guidance. **True/False**

_____

_____

15. Jesus taught us that we cannot have the Kingdom without justice. **True/False**

_____

_____

16. The Lord's Prayer is often called the perfect prayer because it sums up the message of the Gospels. **True/False**

_____

_____

17. Hell is defined as being apart from the people you love forever. **True/False**

_____

_____

18. In the Gospel according to John, when Jesus goes to raise Lazarus from the dead, he says he is the sacrifice and the life. **True/False**

_____

_____

19. At the Last Judgment, those who have died in God's friendship will be glorified in body and soul. **True/False**

_____

_____

C **Make Connections**   Write a short answer to the questions below.

20. How can your school community actively work toward the Kingdom of God—God's love, peace, and justice—on campus?

_____

_____

_____

_____

21. Imagine you are a reporter at the Last Judgment. What do you see happening? How are people responding? What are your reactions?

_____

_____

_____

_____

22. Name two Corporal Works of Mercy and describe how you could perform them in your everyday life.

_____

_____

_____

_____

23. Name two Spiritual Works of Mercy you have performed in your everyday life and what effect they had.

_____

_____

_____

_____

24. Of the three vows taken in consecrated religious life—poverty, celibacy, and obedience—which do you think is the hardest? Why?

_____

_____

_____

_____

25. How does the Church describe Heaven?

_____

_____

_____

_____

Circle the letter of the response that correctly completes the statement.

1. The ___ is the term for the mystery of the Son of God taking on human nature.

   a. Annunciation

   b. Nativity

   c. Miracle

   d. Incarnation

2. Jesus instructed the Apostles to travel in such a way that they ___ .

   a. would meet with important people

   b. could gather monetary treasures for the Church

   c. would trust in God to provide for them

   d. could leave a place quickly if they were persecuted

3. Jesus' ___ teach us about the meaning and path to true happiness and the ways to live in the Kingdom of God.

   a. Ten Commandments

   b. miracles

   c. Beatitudes

   d. first books of the Bible

4. The process by which, through the power of the Holy Spirit and the words and actions of the priest, the bread and wine are transformed into the Body and Blood of Christ is known as ___ .

   a. discernment

   b. conversion

   c. transubstantiation

   d. transfiguration

5. The deliberate ending of a pregnancy by killing the unborn child is known as ___ .

   a. suicide

   b. scandal

   c. abortion

   d. euthanasia

6. Much of Catholic liturgy has its roots in the ___ traditions that Jesus took part in as he grew up.

   a. Jewish

   b. Roman

   c. Apostolic

   d. Gentile

7. A ___ is a the purpose for which God made us and the particular way to answer and live out his call.

   a. spirituality

   b. vocation

   c. reparation

   d. covenant

8. A soul that is in Purgatory is in the process of being ___ .

   a. judged

   b. punished

   c. rewarded

   d. cleansed

9. Contemplative prayer is ___ .

   a. based on songs

   b. group prayer

   c. part of the Mass

   d. wordless prayer

10. ____ is the God-given ability that helps individuals judge whether actions are right or wrong.

   a. Free will

   b. Conscience

   c. Reason

   d. Judgment

11. When we attempt to indirectly correct the damage caused by sin, we are making ____.

   a. reparation

   b. contrition

   c. conscience formation

   d. reconciliation

12. The ____ Commandment identifies lying as a sin that damages our character and integrity.

   a. Tenth

   b. Eighth

   c. Fourth

   d. Sixth

13. Jesus told the Beatitudes during the ____.

   a. Last Supper

   b. journey to Jerusalem

   c. Sermon on the Mount

   d. wedding at Cana

14. Letters from the Pope to the Church community are known as ____.

   a. spiritual treasury

   b. encyclicals

   c. evangelical counsels

   d. spiritualities

15. God is ____, which means he always was, is now, and always will be.

   a. faithful

   b. eternal

   c. holy

   d. love

16. A prayer that acclaims God for his nature is a prayer of ____.

   a. intercession

   b. thanksgiving

   c. blessing

   d. praise

17. Through ____, God promised to remain in a relationship with his People.

   a. his law

   b. his grace

   c. the covenant

   d. the spiritualities

18. The Church's complete list of inspired books included in Sacred Scripture is called ____.

   a. the canon of Scripture

   b. Sacred Tradition

   c. Church doctrine

   d. natural law

19. ____ is the free, loving gift of God's life and help.

   a. Solidarity

   b. Inspiration

   c. Grace

   d. Conscience

20. The Church is organized into ___ that has different levels of leadership and membership.

    a. a hierarchy

    b. the Magisterium

    c. a canon

    d. an encyclical

21. The Cardinal Virtues include all of the following **except** ___.

    a. prudence

    b. justice

    c. charity

    d. fortitude

22. We show our ___ when we are sorry for our sins and pledge to try to not sin again.

    a. contrition

    b. forgiveness

    c. suffering

    d. confession

23. ___ is the courage to do what is right even if others disagree with or challenge you.

    a. Justice

    b. Temperance

    c. Fortitude

    d. Prudence

24. When we act with ___, we give God and our neighbor what is due to them.

    a. prudence

    b. hope

    c. justice

    d. temperance

25. The ___ is the event of the Angel Gabriel telling Mary she would be the Mother of God.

    a. Assumption

    b. Annunciation

    c. Ascension

    d. Attribution

26. The ___ Commandment instructs us not to kill another person.

    a. First

    b. Tenth

    c. Third

    d. Fifth

27. Jesus told ___, or stories that taught moral or spiritual truths.

    a. passages

    b. parables

    c. poems

    d. pastiches

Write a short answer to the questions or statements below.

Name the Marks of the Church, and describe what each means, in your own words.

28. _____

29. _____

30. _____

31. _____

32. Describe the Kingdom of God in your own words.

_____

_____

_____

33. What is the Paschal Mystery?

_____

_____

34. What is the mission of the Catholic Church?

_____

_____

35. Define _Sacrament_ and list the Seven Sacraments.

_____

_____

_____

_____

36. How does your conscience help you make good decisions?

_____

_____

_____

How are the three Divine Persons of the Trinity related to one another?

37. _____

38. _____

39. _____

40. Who are the Saints and why are they important to us?

_____

_____

_____

Live Your Faith

Catholic Social Teaching

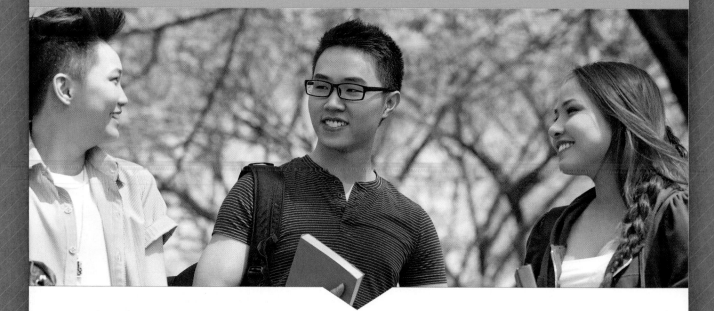

Life and Dignity of the Human Person

In Scripture God tells us, "Before I formed you in the womb I knew you" (Jeremiah 1:5). God created each one of us. Every person is unique and unrepeatable. He has a special plan for each of our lives. He knows what he made us to be.

Because God made each person, we are called to treat each person with human dignity. Every life is valuable to God. We should take care of the bodies and minds God gave us and use them to do good things. We are meant to be kind toward others, and solve problems peacefully instead of fighting. If we see someone else being bullied, teased, or disrespected, we are called to speak up and defend that person, and get help if necessary. It is our responsibility to help to protect others, because every single life is important to God.

Each one of us, every person on Earth, is created in the image and likeness of God and is equally precious in the eyes of God. That's the basis of our dignity as human persons. Because God is love and loves all persons, we too are called to love everyone, even those who may seem difficult to love.

It almost seems easy to tease certain kids, to make fun of strange-looking adults, or to hang out only with people like ourselves. Everybody does it, right? There are some wonderful movies about kids who are "different," whether in size or ability. These show us the beauty and dignity of people we don't usually respect. What about your own experiences of being disrespected? Most kids have been teased, picked on, or talked about at some point. You know how it feels.

Stand Up for Dignity

One of the most basic aspects of respect is a person's reputation. We all want others to think highly of us. Sometimes the meanest thing we can do to people is to tell half-truths about them. Sometimes we do this to look good in the eyes of others. Sometimes we do it because we want to get even with someone or maybe because we're hurting, too. No matter what the reason, the Church is clear that this is sinful.

You might sometimes hear other kids teasing or telling lies about someone. That's when you are called to stand up for the person being talked about. The Holy Spirit is there to give all of us the courage to challenge friends, classmates, or others who are not respecting human dignity. God and the Church call us to speak up and show the love of Christ every day.

> **Why is it often easier to disrespect people than to stand up for them?**

Personal Action

Identify and write down at least one time you remember disrespecting someone else or watching it happen and doing nothing.

_____

_____

_____

_____

_____

Write down at least one time when you stood up for someone who was being disrespected.

_____

_____

_____

_____

_____

Group Action

In small groups, select one of the following groups of people who are often excluded or are among the least respected: people who have physical challenges, people with mental illness, people who have less common interests, and people who dress differently or have distinctive head wear.

Draw a tree. On the trunk, write the name of the excluded group. On the branches, write the actions some people take that are disrespectful. On the roots of the tree, write the reasons or things that might motivate people to act disrespectfully to this group.

Live Your Faith

Catholic Social Teaching

Call to Family, Community, and Participation

From the very beginning, God made people to be in relationship with one another. Scripture tells us, "The LORD God said: It is not good for the man to be alone. I will make a helper suited to him" (Genesis 2:18). God gave us communities of persons so that we could take care of one another.

The family is a very special type of community. The Catholic Church teaches that the family is the "school of holiness" and the "domestic Church." These names reflect the Catholic teaching that the family is where we first learn who God is and how to live a Christian life. It is in our families that we learn what it means to live in a community and how to love and respect others. This love and respect extends to other communities.

In the Sacrament of Baptism, we are welcomed to and included in the Church. Now who needs us to be more welcoming or inclusive to them? Exactly how can you do so? In the Eucharist, we are nourished. Now who needs us to nourish them? Exactly how can we be more nourishing to this person? In the Sacrament of Confirmation, we affirm our call to discipleship. Now what do we need to work on to improve the way we live as disciples?

We are the Church, the Body of Christ. With our different gifts, we form one Body in Christ, made of many parts. Created in the image of God who is a Communion of three Divine Persons, we are all created to develop and participate in community.

You and Your Community

Today, so many people seem to spend more time at work or in front of the TV or computers, while fewer people seem to care or participate at school or in their parish. In most elections, the percentage of people who vote is going down rather than up. Are people giving up? Are they finding other things to give their time to? It's a huge challenge. But people called, confirmed, and sent forth by God's Spirit of courage and love have a responsibility to say "yes, we truly are Christ's disciples in our world."

You are sent to school to help build a community of learners who care about others, including your classmates. At home, you are called to help create a family community. Your parish needs your talents and your ideas. And your country needs you to care about others and your ideals enough that you will speak out when something's wrong. The Church is clear—political authority must be consistent with morality and promote the common good.

> **Why do you think so many people don't participate in their community?**

Personal Action

List some things you can do to help build a greater sense of community in the following areas.

At home:

_____

_____

_____

At school:

_____

_____

_____

In my neighborhood:

_____

_____

_____

Group Action

With your classmates make a list of reasons why people do not get involved at school, in your neighborhood, and in the broader community. Then create a response to each of the reasons. Put a star next to the more significant reasons and discuss which would need a change of perspective or priority.

Rights and Responsibilities of the Human Person

Because God made every person, each of us has rights and responsibilities. Rights are the freedoms or things every person needs and should have. Responsibilities are our duties, or the things we must do.

Jesus tells us to "love your neighbor as yourself" (**Mark 12:31**). The *Catechism* teaches that when we respect the dignity of another person, we treat them as "another self." We respect the rights that come from their dignity as a human being (CCC, 1943–44). Everyone has a basic human right to food, shelter, clothing, rest, and the right to see a doctor if they need one. While we work for individual rights, we also have a responsibility to treat others well and work together for the good of everyone.

"All men [and women] are created equal and endowed with certain inalienable rights. . . ." This basic principle of the United States Declaration of Independence is found first in Church teaching. But the Church goes a step further. Yes, we are all endowed with rights and freedom, but we are also called to use this freedom constructively, for the common good.

Governments, too, are meant to respect the fundamental rights of the human person, promote freedom, and defend the common good. Public authority is part of God's plan for promoting positive values in society and the well-being of all. The Church, too, gets involved in political affairs whenever economic and social issues affect peoples' fundamental human rights.

Our Human Rights

What are these fundamental human rights? They start with the right to life and the basic necessities of life—food, shelter, clothing, health care, education, and work.

Second, all people have the right to their own dignity and religious and cultural expression. This means being respected and appreciated for how unique each one of us is. It also means developing relationships with people—learning from them as well as helping them.

Third, all have a right to participate in decisions that affect their lives. With rights go responsibilities. We all have the responsibility to exercise our own rights and to work with others to gain, support, and expand their human rights. Too often the voices of people who need our support are silenced, and we are called to help them make their voices heard. Disciples of Jesus are called to bring the light of the Gospel to unjust situations, and help make them right.

> **How does the Church support human rights in the world?**

Personal Action

As you read about current events, listen to the news, or observe how different people live or are treated in your community or in other parts of the world, who are the people that are treated unfairly?

_____

_____

_____

_____

Which of these people do you want to stand up for and help?

_____

_____

_____

_____

_____

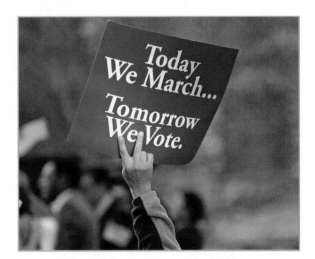

Group Action

Work in groups to identify human rights issues that interest you, and learn how organizations are working on behalf of these issues. Then, consider making some kind of slogan, button, or badge members of your class can use or wear to express your concern and invite others to join you in action.

Option for the Poor and Vulnerable

In Scripture, Jesus says that whatever we have done for people who are poor or needy, we have also done for him and what we have not done for them, we haven't done for Jesus (see Matthew 25:40–45). This means we should treat people in need the same way we would treat Jesus himself. We should give special priority to people who are hungry, thirsty, homeless or alone.

Pope Francis has said, "Among our tasks as witnesses to the love of Christ is that of giving a voice to the cry of the poor." Our Church teaches that we should put the needs of those who are poor first. This is called the preferential option for the poor. The *Catechism* teaches that "God blesses those who come to the aid of the poor" (CCC, 2443).

We can clearly see in the life of Jesus his love for the poor and others considered outcasts by society. In fact, the Church says that Jesus had a "preferential love" for these people.

Saint Rose of Lima also put it this way: "When we serve the poor and the sick, we serve Jesus. We must not fail to help our neighbors, because in them we serve Jesus, (P. Hansen, *Vita mirablis* [Louvain, 1668])." No wonder the Church tells us that among the options we face when we decide what to do with our time, with our talents, and with our possessions and money, our first option, perhaps after our own family, should be the poor. We should prefer (show "preferential love" for) them more than we do others.

Sacrificial Love

This may be easy to say, but it is certainly difficult to do. Everyone wants to hang out with his or her friends and take care of their own needs. Spending time with those who don't have lots of friends or things, sharing with them, or helping them in some way—that's sacrificial love. But that's our mission: to be the sacrificial love of Jesus for others.

An American soldier during World War II was marching with his unit across an Italian hillside. When they stopped for a break, he wandered into some tall bushes, where he discovered a statue of Jesus, but the hands were missing. He stared at that statue for a long time. Then he took out a piece of paper and wrote these words: "I have no hands but yours." Jesus tells each of us the same thing. He has no hands but ours, and we are called to use them to show his love in the world.

> How can you show Jesus' preferential love for the poor in your own life and community?

Personal Action

Figure out how much "free time" you have each month and how you could choose to spend at least one or two hours a month with those around you who have no home, are sick, or are lonely.

_____

_____

_____

_____

Figure out how much "spending money" you have each month (or week) and what ten percent of that would be. Then decide how best to use that ten percent on behalf of others who are in need.

_____

_____

_____

_____

Group Action

As a class identify organizations in your community that serve people struggling to meet their needs. Which groups might be able to use students' artwork for their facilities? Assign a person or team to contact each group and report their findings. Choose which groups you want to work with and then create a plan for providing the artwork.

Live Your Faith

Catholic Social Teaching

Dignity of Work and the Rights of Workers

All adults have a right and responsibility to work. Work helps people earn money to buy food and other necessities. It also helps to give their lives meaning as they cooperate with God's creation. Everyone should have access to meaningful work, whether that work is within the home or outside the home.

Sacred Scripture and Sacred Tradition teach that workers deserve to be treated with justice by their employers (see Deuteronomy 24:14). Employees also have a right to a fair wage for their work (see Leviticus 19:13 and Deuteronomy 24:15). When there is a conflict between workers and employers, workers have a right to get together and express their opinion.

Workers and their employers should treat one another with respect and solve those conflicts peacefully.

Part of spreading God's love is working for justice for those who are treated unfairly. Workers in our own country as well as the rest of the world are sometimes treated unfairly. Because of our oneness in God's family, such unfair treatment is a sin against human solidarity.

The equal dignity of all people, no matter what kind of work they do or whether they are able to work at all, calls Catholics to work to eliminate these sinful inequalities, and promote the dignity and respect of all workers.

Supporting the Workers

We can support the right of workers to form unions to protect their rights. When unions go on strike, we can refuse to cross their picket lines, even when that is inconvenient. Many people and some dioceses joined boycotts to support farm workers in receiving a living wage. Some have boycotted companies who use sweatshop labor or refuse to pay their workers fairly.

Some people support workers by buying directly from farmers at markets, rather than buying produce in giant supermarkets. Others choose to patronize locally owned restaurants and stores rather than large chains, even if they have to pay more. Communities have challenged superstores because they put some local stores out of business and pay nonunion-level wages. There are many ways to help. For example, buying "Fair Trade Coffee" supports coffee cooperatives that pay their workers a fair wage.

> **Which of these ways to help appeals to you the most?**

Personal Action

Make a list of all the places you shop or eat. Put an "L" next to those that are locally owned. Put a "C" next to those that are out-of-town chains. For each chain store you list, identify at least one locally owned alternative that is not too inconvenient for you.

_____

_____

_____

_____

_____

_____

Make a decision to change one of your shopping habits in order to support workers in your community. Share this decision with others you trust, and invite them to join you.

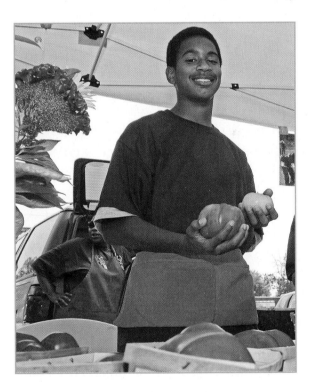

Group Action

Research with your classmates any consumer boycotts going on in your area. Share your findings, choose one of these boycotts to participate in, and create a plan for doing so.

Solidarity of the Human Family

Our world includes people of different nations, races, cultures, beliefs, and economic levels. But God created each one of us. We are one human family. In fact, Sacred Scripture tells us that the differences that we see between ourselves and others are not important to God (see Romans 2:11). God calls everyone to be his children.

Because God created all people, we have an obligation to treat everyone with love, kindness, and justice. In the Beatitudes, Jesus tells us "Blessed are the peacemakers" (Matthew 5:9). Working for justice between people will help us to live in peace with one another.

This principle of Catholic Social Teaching makes it clear that it's not just those around us for whom we should be advocating, but for people throughout the world. It is God's love of all persons that motivates us to care globally. We share in the Church's missionary mandate to bring the Gospel to all nations.

Jean Donovan of Cleveland, Ohio, heard this missionary mandate as a young businesswoman in the mid-1970s. She left her job and family to go to El Salvador to work with the poor. Realizing that "solidarity" means sharing both spiritual goods and material goods, Jean brought both to her ministry. She shared her faith and found her own faith deepened by the heroic faith of the people of El Salvador. Her friends in Cleveland sent material goods in response to Jean's appeals.

Sacrifice and Solidarity

Each day in the midst of poverty and civil war, Jean Donovan grew in her understanding of her mission—to be the sacrificial love of Jesus for others. As the danger in the country increased, her fiancé and family begged Jean to come home. But she kept thinking about the children she cared for there. On December 2, 1980, Jean was assassinated along with Maura Clarke, Ita Ford, and Dorothy Kazel, three other American Catholic religious women who worked with the poor and refugees in El Salvador.

Although Jean sacrificed her life completely, you are asked to consider other ways of sacrificing in solidarity with others suffering around the world. It starts with taking the time to read about others and learn their realities. It includes sharing your money, not only during Lent, but year-round. And it includes using your talents to raise the awareness about the needs of others, and showing how others can help.

> **Why would Jean Donovan stay in El Salvador, especially with her fiancé asking her to come home? Explain your answer.**

Personal Action

Research several groups in other countries that need help and discuss with the rest of your family how you might be able to act in solidarity with one or more of the groups. List who you might help, and how.

_____

_____

_____

_____

_____

_____

_____

_____

Create some reminder (like a note or picture on your mirror) to pray for this group every day and suggest that your family add a prayer for them at dinner.

Group Action

Research as a class a variety of groups or programs in other countries that could use your help. Missionary groups like Maryknoll and the Columban Fathers, aid groups like Catholic Relief Services, and the USCCB Offices of Domestic Social Development and International Justice and Peace can be very helpful. Choose one group or program and create a plan to help. Consider sharing your plan with other classrooms, or other groups in your parish or local community, and invite them to help.

Care for God's Creation

When God created the world—the animals, plants, and all natural things, he looked upon what he had made and called it "very good" (**Genesis 1:31**). God made people the stewards of the "fish of the sea, the birds of the air, and all the living things that crawl on the earth" (**Genesis 1:28b**). That means humans have a special responsibility to care for all of God's creation.

Sacred Tradition teaches us that God created the earth and all living things for the common good—the good of everyone. We should work to take care of the environment and all living things, so they can be enjoyed by everyone today and in future generations. The *Catechism* teaches us that we owe animals kindness, because they give

glory to God just by being what they were made to be.

Our response to God's sharing all this goodness and beauty with us involves several steps. First, God wants us to enjoy it. God invites us to pause every day to notice the beauty around us and just enjoy it—see it, smell it, touch it, listen to it, taste it. It could be a sunset, a flower, a creek, a bird, a mountain, a sky full of stars, a baby. Just enjoy them! Second, God wants us to realize that he is there in all that beauty and to say "thank you, God." Yes, we are made to live in communion with God in his "garden of paradise" on Earth. This is real happiness. Third, God wants us to take care of this garden, to make it even more beautiful, and to share it with others.

Generosity and Creation

In the Book of Genesis, God tells us to "have dominion" over the Earth. This doesn't mean we can do anything we want to the Earth. Even if something is "our property," we are not free to destroy it or harm it. We have to take care of the beauty and resources of the Earth for future generations and to share it with others now. God made it for everyone.

Just because God meant his creation to be for everyone doesn't mean we have the right to take property from someone else. That would be stealing, which is against the Seventh Commandment. But it means that if we see that someone has been kept from enjoying God's blessings, either because their property has been stolen or because they have been unfairly kept from having anything, we should try to help them. God calls us to be generous and fair. He wants us to make a difference in the way the world operates by speaking up for others and helping all people to enjoy his blessings together.

> **How do you say "thank you, God" when you enjoy his gifts of beauty?**

Personal Action

Take a trip around your neighborhood (or a special place in your community) and make a list of the forms of natural beauty you find.

_____

_____

_____

_____

Choose your favorite and spend ten minutes enjoying it with all your senses. Say a prayer of thanks to God for this beauty. Then decide what you can do to protect this place. List your ideas here.

_____

_____

_____

_____

Group Action

Discuss with your classmates different ways that your school could improve its recycling program (or other ways that the area around your school or neighborhood could be made more beautiful) or another project that honors God's creation. You may want to organize a group to promote the recycling efforts or ask a speaker to explain its use. Then create a plan for putting your group's work into practice.

33 Death of Jesus
Pentecost

50 *Council of Jerusalem* Saint Paul writes first Epistle, beginning of New Testament writings

A.D. 0   A.D. 20   A.D. 35   A.D. 50   A.D. 65

34 *Death of Stephen, first Christian martyr*

54 First persecution of Christians under Herod Agrippa

35 *Conversion of Saint Paul*

64 *Emperor Nero begins to persecute Christians.* Execution of Saints Peter and Paul in Rome.

● Pentecost, A.D. 33

A most astonishing event occurred around the year 30 during Shavu'ot, the Jewish harvest Festival of Weeks, so called because it took place fifty days—or a week of weeks—after Passover. The Greek name for Shavu'ot was Pentecost, a word that means "fiftieth day."

Many people gathered in Jerusalem for this feast. A small group of Jesus' Apostles and disciples were meeting in an upper room of a house there and suddenly the Holy Spirit entered the room and filled them with the power and grace to begin boldly preaching the Gospel message. This event is said to mark the beginning of the Church.

Go to the Source

Read Acts 2:2–4 to find out more about the events of Pentecost.

● Death of Stephen, A.D. 34

Stephen was a deacon, or assistant, of the Apostles. In addition to preaching and serving the needs of widows and the poor, he also worked miracles. The Jewish leaders denounced him as a blasphemer and when he reproached them for their part in putting Jesus to death, the crowd stoned him to death. Saul, later to become Saint Paul, took part in the stoning.

Go to the Source

Read Acts 6–7 to learn more about Stephen's martyrdom.

● Conversion of Saint Paul, A.D. 35

Saul, a member of the Pharisees, was an ardent persecutor of early Christians. As he traveled to Damascus to obtain authority to arrest followers of Jesus, a light from Heaven blinded him and he heard a voice saying, "Why do you persecute me?" When the voice revealed himself to be Jesus, Saul converted, changed his name and became one of the great leaders of the early Church. He is noted especially for his missions to the Gentiles and the many letters, called Epistles, that he wrote to churches he helped found throughout Asia Minor.

Go to the Source

Read Acts 9:3-6 for the events of Paul's conversion.

● Council of Jerusalem, A.D. 50

An account of the meeting Peter had with other Christians is often called the Council of Jerusalem. This meeting occurred because some Christian Jews at Antioch taught that Gentile converts had to be circumcised. Paul, Barnabas, and others traveled to Jerusalem to consider this matter with the Apostles and presbyters ("elders") there. The leaders of the Church announced the decision to free the Gentiles from this Jewish regulation and other Jewish dietary laws.

Go to the Source

Read Acts 15:28-30 to read more about the Council of Jerusalem.

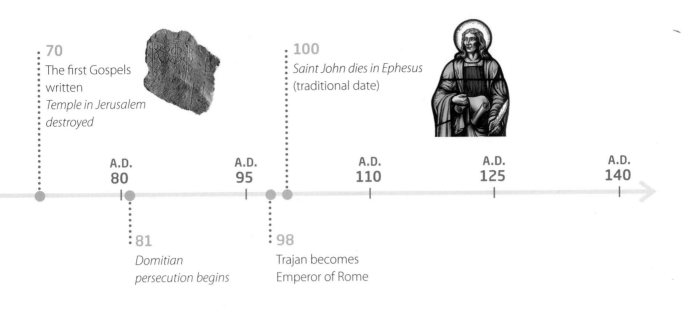

70

The first Gospels written

Temple in Jerusalem destroyed

100

Saint John dies in Ephesus (traditional date)

A.D. **80**

A.D. **95**

A.D. **110**

A.D. **125**

A.D. **140**

81

Domitian persecution begins

98

Trajan becomes Emperor of Rome

● **Emperor Nero's Persecution,** A.D. 64–67

On July 19, 64, a huge fire destroyed much of Rome. Although Emperor Nero may have set the fire himself in order to rebuild the city, when he realized how angry the citizens were, he blamed the new religion of Christianity and began a massive persecution of Christians. Saints Peter and Paul are believed to have died during this period. Saint Peter was crucified head-down and Saint Paul was beheaded.

● **Temple in Jerusalem Destroyed,** A.D. 70

In A.D. 70, the Roman army, under the command of the future Emperor Titus, attacked and conquered the city of Jerusalem, laying waste to the Jewish Temple. Before his Death, Jesus predicted the destruction, saying, "Do you see all these great buildings? Not one stone here will be left on another; everyone will be thrown down."

✏ **Go to the Source**

Mark 13:1-2 relates Jesus' prophecy regarding the Temple.

● **Domitian Persecution,** A.D. 81–96

The Emperor Domitian began an empire-wide persecution of all those who did not worship him as "lord and god." Many accounts of the early Church persecutions of Christians come from this period. He also taxed the Jews and then claimed that Christians pretended not to be Jews to avoid taxation.

● **Saint John dies in Ephesus,** A.D. 100

Saint John the Evangelist was a follower of John the Baptist and a fisherman before Jesus called him to be an Apostle. Saint John was with Jesus for three years and was the only Apostle known to have been present at the Crucifixion. John is said to be the author of the Book of Revelation, the final book of the Bible, as well as the Gospel according to John and three Epistles.

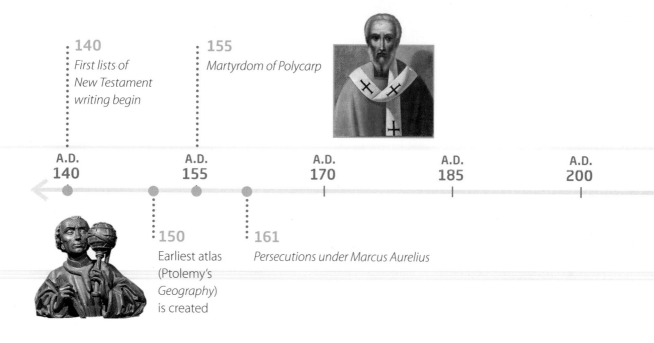

140
First lists of New Testament writing begin

155
Martyrdom of Polycarp

A.D. **140** A.D. **155** A.D. **170** A.D. **185** A.D. **200**

150
Earliest atlas (Ptolemy's *Geography*) is created

161
Persecutions under Marcus Aurelius

● **First lists of New Testament writing begin,** A.D. 140

Beginning approximately 50 years after Jesus' Death, Gospels, letters (called Epistles), memoirs, teachings, and other documents were shared among Christian churches to help explain the saving work of Jesus and the mission of early Church leaders. Over the next century, more Epistles were written. A list of these writings became part of the canon of Scripture, joining the Old Testament writings as a New Testament. The order of New Testament books is consistent in the Roman Catholic, Orthodox, and Protestant churches. The first translations of the New Testament had already been made by the end of the Second Century.

● **Martyrdom of Polycarp,** A.D. 155

Saint Polycarp is considered one of the "apostolic fathers of the Church," one of the first- and second-century writers who give us information about the early Christian Church. They are called apostolic because it is believed they had a historical connection to the Apostles. Polycarp was the author of the Epistle of Barnabas and the Didache, which contains several important teachings of the early Church. He was martyred after refusing to burn incense in honor of the Roman Emperor. Though he had been sentenced to be burned at the stake, it is said that the fire would not touch him, and he was stabbed to death.

● **Persecutions under Marcus Aurelius,** A.D. 161–180

Marcus Aurelius was the Emperor of Rome between 161 to 180. He was known as a strong proponent of Stoicism, a philosophy which conflicted with the Christian teachings of the time. In the early years of his reign as Emperor, Marcus Aurelius continued a policy of allowing Christian to worship, but after a time he upheld that the Church's belief in an immortal soul and life after death was dangerous to the state, and began persecutions of Christians in A.D. 161.

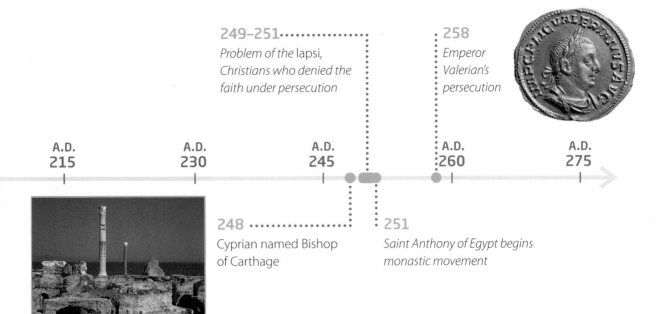

249–251

Problem of the lapsi, *Christians who denied the faith under persecution*

258

Emperor Valerian's persecution

| A.D. 215 | A.D. 230 | A.D. 245 | A.D. 260 | A.D. 275 |

248

Cyprian named Bishop of Carthage

251

Saint Anthony of Egypt begins monastic movement

● **Problem of the lapsi,** A.D. 249–251

In the first years of Christianity, people expected the immediate return of Jesus. As time wore on and the Second Coming didn't happen, some people began to fall away from the faith and resume old pagan practices or deny the faith under the pressure of persecution. When these people wanted to return at a later date, the Church was forced to decide how to handle the situation. Sanctions ranged from severe penance to denial of absolution until the time of death.

● **Saint Anthony of Egypt begins monastic movement,** A.D. 251–356

The first monk in the Catholic Church was Saint Anthony of Egypt. He was inspired by two passages in Scripture to sell all he had and give to the poor, and to not be concerned about tomorrow. A brilliant scholar, he lived as a hermit in modern-day Libya. Eventually, his reputation for holiness attracted many to him and he was convinced to establish a community of monks. Preferring to live alone, he visited the community now and then to be sure they were following his rules.

Go to the Document

Read *Life of Saint Anthony* by Athanasius, Bishop of Alexandria.

● **Emperor Valerian's persecution,** A.D. 258

During his reign as Emperor of Rome, Valerian first ordered Christian clergy members to make sacrifices to Roman gods under threat of banishment from the empire. A year later, he demanded that Christian leaders be executed, and forced Roman Christians in authority to renounce their faith or lose their positions. Cyprian, the Bishop of Carthage and an early Christian writer, was executed under Valerian's order for refusing to worship the Roman gods.

284 · · · · · · · · · · ·
Diocletian becomes
emperor

313 · · · · · · · · · · · ·
*Edict of Milan
establishes religious
freedom for Christians*

315 · · · · · · ·
*Arian
controversy
begins*

326 · · · · · · · ·
The Basilica of Saint
Peter consecrated

A.D.
275

A.D.
290

A.D.
305

A.D.
320

A.D.
335

303 · · · · · · · · · · · · · ·
Diocletian's Great
Persecution begins

325
*The First
Council
of Nicaea*

312
Battle of Milvian Bridge
and Constantine's vision

● **Edict of Milan establishes religious freedom for Christians,** A.D. 313

One of the most important events in the life of the Church occurred in 313 when the Emperor Constantine issued the Edict of Milan granting religious freedom to Christians. This edict allowed Christians to practice their faith openly without fear of persecution. In addition, it meant that Christians could be involved in secular affairs, Christian worship became public, and Christian missionaries would help spread both the faith and the Roman civilization throughout the Empire.

● **Arian controversy begins,** A.D. 315

One of the first major threats to Christianity began shortly after the Edict of Milan, when an Alexandrian priest named Arius taught that Jesus was not of the same substance as the Father, and while he was like the Father, Jesus was not truly God. Arius' teachings became popular because they reflected earlier pagan beliefs about the gods. Debate over the nature of Jesus got so heated, riots even broke out in Egypt and the Emperor became embroiled in the controversy.

Go to the Document

Read more about early heresies in the *Catechism of the Catholic Church*, 464-465.

● **The First Council of Nicaea,** A.D. 325

In order to address the controversy created by Arius, Emperor Constantine brought all Church leaders together in Nicaea, a town outside present-day Istanbul, Turkey. This gathering is considered the first ecumenical council or meeting of Catholic bishops. At this council, the bishops combated the Arian heresy by formulating the Nicene Creed, which is used in Catholic masses to this day. In it, we affirm that Jesus is truly divine by proclaiming that he is "the Only Begotten Son of God, born of the Father before all ages. God from God, Light from Light, true God from true God, begotten, not made, consubstantial with the Father; through him all things were made."

Go to the Document

Read more about the Creed in the *Catechism of the Catholic Church*, 198.

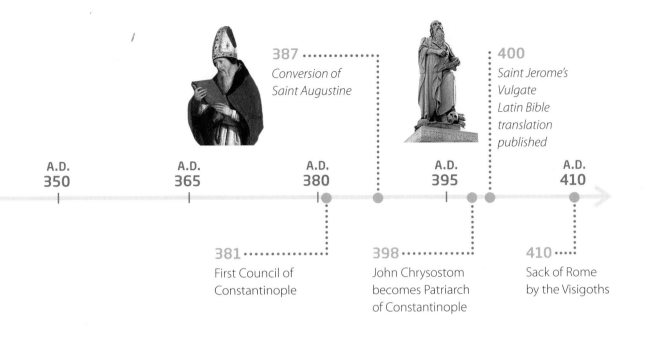

387 ·········
*Conversion of
Saint Augustine*

400
*Saint Jerome's
Vulgate
Latin Bible
translation
published*

| A.D. 350 | A.D. 365 | A.D. 380 | A.D. 395 | A.D. 410 |

381 ··············
First Council of
Constantinople

398 ············
John Chrysostom
becomes Patriarch
of Constantinople

410 ·····
Sack of Rome
by the Visigoths

● Conversion of Augustine, A.D. 387

Saint Augustine was the bishop of Hippo, located in present-day Algeria. One of the most important early Church Fathers, his early youth was marked with a libertine lifestyle. His mother, Saint Monica, prayed for his conversion and, at age 32, he became a Christian. Augustine was heavily influenced by Saint Ambrose, Bishop of Milan. Through his writings, Augustine challenged Christians to see a deeper spiritual meaning in everything, reassuring his readers that eternal life is more important than anything happening in the present day. This perspective became a dominant worldview in the medieval period. Saint Augustine's writings continue to inspire and influence theologians to the present time. Pope Boniface VIII named him a Doctor of the Church in 1298.

Go to the Document

Read Augustine's most important works: *City of God* and *Confessions.*

● Jerome's Vulgate Latin Bible translation published, A.D. 400

In 382, Pope Damasus I commissioned Saint Jerome to begin work on a Latin version of Scripture. He corrected earlier Latin text of the New Testament and in 390 began translating the Old Testament from the original Hebrew. By the 13th century, his Bible became known as the *versio vulgata,* "commonly used translation," generally referred to as the Vulgate. It was the official Latin text of Scripture in the Church and was often used until more modern translations were made in the 20th century. One of Jerome's most famous sayings is, "Ignorance of the Scriptures is ignorance of Christ."

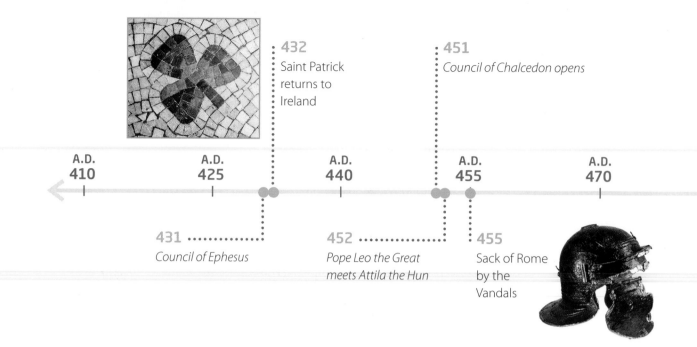

432
Saint Patrick returns to Ireland

451
Council of Chalcedon opens

A.D. **410** A.D. **425** A.D. **440** A.D. **455** A.D. **470**

431 ....
Council of Ephesus

452 ....
Pope Leo the Great meets Attila the Hun

455
Sack of Rome by the Vandals

● **Council of Ephesus,** A.D. 431

The third ecumenical council, the Council of Ephesus, was convened by the Roman Emperor Theodosius II. It reconfirmed the wording of the Nicene Creed, forever establishing that Jesus is both God and man. It also affirmed Mary's title as the *Theotokos,* "Mother of God." Approximately 250 bishops took part in the gathering, which was held in the Church of Mary in Ephesus in present-day Turkey.

● **Council of Chalcedon,** A.D. 451

The Council of Chalcedon, the fourth ecumenical council, declared Christ's two natures were unmixed, unchanged, undivided and inseparable in refutation of the heresy of Monophysitism, which said the human nature of Jesus was lost in the Divine. The Council was held near modern-day Istanbul.

Go to the Document

Read more about the teachings of the Council in *Catechism of the Catholic Church,* 467.

● **Pope Leo I (the Great) meets Attila the Hun,** A.D. 452

Attila the Hun invaded Italy, sacking cities on his way to overtake the city of Rome. The Emperor sent an envoy that included Pope Leo to try to prevent Attila from attacking the Eternal City. Although the exact details of the negotiations are lost, historians agree that as a result of Pope Leo's intervention, Attila agreed to withdraw. Three years later, when Genseric did occupy Rome, Leo was able to mitigate the effects of the invasion, persuading the Vandals not to harm the citizens or plunder the city.

496
Clovis I converts to the Catholic faith

CLOVIS.I.

533
Mercurius becomes Pope John II, the first Pope to change his name

A.D. **485**

A.D. **500**

A.D. **515**

A.D. **530**

A.D. **545**

528 ....
Benedict begins monastery at Monte Cassino

545 ....
Saint Ciarán founds monastery of Clonmacnoise in Ireland.

● **Benedict begins monastery at Monte Cassino,** A.D. 528

Saint Benedict of Nursia is widely recognized as the father of Western monasticism. He founded 12 monasteries in Subiaco, before finally settling at Monte Cassino. His twin sister, Saint Scholastica, lived in a nearby convent. He is best known for his "Rule of Saint Benedict," a list of guidelines for monastic life that continues to guide and influence monastic life today with its principles of moderation and reasonableness. He is the patron Saint of Europe and of students.

Go to the Document
Find the original Rule of Saint Benedict and read about three of the guidelines.

● **Saint Ciarán founds monastery of Clonmacnoise,** A.D. 545

Saint Ciarán is considered one of the Twelve Apostles of Ireland, early monastic Saints of the country. Ciarán studied as a monk on Aran Island in Ireland, where he was eventually ordained as a priest. After some traveling he settled in the area of Clonmacnoise and founded a monastery whose ruins are still visible today. He was known as a humble man whose monastery became renowned as a place of spiritual and intellectual learning. The site served as a monastery until 1552, when it was dissolved under the rule of King Henry VIII of England and his Suppression of the Monasteries. Pope Saint John Paul II visited the site of the monastery during his visit to Ireland in 1979.

553
Second Ecumenical Council of Constantinople

571
The Monophysites reject the Council of Chalcedon, causing a further schism in the Church

596
Saint Augustine of Canterbury evangelizes the English

A.D. **545**   A.D. **560**   A.D. **575**   A.D. **590**   A.D. **605**

569
John of Ephesus completes *Biographies of Eastern Saints*

590
Pope Saint Gregory the Great elected

● Pope Saint Gregory the Great, A.D. 590

Pope Saint Gregory, one of the Doctors of the Church, was a strong supporter of monasticism and an organizer of missionary activity, especially to England. During his reign, he reformed the liturgy and clarified doctrines. Although he would have personally preferred to remain a monk, he willingly agreed when he was elected Pope. The Gregorian chant is named after him because he promoted its use and even wrote some chants for parts of the Mass, although it probably existed as an earlier musical form. He was the first Pope to call himself "Servant of the Servants of God." His *Dialogues,* a collection of four books, including a biography of Saint Benedict, are still read today.

Go to the Document
Read Pope Saint Gregory's *Dialogues* for insight into sixth-century Italian religious life.

● Saint Augustine of Canterbury evangelizes the English, A.D. 596

A Benedictine monk, Saint Augustine is considered the "Apostle to the English." In 595, Pope Saint Gregory the Great chose him to lead a band of missionaries to Britain to bring the Gospel message to King Æthelberht and his kingdom. Augustine, along with Laurence of Canterbury, and a group of about 40 companions, landed on Isle of Thanet in 597. Their missionary activity met with success and thousands were baptized. Saint Augustine was named the first Archbishop of Canterbury. He died in 604 and was soon afterwards declared a Saint.

Go to the Document
Some of the early history of the missions to the English is recorded in Venerable Bede's *Ecclesiastical History of the English People.*

638
Muslim Conquest of
Syria and Jerusalem

680 ·········
Third Ecumenical Council of
Constantinople condemns
Monothelitism

A.D.	A.D.	A.D.	A.D.	A.D.
620	**635**	**650**	**665**	**680**

622
Medina accepts Islam
as official religion

664
The Synod of Whitby

● The Synod of Whitby, A.D. 664

The Celtic priest Saint Aidan introduced some practices into the English church that were different from those in Rome. The Synod of Whitby determined that the Pope was appointed to head the entire Church and that the English Church would follow Rome in matters such as the date for the celebration of Easter. This decision cleared the way for the whole English Church to be united in doctrine and practice under one head. Saint Hilda, who was a pupil of Saint Aidan and had founded a double monastery for men and women at Whitby in 657, had a prominent role during this Synod, supervising the discussions. Though she had initially followed Saint Aidan, Hilda accepted the decision of the Synod in favor of Rome. Following the Synod, the Church in England flourished, and monks from Rome brought many famous manuscripts to English monasteries, where they were copied and made available to many.

● Third Ecumenical Council of Constantinople condemns Monothelitism, A.D. 680

Convened by Emperor Constantine IV, this Council further clarified the nature of Jesus by declaring that monothelitism, the teaching that Jesus has two natures but only one will, is heretical. It affirmed that Jesus has two wills (human and Divine) that correspond to his two natures, although his human will was "in subjection to his divine and all-powerful will."

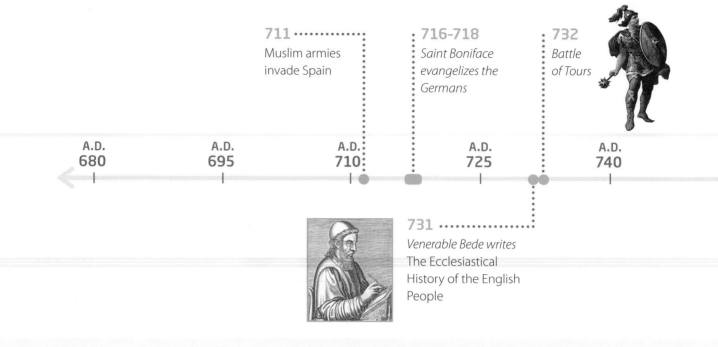

711 ·········
Muslim armies
invade Spain

716–718
*Saint Boniface
evangelizes the
Germans*

732
*Battle
of Tours*

A.D. **680**   A.D. **695**   A.D. **710**   A.D. **725**   A.D. **740**

731 ·········
Venerable Bede writes
The Ecclesiastical
History of the English
People

● **Saint Boniface evangelizes the Germans,** A.D. 716–718

Boniface, also known as Winifred, was an English Benedictine priest. He traveled to what is now present-day Germany to convert the native peoples to Christianity. The story is told that when Boniface started to chop down an oak that was sacred to the pagan population, a great wind finished the job. When Boniface was not punished by the god, the townsfolk converted and Boniface used the wood to build a chapel dedicated to Saint Peter.

Go to the Document

Some of Boniface's works include: *Collection of Letters; Poems and Riddles; Poenitentiale; Compendium of the Latin Language* and *Compendium of Latin Prosody.*

● **Venerable Bede writes** *The Ecclesiastical History of the English People,* A.D. 731

An author and scholar, Venerable Bede was given the title of "The Father of English History" based on his most famous writing, *The Ecclesiastical History of the English People,* which he wrote to demonstrate the growth and history of the English Catholic Church. About 160 manuscript copies of his work still exist today. A skilled linguist and translator of both Latin and Greek, he was named a Doctor of the Church by Pope Leo XIII in 1899, the first native Briton to be so designated.

● **Battle of Tours,** A.D. 732

By this time in history, the Muslims ruled much of Spain and were beginning to make inroads into the rest of Europe. Charles Martel, a Christian prince who had already united the kingdom of the Franks after two centuries of weakened rulers, defeated a Muslim force that had invaded present-day France as far as Tours. Most historians agree that if Martel hadn't defeated the Muslim army, all of Europe might have fallen under Islamic rule, effectively ending the Christianization of Europe. Because of his role in the battle, Charles was given the nickname *Martellus,* "The Hammer." He was the father of Pepin the Short, king of the Franks, and the grandfather of Emperor Charlemagne.

793
Beginning of Viking raids on Christian Europe

| A.D. 755 | A.D. 770 | A.D. 785 | A.D. 800 | A.D. 815 |

756
Birth of the Papal States

787
Second Ecumenical Council of Nicaea

800
Charlemagne crowned Holy Roman Emperor

● Birth of the Papal States, A.D. 756

In 751, Pepin the Short (the son of Charles Martel) was crowned King of the Franks, beginning the Carolingian dynasty. Five years later, in the Donation of Pepin, he gave Pope Stephen III control over the middle part of Italy, founding the Papal States, which existed until 1870. Today Vatican City is all that remains. It is a separate city-state, independent from Italy, even though it lies in the heart of Rome.

● Second Ecumenical Council of Nicaea resolves iconoclasm, A.D. 787

Iconoclasm refers to the destruction of religious images. Around 730, the Byzantine Emperor Leo III ordered the removal of an image of Jesus over the ceremonial entrance to the Great Palace of Constantinople to be replaced by a cross. This began a systematic removal of holy images and a quarrel between those who venerated "icons" and those who wanted them removed. The Second Council of Nicaea ended the conflict by stating: "we decree with full precision and care that, like the figure of the honoured and life-giving cross, the revered and holy images, whether painted or made of mosaic or of other suitable material, are to be exposed in the holy churches of God, on sacred instruments and vestments, on walls and panels, in houses and by public ways; these are the images of our Lord, God and saviour, Jesus Christ, and of our Lady without blemish, the holy God-bearer, and of the revered angels and of any of the saintly holy men…"

● Charlemagne crowned Holy Roman Emperor of the West, A.D. 800

On Christmas Day, 800, Pope Leo III crowned Charlemagne, or Charles the Great, Holy Roman Emperor of the West. Possessing both great political power and enormous personal charisma, Charlemagne was accepted as ruler of Europe from the Baltic to the Mediterranean. He is sometimes called the "second Constantine" because he united all of Europe under the Catholic faith. Believing he ruled by divine right, Charlemagne refused to be subject to the Pope, and actively involved himself in Church affairs, even instituting rules for members of the clergy and enacting laws against heresy. His coronation symbolized the union of Church and state in Western Europe, leading to a growing discontent between the Western Church and the emperor in the East, which eventually led to the split between Eastern and Western Christianity.

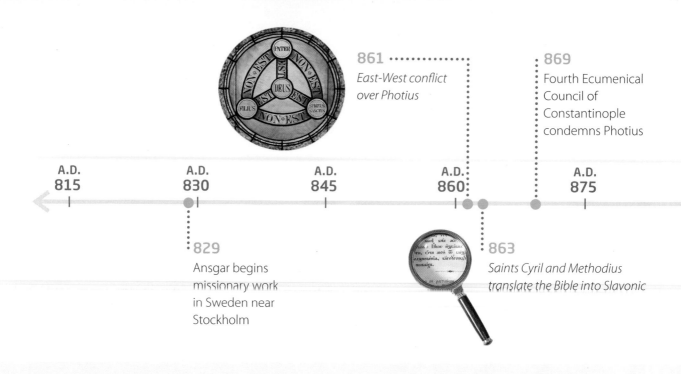

861

East-West conflict over Photius

869

Fourth Ecumenical Council of Constantinople condemns Photius

| A.D. 815 | A.D. 830 | A.D. 845 | A.D. 860 | A.D. 875 |

829

Ansgar begins missionary work in Sweden near Stockholm

863

Saints Cyril and Methodius translate the Bible into Slavonic

● East-West conflict over Photius, A.D. 861

Photius I was a layman who was named the Patriach of Constantinople from 858 through 867, and then again from 877 through 886. Photius was first named Patriarch after the Emperor deposed the previous man in the position, the Patriarch Ignatius. At first the reigning Pope Nicholas expressed support for the new Patriarch, but then Photius declared he could not accept the Pope's supremacy over the Catholic Church in the East. Separate synods were held in Rome and Constantinople (now Istanbul), and what became known as the Photian Schism between the Church in the East and in the West was created.

Go to the Document

Read more about the Church's definition of *schism* in the *Catechism of the Catholic Church*, 2589.

● Saints Cyril and Methodius translate the Bible into Slavonic, A.D. 863

The Byzantine Greek brothers Cyril and Methodius were sent by the Patriarch of Constantinople as missionaries to the Slavic people in what is now near present day Hungary, Slovakia, Bosnia, Herzegovina and the Czech Republic. Given the title "Apostles to the Slavs," they helped devise the Glagolitic alphabet whose descendant script, Cyrillic, is still used today. They translated the Bible into Slavonic and were quite successful in their efforts to promote their new translation. Pope Saint John Paul II named them co-patrons of Europe, along with Saint Benedict of Nursia.

899
Death of
English
King Alfred
the Great

910
*Monastery of Cluny
founded*

935
*Death of
Saint Wenceslaus*

**A.D.
890**

**A.D.
905**

**A.D.
920**

**A.D.
935**

**A.D.
950**

909 ....
Birth of Saint Dunstan,
Archbishop of Canterbury

950 ....
Olga of
Russia
converts to
Christianity

● Monastery of Cluny founded,
A.D. 910

William the Pious, Duke of Aquitaine, donated land in Cluny, France to a monk named Berno to found a Benedictine monastery with the proviso that it would report directly to the Pope, although the monks would choose their own abbot. This centralization under the Pope was the beginning of a campaign to address abuses that had crept into the monastic system. The monks at Cluny emphasized prayer over all else, praying the Divine Office or Liturgy of the Hours five or six times a day. The Cluniac reform, as it came to be known, spread throughout France, England, Italy, and Spain. New monasteries sprang up all over Europe, with the result that after the Pope himself, the Abbot of Cluny was the most important Church figure in the Western world. By the twelfth century the Congregation of Cluny included more than one thousand monasteries.

● Death of Saint Wenceslaus, A.D. 935

Wenceslaus was one of two grandsons of Saint Ludmilla. His twin brother was known as Boleslaus the Cruel, but Wenceslaus was influenced to such an extent by his grandmother Ludmilla that he became a Christian. He became ruler of Bohemia when he was eight years old, and as he grew older, he helped spread Christianity throughout Bohemia. It is still the major religion of the region, located primarily in the Czech Republic. Wenceslaus was murdered by supporters of his brother when he was on his way to church. Though in his lifetime he was known as a Duke, after his death he was given the title King by Holy Roman Emperor Otto I. He is the king referred to in the Christmas carol "Good King Wenceslaus."

962
Otto I crowned Holy Roman Emperor by Pope John XII

966
Mieszko I of Poland converts to Catholicism

1009
Muslims destroy Holy Sepulchre in Jerusalem

| A.D. 950 | A.D. 965 | A.D. 980 | A.D. 995 | A.D. 1010 |

982
Eric the Red establishes first Viking colony in Greenland

988
Saint Vladimir I the Great becomes the first Christian Grand Duke of Kiev

● **Otto I crowned Holy Roman Emperor by Pope John XII,** A.D. 962

Otto I was a German king who founded the Holy Roman Empire. Otto was known for associating himself with Catholic Church leaders, often placing bishops in positions of secular leadership rather than allowing other men who disagreed with him to come to power. Otto considered himself a protector of the Church, but many believed that by controlling Church leaders, Otto was establishing more power for himself. He also became known for appointing men who had little ecclesiastical background as leaders of monasteries and churches. After helping protect the city of Rome and the Papal States from an attack by Berengar II, Otto was eventually crowned Emperor by Pope John XII, and this event joined the kingdoms of Germany and Italy as the Holy Roman Empire. This Empire lasted from 962 until 1806.

● **Muslims destroy Holy Sepulchre in Jerusalem,** A.D. 1009

Although Jerusalem was under Muslim rule, most Christian places of worship were left alone. That changed on October 18, 1009 when Fatimid Caliph Al-Hakim bi-Amr Allah ordered the destruction of the Church of the Holy Sepulchre, long believed to be built over the burial place of Jesus. One Christian writer wrote at the time that everything was destroyed "except those parts which were impossible to destroy or would have been too difficult to carry away." A few repairs were attempted but restoration would take decades. Ultimately this act of desecration gave fuel to the later Crusades.

1012
Burchard of Worms completes his twenty-volume *Decretum* of canon law

1040
Macbeth murders Duncan, King of Scotland

A.D. 1025

A.D. 1040

A.D. 1055

A.D. 1070

A.D. 1085

1027
Truce of God

1054
The Great East-West Schism

● Truce of God, A.D. 1027

One of the world's first "peace movements," the Peace of God, or *Pax Dei,* used spiritual sanctions to limit violence against those who could not defend themselves, beginning with peasants and clergy. The Truce of God, or *Treuga Dei,* was an extension of the movement that asked Christian soldiers to abstain from fighting on Sundays, holy days, Lent and eventually all Fridays. Its goal was to reduce the private wars and fighting that had become rampant in feudal society.

● The Great East-West Schism, A.D. 1054

Over the first 1,000 years of Church history, differences began to develop between the Western and the Eastern Churches. For instance, Western bishops added the words "from the Father *and the Son,*" to the Creed over the objections of Eastern leaders. Other conflicts, including the use of icons and sacred images, as well as some doctrinal points continued to foment until finally, in 1054 both the Eastern and the Western Church excommunicated each other. The Eastern Churches, which were no longer in union with Rome, are known as the Orthodox Churches. Those Eastern Churches that remained in communion with the Pope are known as Eastern Rite Catholic Churches. In 2013, the Ecumenical Patriarch Bartholomew, head of the Orthodox Churches, attended Pope Francis' installation as Bishop of Rome, something that had not happened since the Great East-West Schism.

Scripture

Catholic Bibles

Catholic Bibles have seven Old Testament books or parts of books not included in other Christian Bibles. When these books are included in a Protestant Bible, they are usually found in a section called the Apocrypha or Deutero-canonical Books. The word *apocrypha* comes from a Greek word that means, "hidden things."

Catholic translations of the Bible include The New American Bible Revised Edition and The New Jerusalem Bible. Some translations, such as The New Revised Standard Version, are accepted by Catholics and Protestants.

Senses of Scripture

There are many layers, or senses, of Scripture.

- The **literal** sense of Scripture refers to the actual words recorded. We understand the literal sense by studying the culture in which the words were written and the meaning of the words at that time.
- The **allegorical** sense of Scripture shows how certain events pointed to Christ, even before his birth. The crossing of the Red Sea, for example, is a sign of Christ's victory over death.
- The **moral** sense of Scripture gives instruction on how to live justly before God.
- The **anagogical** sense of Scripture shows how human events and realities are signs of our heavenly future. The word *anagogical* comes from the Greek word *anagoge*, which means "leading." The Church, for example, is understood as leading to the New Jerusalem of Heaven.

You should always rely on the guidance of the Holy Spirit and the Church to help you understand the Word of God in Scripture.

Gospel Formation

The Gospels according to Matthew, Mark, Luke, and John announce the Good News of Jesus to Christians today. These books were formed in three stages:

1. **The life and teaching of Jesus**
   Jesus' whole life and teaching proclaimed the Good News.

2. **Oral tradition**
   After the Resurrection, the Apostles preached the Good News. Then the early Christians passed on what Jesus preached. They told and retold the teachings of Jesus and the story of his life, Death, Resurrection, and Ascension.

3. **The written Gospels**
   The stories, teachings, and sayings of Jesus were collected and written in the Gospels according to Matthew, Mark, Luke (the synoptic, or similar Gospels), and John.

The Apostles

You can find the names of the Twelve Apostles in Matthew 10:1−4, Mark 3:13−19, and Luke 6:12−16.

Simon Peter: The leader of the Apostles, Simon was renamed "Peter" by Jesus. A fisherman from Galilee, he was introduced to Jesus by his brother Andrew. Peter was the first to proclaim Jesus as "the Christ, the Son of the Living God." He is said to have been crucified upside down in Rome under the Emperor Nero. Considered the first Pope, he is believed to be buried under St. Peter's Basilica at the Vatican.

Andrew: Andrew was originally a follower of John the Baptist. A fisherman like his brother Simon Peter, he is the disciple who brought the young boy with the loaves and fishes to Jesus to feed the crowds. According to tradition, he founded the church in Constantinople, present-day Istanbul, Turkey, and was martyred in Southern Greece.

James: Considered the first Apostle to be martyred, he was a son of Zebedee and Salome and brother of John. He and his brother were called *Boanerges* or "Sons of Thunder" by Jesus, perhaps because of their tempers.

John: Traditionally known as the author of the Fourth Gospel, John is the brother of James. Jesus entrusted his mother Mary to John's care during the Crucifixion. He is the only Apostle to live into old age and not be martyred.

Philip: Originally from the town of Bethsaida, Philip introduces Nathanael (Bartholomew) to Jesus. At the Feeding of the 5,000, Jesus tested him, asking, "Where can we buy enough food for them to eat?" At the Last Supper, he asks Jesus to show them the Father, prompting Jesus' teaching about the Father and the Son being one. He was martyred in what is now Turkey.

Bartholomew: Often identified as Nathanael, he was a friend of Philip. When he learned about Jesus, he had a hard time believing the Messiah could come from Nazareth, saying, "Can anything good come out of Nazareth?" He is said to have traveled to India and was later killed in Armenia.

Matthew: Matthew calls himself "the tax collector" in his Gospel and the Gospel according to Mark says his name was "Levi." After Jesus called him, he went to Matthew's house and shared a meal with him.

Nothing specific is known about the end of Matthew's life.

Thomas: The Gospel according to John calls Thomas "Didymus," which means "the twin." He is sometimes called "Doubting Thomas" because he said he would not believe Jesus had risen from the dead unless he could put his fingers in Jesus' wounds. When Jesus appeared and invited him to do just that, Thomas proclaimed, "My Lord and my God." He is believed to have been martyred in India.

James: Some called him the "son of Alphaeus" to show he is a different James from John's brother. Sometimes he is called "James the Lesser." His name appears four times in the New Testament, in lists of the Apostles. Tradition says that he was martyred in Egypt where he was preaching the Gospel.

Simon: Matthew and Mark calle him "the Cananean," and Luke called him a "Zealot," to make sure we know he is not Simon Peter. Other than that, nothing specific is known about him. He is traditionally believed to have traveled and preached with Saint Jude Thaddeus and been martyred with him in the area around present-day Lebanon.

Thaddeus: He is also called "Jude Thaddeus." He is not to be confused with Judas, who betrayed Jesus. Jude Thaddeus is the patron Saint of lost or hopeless causes. According to legend, he was the son of a cousin of the Virgin Mary and a close friend of Simon the Zealot.

Judas Iscariot: Judas handed Jesus to the authorities to be crucified for thirty coins. He is said to have hanged himself in remorse for his betrayal. Matthias was later chosen to take his place among the Twelve Apostles.

The Holy Trinity

God is a communion of three Divine Persons: Father, Son, and Holy Spirit. God the Father is the Creator and source of all things. God the Son, Jesus, is the Savior of all people. God the Holy Spirit guides and makes holy all people and the Church.

The Holy Trinity is honored in the Sign of the Cross, in the Doxology, and in the liturgy of the Church. Christians are baptized "In the name of the Father, and of the Son, and of the Holy Spirit." In the blessings and in the Eucharistic Prayer of the Mass, prayers are directed to God the Father, through the Son, in the Holy Spirit.

God the Father

The First Person of the Holy Trinity, God the Father, is Creator of all that is. He is all-powerful and all-knowing. He is the one who journeys with you. He is the faithful and compassionate God who freed his People from slavery. He is as revealed to Moses, "I am who I am." God is gracious and merciful and steadfast in his love.

He is a God whom you can call Father, as Jesus taught in the Lord's Prayer. And, as Jesus also taught, God is love.

God the Son

Through the power of the Holy Spirit, the Second Person of the Trinity took on human nature and was born of the Virgin Mary. This is known as the Incarnation. Jesus is both true God and true man.

The Paschal Mystery includes Jesus' suffering, Death, Resurrection, and Ascension. By the Paschal Mystery, Jesus completed the work of salvation and won for all people the promise of eternal life. The Paschal Mystery is celebrated in each of the Sacraments, particularly in the Mass, and in Lent, the Triduum, and Easter. Jesus' whole life can be said to be a Sacrament, a sign of God, a sign of God's salvation and love. At the Last Supper, Jesus said, "Whoever has seen me has seen the Father. . . . Believe me that I am in the Father and the Father is in me. . ." (John 14:9, 11).

- In each Sacrament, Jesus is priest. For example, in the Eucharist, Jesus brings the people's prayers to God and offers himself as a sacrifice.
- Jesus is prophet because he speaks for God. Jesus announced the Good News of God's mercy and forgiveness. He calls people to love God and one another, to be sorry for their sins, and to live justly.
- Jesus is King, the judge of everything in Heaven and on Earth. His judgments are merciful and just.

God the Holy Spirit

The Third Person of the Trinity, the Holy Spirit, is the guide who helps people to know God as he is revealed in Sacred Scripture and the living Word, Jesus. It is through the power of the Spirit that you come to know the Father and the Son.

The Spirit makes the Paschal Mystery real and present in the Sacraments and the Mass. At Mass it is the Spirit who is called on to transform the bread and wine into the Body and Blood of Jesus. Finally, in the Eucharist, the Spirit unites the faithful with one another and with God in Christ. The Holy Spirit brings joy, peace, and reconciliation into the lives of the faithful.

Creed

A creed is a summary of the Christian faith. The word *creed* means "I believe." There are two main creeds in the Church: The Nicene Creed and the Apostles' Creed.

Nicene Creed

This creed which is prayed at Mass was written over a thousand years ago by leaders of the Church who met at a city named Nicaea. It is a summary of basic beliefs about God the Father, God the Son, and God the Holy Spirit, the Church, and other teachings.

I believe in one God,
the Father almighty,
maker of heaven and earth,
of all things visible and invisible.

I believe in one Lord Jesus Christ,
the Only Begotten Son of God,
born of the Father before all ages.
God from God, Light from Light,
true God from true God,
begotten, not made, consubstantial with
   the Father;
through him all things were made.
For us men and for our salvation
he came down from heaven,

*At the words that follow up to and including
and became man, all bow.*

and by the Holy Spirit was incarnate of the
   Virgin Mary,
and became man.

For our sake he was crucified under
   Pontius Pilate,
he suffered death and was buried,
and rose again on the third day
in accordance with the Scriptures.
He ascended into heaven
and is seated at the right hand of the Father.
He will come again in glory
to judge the living and the dead
and his kingdom will have no end.

I believe in the Holy Spirit, the Lord,
   the giver of life,
who proceeds from the Father and the Son,
who with the Father and the Son is adored
   and glorified,
who has spoken through the prophets.

I believe in one, holy, catholic and
   apostolic Church.
I confess one Baptism for the forgiveness
   of sins
and I look forward to the resurrection
   of the dead
and the life of the world to come. Amen.

Apostles' Creed

This summary of Christian beliefs has been taught since the time of the Apostles. It is used in the celebration of Baptism and is often used at Mass during the Season of Easter and in Masses with children. This creed is part of the Rosary.

I believe in God,
the Father almighty,
Creator of heaven and earth,
and in Jesus Christ, his only Son, our Lord,

*At the words that follow, up to and including
the Virgin Mary, all bow.*

who was conceived by the Holy Spirit,
born of the Virgin Mary,
suffered under Pontius Pilate,
was crucified, died and was buried;
he descended into hell;
on the third day he rose again from the dead;
he ascended into heaven,
and is seated at the right hand
   of God the Father almighty;
from there he will come to judge
   the living and the dead.
I believe in the Holy Spirit,
the holy catholic Church,
the communion of saints,
the forgiveness of sins,
the resurrection of the body,
and life everlasting. Amen.

The Church

The Catholic Church is the Church founded by Christ and his Apostles. There are four marks, or essential characteristics, that distinguish Christ's Church and her mission: one, holy, catholic, and apostolic. These marks are mentioned in the Nicene Creed.

Marks of the Church

One means all the members are united as the Body of Christ, given life by the one Spirit. They acknowledge one Lord, one faith, one Baptism.

Holy means the Church is centered in God. It is Christ who, by his sacrifice, makes the Church holy.

Catholic means universal. The Church has the fullness of faith and is the means of salvation for all. The Church is for all times and all people.

Apostolic means the Church is built on the foundation of the Apostles. It teaches the doctrine of Jesus as it has been handed down through the Apostles and their successors, the Pope and bishops.

The Church's Mission

The Church's mission is to proclaim and further God's Reign in the world. She continues the mission, or work, of Christ through the Holy Spirit, according to God's plan until Jesus comes again in glory. This work is done by all Catholics—clergy, laity, and religious.

Ecumenism is a movement that seeks to bring about the unity of all Christian churches. The word *ecumenism* comes from a scriptural phrase in Greek that means "the whole household of God."

The Pope

The Pope's title of "Servant of the Servants" began with Pope Gregory the Great. It is stated that "[W]hoever wishes to be first among you will be the slave of all" **(Mark 10:44)**.

The many titles for the Pope include: Bishop of Rome, Vicar of Christ, Supreme Pontiff of the Universal Church, Patriarch of the West, Primate of Italy, Successor of Saint Peter, Prince of the Apostles, Servant of the Servants of God, and Sovereign of Vatican City.

The Church as Community

The church is a building in which God's people come together to worship. But the Church is the community of people. It was the plan of God the Father to call together those who believe in Christ. The Church is a gift from God, brought into being by the Holy Spirit to serve the mission of Jesus. The Church, in Christ, can be called a Sacrament, a sign of the communion of the Trinity, the union of all people with God, and the unity among people that will reach completion in the fullness of the Kingdom of God.

The Catholic Church is united in her faith, leadership structure, and Seven Sacraments. She is made up of Eastern Rite Catholics (Middle East and Eastern Europe) and Latin Rite Catholics (Rome and Western Europe).

The Catholic Church is governed by the Pope in union with all the bishops. Through the Sacrament of Holy Orders, bishops, priests, and deacons are ordained to serve the Church. Between fifteen and twenty days after the death of a Pope, the cardinals who are under the age of 80 meet in the Sistine Chapel in Rome to vote for a new Pope. Each cardinal writes on a sheet of paper the name of the man (usually one of the cardinals) he wishes to elect. If a candidate does not receive a majority of votes, the papers are burned with straw to produce black smoke. If a new Pope has been chosen, the papers alone are burned, producing white smoke.

The resignation of Pope Benedict XVI in 2013 was the first papal resignation in nearly 600 years. Following his resignation, Benedict XVI's official title became Pope Emeritus (a word that means retired but retaining a title). His successor, Cardinal Jorge Maria Bergoglio, took the name Pope Francis. Because he was the Cardinal Archbishop of Buenos Aires, Argentina, Pope Francis became the first Pope from the New World.

The Saints

The Saints are holy people who loved God, did his work on Earth, cooperated with his grace, and are now with him in Heaven. Catholics honor the Saints for their virtue and try to imitate them. They also ask that the Saints join with them in praying to God for special blessings. Saints are remembered in the Eucharistic Prayer and in the Litany of the Saints at Baptisms. Statues and images of the Saints on medals and holy cards are reminders that these "friends of God" can help believers grow in their own friendship with God.

Mary is honored above all other Saints. She is the Mother of God because she is the mother of the Son of God who became a human being. When the Angel Gabriel told Mary that she would be the mother of the Son of God, Mary believed and accepted God's plan. Her "yes" sets the example for all believers.

Throughout the liturgical year, the Church celebrates Mary's place in Christian history. Among different cultures and traditions, devotion to Mary takes many forms.

Life after Death

At the end of the Nicene Creed we profess, "and I look forward to the resurrection of the dead and the life of the world to come." The Church sometimes refers to teaching about this topic as the Last Things.

The Particular Judgment is the judgment made at the moment of a person's death. At this judgment the soul is rewarded with the blessings of Heaven, given a time of purification, or condemned to Hell.

- Heaven is the state in which souls of the just experience the full joy of living in God's presence forever.
- Purgatory is a time after death for those who are in God's friendship but need to be purified to be with him in Heaven. It is a state of final cleansing after death and before entering into Heaven.
- Hell is the state of eternal separation from God because of a choice to turn away from him and not seek forgiveness

The Last Judgment is also called the General Judgment. This refers to God's final triumph over evil that will occur at the end of time when Christ returns and judges all the living and the dead. Then, all will fully see and understand God's plan for creation.

The new Heaven and new Earth is the Kingdom of God (or new Jerusalem) that will come in its fullness at the end of time.

The Seven Sacraments

The Sacraments of Initiation

The Sacraments of Initiation—Baptism, Confirmation, and Eucharist—celebrate membership into the Catholic Church.

Through the words and waters of **Baptism**, God forgives all sin and gives new life in Christ.

In emergencies and other times of necessity, anyone can baptize another person. The person baptizing must intend to do what the Church does in this Sacrament. He or she needs to pour water over the head of the person being baptized while saying, "I baptize you in the name of the Father, and of the Son, and of the Holy Spirit."

Confirmation completes the baptismal grace and strengthens a person to be a witness to the faith through the power of the Spirit.

Catholics in different dioceses in the United States receive the Sacrament of Confirmation at different ages. In the Roman, or Latin, Rite candidates for Confirmation must meet certain criteria. They must believe in the faith of the Church, be in a state of grace, and want to receive the Sacrament. Candidates must be prepared and willing to be a witness to Christ in their daily lives and take an active part in the life of the Church.

Eucharist completes the Sacraments of Initiation, nourishing the baptized with Christ's own Body and Blood and uniting the new Christians with God and one another in Jesus.

The Eucharist is known by several different names. These include the Blessed Sacrament, Holy Communion, the Bread of Heaven, Breaking of Bread, the Lord's Supper, Holy Sacrifice, Holy Mass, and the Body of Christ.

The Sacraments of Healing

In the Sacraments of Healing—Penance and Reconciliation and Anointing of the Sick— God's forgiveness and healing are given to those suffering physical and spiritual sickness.

In **Penance and Reconciliation**, through the words of absolution, personal sins are forgiven and relationships with God and the Church are healed.

In the **Anointing of the Sick**, one who is sick or dying is anointed with oil and with the laying on of hands. The person unites his or her suffering with that of Jesus. The Sacrament gives spiritual strength and God's grace. Physical healing also may take place.

The Sacraments at the Service of Communion

The Sacraments at the Service of Communion— Holy Orders and Matrimony—celebrate people's commitment to serve God and the community and help build up the People of God.

In **Holy Orders**, the bishop lays hands on a man and anoints him with Sacred Chrism. The man is empowered to serve the Church as deacon, priest, or bishop.

In **Matrimony**, a baptized man and a baptized woman, through their words of consent, make a covenant with God and one another. Marriage is for the sake of their love and any children God blesses them with.

Order of Mass

Introductory Rites

Entrance Chant

Greeting

Rite for the Blessing and Sprinkling of Water

Penitential Act

Kyrie

Gloria

Collect

Liturgy of the Word

First Reading

Responsorial Psalm

Second Reading

Gospel Acclamation

Dialogue at the Gospel (*or* Gospel Dialogue)

Gospel Reading

Homily

Profession of Faith (*or* Creed—Nicene Creed or Apostles' Creed)

Prayer of the Faithful

Liturgy of the Eucharist

Preparation of the Gifts

Invitation to Prayer

Prayer over the Offerings

Eucharistic Prayer

Preface Dialogue

Preface

Preface Acclamation

Consecration

Mystery of Faith

Concluding Doxology

Amen

Communion Rite

The Lord's Prayer

Sign of Peace

Lamb of God

Invitation to Communion

Communion

Prayer after Communion

Concluding Rites

Solemn Blessing or Prayer over the People

Final Blessing

Dismissal

Order of Rite for Reconciliation of Individual Recipients

1. Reception of the Penitent (Welcome)

2. Reading of the Word of God

3. Confession of Sins and Acceptance of Satisfaction (a Penance)

4. Prayer of the Penitent (beginning with the Act of Contrition; see page 387)

5. Absolution, including the words of absolution from the priest:

> God, the Father of Mercies,
> through the death and resurrection of his Son
> has reconciled the world to himself
> and sent the Holy Spirit among us
> for the forgiveness of sins;
> through the ministry of the Church
> may God give you pardon and peace,
> and I absolve you from your sins
> in the name of the Father, and of the Son,
> and of the Holy Spirit.

6. Closing Prayer

The Liturgical Year

The liturgical year celebrates Jesus' life and work for the salvation of the world. During Advent and Christmas, the Church celebrates the Incarnation. The Seasons of Lent, Triduum, and Easter explore the Paschal Mystery. Easter is the high point of the liturgical year because it is the greatest celebration of the Resurrection. The life and ministry of Jesus are the focus of Ordinary Time. Mary and the Saints are also remembered throughout the year in what is known as the sanctoral cycle.

Holy Days of Obligation

Catholics must attend Mass on Sunday unless a serious reason prevents their doing so. They must also go to Mass on certain holy days. United States Holy Days of Obligation are

- Mary, Mother of God (January 1)
- Ascension (forty days after Easter or the Sunday nearest the end of the forty-day period)
- Assumption (August 15)
- All Saints Day (November 1)
- Immaculate Conception (December 8)
- Christmas (December 25)

Fasting and Abstinence

To help prepare spiritually for the Eucharist, Catholics fast for one hour before Holy Communion. They take no food or drink except water. (Exceptions are made for those who are sick and for those of advanced age.)

To fast means to eat only one full meal and two smaller meals during the course of a day. All Catholics, from their eighteenth birthday until their fifty-ninth birthday, are required to fast on Ash Wednesday and Good Friday unless a serious reason prevents them from doing so. Another discipline of self-denial is abstinence. Catholics who are fourteen years of age or older are expected to abstain from eating meat on Ash Wednesday, Good Friday, and, in the United States, on all of the Fridays in Lent.

Examination of Conscience

Examining your conscience should be done daily and especially in preparation for the Sacrament of Penance and Reconciliation.

1. Pray to the Holy Spirit to help you examine your conscience.

2. Look at your life in light of the Beatitudes, the Ten Commandments, the Great Commandment, and the Precepts of the Church.

3. Ask yourself:
   Where have I fallen short of what God wants for me?
   Whom have I hurt?
   What have I done that I knew was wrong?
   Have I done penance and tried as hard as I could to make up for past sins?
   Am I working to change my bad habits?
   With what areas am I still having trouble?
   Am I sincerely sorry for all my sins?

4. In addition to confessing your sins, you may wish to talk with the priest about one or more of the above questions.

The Law

Divine law is the eternal law of God. It includes:

physical law: the law of gravity is an example of physical law.

natural moral law: a moral law is one that humans understand through reasoning (stealing is wrong) and through Divine Revelation (keep holy the Lord's Day).

Natural moral law refers to the precepts about goodness that are written by God in our hearts and accessible through our God-given reason. For example, people everywhere understand that no person may kill another unjustly. Everyone must obey natural moral law because everyone is created by God. God's Commandments are based on natural moral law.

The Ten Commandments	
1.	I am the Lord your God. You shall not have strange gods before me.
2.	You shall not take the name of the Lord your God in vain.
3.	Remember to keep holy the Lord's Day.
4.	Honor your father and your mother.
5.	You shall not kill.
6.	You shall not commit adultery.
7.	You shall not steal.
8.	You shall not bear false witness against your neighbor.
9.	You shall not covet your neighbor's wife.
10.	You shall not covet your neighbor's goods.

The Great Commandment

"You shall love the Lord, your God, with all your heart, with all your being, with all your strength, and with all your mind, and your neighbor as yourself." **(Luke 10:27)**

The New Commandment

"Love one another. As I have loved you, so you also should love one another." **(John 13:34)**

Precepts of the Church

The Precepts of the Church are some of the minimum requirements given by Church leaders for deepening our relationship with God and the Church. They name specific actions that all Catholics are obligated to carry out.

1. Take part in the Mass on Sundays and holy days. Keep these days holy and avoid unnecessary work.

2. Celebrate the Sacrament of Penance and Reconciliation at least once a year if there is serious sin.

3. Receive Holy Communion at least once a year during the Easter Season.

4. Fast and/or abstain on days of penance.

5. Give your time, gifts, and money to support the Church.

The Beatitudes

The Beatitudes are Jesus' eight teachings about the meaning and path to true happiness. They depict the way to live in God's Kingdom now and always, working toward the eternal holiness to which God calls all people. Jesus spoke them during his Sermon on the Mount, and his words lead us on a new path of discipleship, explaining how we are to live with each other.

Blessed are the poor in spirit,
for theirs is the kingdom of heaven.
Blessed are they who mourn,
for they will be comforted.
Blessed are the meek,
for they will inherit the land.
Blessed are they who hunger and thirst for righteousness,
for they will be satisfied.
Blessed are the merciful,
for they will be shown mercy.
Blessed are the clean of heart,
for they will see God.
Blessed are the peacemakers,
for they will be called children of God.
Blessed are they who are persecuted for the sake of righteousness,
for theirs is the kingdom of heaven.

Matthew 5:1–12

The Corporal and Spiritual Works of Mercy

The Works of Mercy are "charitable actions by which we come to the aid of our neighbor in his spiritual and bodily necessities" (CCC, 2447). The Corporal Works of Mercy are actions the show care for the physical needs of people, while the Spiritual Works of Mercy are actions that address the needs of the heart, mind, and soul.

The Works of Mercy	
Corporal (for the body)	**Spiritual (for the spirit)**
Feed the hungry.	Warn the sinner.
Give drink to the thirsty.	Teach the ignorant.
Clothe the naked.	Counsel the doubtful.
Shelter the homeless.	Comfort the sorrowful.
Visit the sick.	Bear wrongs patiently.
Visit the imprisoned.	Forgive injuries.
Bury the dead.	Pray for the living and the dead.

Gifts of the Holy Spirit

The Gifts of the Holy Spirit are seven powerful gifts God gives us to follow guidance of the Holy Spirit and live the Christian life. We are sealed with these gifts at the Sacrament of Confirmation, and they strengthen the gifts we receive at Baptism.

Wisdom helps you see yourself as God sees you and act as God wants you to act. Wisdom allows you to live in the image and likeness of God.

Understanding allows you to get to know God, yourself, and others better, and to see how your sometimes make the wrong choices in life. With understanding comes help to make better choices and forgive more freely.

Right judgment (Counsel) helps you give good advice to others and hear the Holy Spirit, who speaks to you through the good advice and good example of others.

Courage (Fortitude) helps you stand up for what is right even doing so it difficult, and allows you to face and overcome your fears, which sometimes lead you to making the wrong choices or failing to love others.

Knowledge allows you to be open to God's loving communication and know God in the way that you come to know someone you love and someone who loves you.

Reverence (Piety) helps you show faithful love and honor to God, and allows you to recognize the importance of spending time talking and listening to God in prayer.

Wonder and awe (Fear of the Lord) allows you to know that God is greater and more wonderful than any created thing, and reminds you to be open to his surprising and powerful goodness.

Fruits of the Holy Spirit		
The Fruits of the Spirit are qualities that can be seen is us when we allow the Holy Spirit to work in our hearts.		
Charity	Faithfulness	Gentleness
Joy	Modesty	Generosity
Peace	Kindness	Self-control
Patience	Goodness	Chastity

Grace and Sin

Sanctifying grace allows you to share in God's own life. It is a permanent gift that builds your friendship with God and assures you of eternal life.

Actual grace is a temporary gift that helps you think or act according to God's will for you in a particular situation. Actual grace helps you understand what is right and strengthens you to turn away from sin.

Sacramental grace is the gift that comes from the Sacraments. Each Sacrament gives its own particular grace.

Sin

Sin is a turning away from God and a failure to love. Sin affects both the individual and the community. A person may be sorry for his or her sin, ask forgiveness for it, accept punishment for it, and resolve to do better. In this case, the experience may actually help the person develop as a Christian and avoid sin in the future. However, a person who makes a habit of sin will harm his or her development, set a poor example, and bring sorrow to others. Society suffers when people disobey God's law and the just laws of society. There are many types of sin.

Original Sin is the sin that the first humans committed by choosing to disobey God. This sin describes the fallen state that caused the human condition of weakness and tendency toward sin. Baptism restores the relationship of loving grace in which all people were created by God.

Personal sin is any thought, word, act, or failure to act that goes against God's law. Sin is a choice, not a mistake.

Mortal sin separates you from God. For a sin to be mortal, it must be a serious matter done with full knowledge and complete consent.

Venial sin weakens or wounds your relationship with God. Continual venial sin can lead to mortal sin.

Social sin results from the effect that personal sin has on a community. People who have been sinned against may sin in return. Violence, injustice, and other wrongs may develop within the community. God created humans in his image and likeness. Because of this, you have dignity and therefore need to respect your dignity and that of others.

Asking forgiveness, accepting punishment, and resolving not to sin again helps a person develop as a Christian. However, one who habitually sins neglects Christian development, sets a poor example, and harms others. When individuals disobey God's law and just civil laws, the entire community suffers.

Virtue

Living a virtuous life is living a holy life. Virtues make it possible for us to relate to God and grow in our understanding of being made in his image and likeness. Virtues are lasting habits or attitudes that lead us to make good decisions and act appropriately. Virtues lead the way to holiness. They strengthen our character, which is uniquely ours but built on the foundation of God's grace and his help.

The Theological Virtues of faith, hope, and charity (love) are gifts from God. These virtues help you live in a loving relationship with God.

The Cardinal Virtues are the principal moral virtues that help you lead a moral life. They help us live as children of God. We strengthen these virtues through God's grace and our own efforts.

Prudence is careful judgment. This virtue helps you be practical and make the right decisions on what is morally good, with the help of the Holy Spirit and an informed conscience.

Fortitude is courage, especially in the face of evil and temptation. Fortitude gives you strength to get through difficulties and helps you not give up when you have chosen to do good.

Justice is giving to God and to each person what is due to them. Justice helps you build up the community by respecting rights and promoting the common good, the conditions that allow people to become who God wants them to become (see page 379).

Temperance means keeping a balance in life. It allows us to use moderation, be disciplined, and have self-control.

Human Dignity

Human dignity is the worth each person has because he or she is made in the image of God. We are all equal in dignity, each and every one of us worthy of respect and love. Because our common human dignity, people have basic human rights, such as food, clothing, and shelter. No government or social group should fail to recognize those rights.

God's image is his likeness that is present in you because you are his creation. You are called to respect the dignity of all people because everyone is made in God's image.

- Freedom means you are able to choose and act with few limitations. We are given freedom by God that we may choose to good things.

- Free will is the gift from God that allows humans to make their own choices. Because you are free to choose between right and wrong, you are responsible for your choices and actions.

- Conscience is a gift from God that helps us judge whether actions are right or wrong. It is important for us to know God's laws so our conscience can help us make good decisions. Conscience helps you choose what is right. It involves free will and reason working together. You must form your conscience properly. If not formed properly, your conscience can lead you to choose what is wrong.

Forming your conscience is a lifelong process. It involves practicing virtues and avoiding sin and people or situations that may lead you to sin. You can turn to good people for advice, to Church teachings for guidance, and to God for help in educating your conscience. It is recommended that Catholics practice an Examination of Conscience (see page 372) before receiving the Sacrament of Penance and Reconciliation.

Justice and Peace

Justice is a Cardinal Virtue. It is the habit and practice of giving God what is due him. It also means to give each person what he or she is due because that person is a child of God.

Social justice is a part of this Cardinal Virtue. It is the part that urges individuals to seek the common good of the whole group rather than just his or her individual good.

Peace is a state of calm and harmony when things are in their proper order and people settle problems with kindness and justice. In the Catholic tradition, peace is not just the absence of conflict. It is the result of right relationships with God and with your neighbor.

Common Good

The common good refers to the good of everyone, with particular concern for those who might be most vulnerable to harm. It means all the conditions that allow people to become who God wants them to become. The common good includes peace, development of groups of people, and respect for every person. These conditions vary from society to society, which is why the Church does not recommend any one country's political or economic system. The Church evaluates each system on the basis of whether or not it provides the conditions for human fulfillment.

Catholic Social Teaching

The Catholic bishops of the United States have named seven themes of Catholic Social Teaching that embrace the Gospel message on how we are to treat others and live in community. For more on each of these themes, read the Live Your Faith section of your book, beginning on page 334.

Life and Dignity of the Human Person: All policies and personal decisions must show a value for human dignity.

Call to Family, Community, and Participation: The well-being of individuals depends on community and family. All people have the right and a duty to participate in society.

Rights and Responsibilities of the Human Person: Human rights must be respected, and responsibilities to others must be met.

Option for the Poor and Vulnerable: Actions must be evaluated in terms of how they affect those who are most vulnerable. A basic moral test is to ask whether an act will help those who are poor or in need.

Dignity of Work and the Rights of Workers: Workers deserve the right to a just wage, to form unions, to hold private property, and to act independently of outside influence or control.

Solidarity of the Human Family: We must be committed to the common good globally as well as locally.

Care for God's Creation: To practice social justice, we must take care of the Earth's natural resources.

Vocations

God calls all of us to share in the life and mission of Jesus. A vocation is the purpose for which God made us, and a particular way to answer his call to service. The word vocation comes the Latin word *vocare*, which means "to call." Our vocation helps us see how everything fits together in our lives. It shows us how God created us to love, serve, and work with each other. Our vocation comes from the grace we receive in the Sacrament of Baptism. Every one of us must answer our call from God to work with him to build up his Kingdom on Earth.

There are three ways you can serve God through your vocation: as a layperson, or member of the laity (see page 295), as a member of a religious community, or as a member of the ordained ministry.

The Laity

The laity is all of the baptized people in the Church who share in God's mission but are not priests or consecrated sisters and brothers. Members of the laity can be single people or married couples. They can perform various roles in the Church, such as lector, altar servers, and musicians at Mass, and also serve their parish by acting as good Catholic role models in their daily lives.

Members of Religious Communities

There are many kinds of communities of religious sisters and brothers. The members of these communities teach, care for the sick, work as missionaries, or do other good works as part of their call from God. Consecrated religious brothers and sisters dedicate their lives to serving God by following the charism, or special grace, of their community and its founder.

Ordained Ministry

Some men are called to ordained ministry through the Sacrament of Holy Orders. This Sacrament gives a sacred power, through the laying on of hands by a bishop, for serving the faithful by teaching, leading people in worship, and pastoral care. Bishops, priests, and deacons share in this Sacrament. A bishop serves the Church as the pastor and teacher of his diocese. They work with other bishops and the Pope for the good of the whole Catholic Church. Priests assist the bishop within a diocese and celebrate the Sacraments with their parish community. Deacons are ministers who serve by helping in liturgical roles and doing works of charity.

You may not know yet about the vocation to which God is calling you. As you get older, you can continue to think about the gifts God has given you, and through them, you will better understand his plan and purpose for you.

Charisms

Charisms are special gifts or graces of the Holy Spirit which benefit the Church and help us lead a Christian life. These gifts build up the community and also help us share Christ's message with others, and serve the common good. Members of religious communities follow the specific charisms given to that community and its founder. For example, some communities are devoted to prayer, because their founders built the foundation of the community's spirituality on the power of this special communication with God. Saint Benedict followed a motto of *prayer and work*, and the Benedictans continue to model their ministry on those things. Other communities may be devoted to service, health care, or missions.

Vows

Members of religious communities profess, or promise aloud, to live three vows, or sacred promises made to or before God, that are found in the Gospel: poverty, chastity, and obedience. These vows are also evangelical counsels that lead to the perfection of the Christian, and therefore apply to all of us.

- **Poverty:** living a simple life and sharing material possessions in community. This helps one free one's self from undue attachment to material things and to rely on God to care for their needs while they provide for others.

- **Chastity:** exercising discipline over sexuality and maintaining the right balance of body and spirit in human sexuality. This shows that for consecrated religious, their love for God is the most important thing in their lives.

- **Obedience:** following and obeying God's will, expressed through the guidance of the community's leaders, the charism of the community, and the person's conscience. Consecrated religious find peace in discerning and following God's will for them.

We are called to live out these counsels, but men and women religious do so in a radical way.

Forms of Prayer

Prayer is talking and listening to God. In prayer, we raise our hearts and minds to God. One of the first prayers we learn in the Church is the Lord's Prayer, which Jesus taught his followers. Jesus prayed when he needed help, when he wanted to help other people, and when he wanted to praise God his Father. Prayer should be an important part of your life as well. You can pray a prayer you have heard before in church or school, or create one yourself with your own words. You can pray out loud or in silence. Your prayers will always be heard by God.

On the next pages, you will find several common prayers of the Catholic Church. You will have heard many of them at Mass, and they fit under the categories of these five principal forms of prayer:

Blessing and Adoration

In this prayer form, we show that we understand God is the Creator of all things, and that we need him. We give him respect and honor his greatness. We bless God, who blesses us. We also bless others who are made in God's image. A blessing is a response to God's gifts. Adoration means giving respect to God by honoring his greatness.

Praise

In this prayer form, we give God honor and thanks because he is God. We give him glory not for what he does, but simply because he is. When we praise God in prayer, we give him glory as his children. Praise holds together all of our prayers, and prayer forms, and raises them toward God, who is the source and goal of all prayer.

Intercession

Intercession, or intercessory prayer, is a form of prayer that involves praying to God on behalf of someone else. We can pray for people who are close to us; for people around the world who suffer from hunger, poverty, disease, war, or other problems; and for those who have died and are not yet with God in Heaven. We use intercessory prayer on behalf of others as Jesus intercedes for us with his Father. Because praying for other is a Work for Mercy, intercessory prayer is vital to the Church and our relationship with God.

Petition

In this prayer form, we ask God for what we need. We turn to God and ask for his help, and recognize that we need him. In prayers of petition, we might pray for God's mercy, forgiveness, and guidance when we are sad, sick, troubled, confused, or in a state of sin. We also ask God to help others.

Thanksgiving

When we pray a prayer of Thanksgiving, we give thanks to God for all he has given us. We express our gratitude to him for the good things in our lives. When we experience a special reason for happiness, such as good grades or someone feeling better after an illness, or even just for a good day, we can thank God for it in prayer.

Basic Prayers

These are essential prayers that every Catholic should know. Latin is the official, universal language of the Church. As members of the Catholic Church, we usually pray in the language that we speak, but we sometimes pray in Latin, the common language of the Church.

Sign of the Cross

In the name of the Father
and of the Son
and of the Holy Spirit. Amen.

Signum Crucis

In nómine Patris
et Fílii
et Spíritus Sancti. Amen.

The Lord's Prayer

Our Father, who art in heaven,
hallowed be thy name;
thy kingdom come,
thy will be done
on earth as it is in heaven.
Give us this day our daily bread,
and forgive us our trespasses,
as we forgive those who trespass
 against us;
and lead us not into temptation,
but deliver us from evil.
Amen.

Pater Noster

Pater noster qui es in cælis:
santificétur Nomen Tuum;
advéniat Regnum Tuum;
fiat volúntas Tua,
sicut in cælo, et in terra.
Panem nostrum
cotidiánum da nobis hódie;
et dimítte nobis débita nostra,
sicut et nos
dimíttus debitóribus nostris;
et ne nos indúcas in tentatiónem;
sed líbera nos a Malo.

Glory Be

Glory be to the Father
and to the Son
and to the Holy Spirit,
as it was in the beginning
is now, and ever shall be
world without end.
Amen.

Gloria Patri

Gloria Patri
et Filio
et Spíritui Sancto.
Sicut erat in princípio,
et nunc et semper
et in sæ´cula sæ´culorem. Amen.

The Hail Mary

Hail, Mary, full of grace,
the Lord is with thee.
Blessed art thou among women
and blessed is the fruit of thy womb, Jesus.
Holy Mary, Mother of God,
pray for us sinners,
now and at the hour of our death.
Amen.

Prayer to the Holy Spirit

Come, Holy Spirit, fill the hearts of
 your faithful.
And kindle in them the fire of your love.
Send forth your Spirit and they shall
 be created.
And you will renew the face of the earth.
Let us pray.
Lord, by the light of the Holy Spirit you
 have taught the hearts of your faithful.
 In the same Spirit help us to relish
 what is right and always rejoice in
 your consolation.
We ask this through Christ our Lord.
Amen.

Ave, Maria

Ave, María, grátia plena,
Dóminus tecum.
Benedícta tu in muliéribus,
et benedíctus fructus ventris tui, Iesus.
Sancta María, Mater Dei,
ora pro nobis peccatóribus,
nunc et in hora mortis nostræ.
Amen.

Memorare

Remember, most loving Virgin Mary,
never was it heard that anyone who turned
 to you for help was left unaided.
Inspired by this confidence, though
 burdened by my sins, I run to your
 protection for you are my mother.
Mother of the Word of God, do not despise
 my words of pleading but be merciful
 and hear my prayer.
Amen.

Hail, Holy Queen

Hail, holy Queen, Mother of mercy,
hail, our life, our sweetness, and our hope.
To you we cry, the children of Eve;
to you we send up our sighs,
mourning and weeping in this land of exile.
Turn, then, most gracious advocate,
your eyes of mercy toward us;
lead us home at last
and show us the blessed fruit of your womb,
Jesus:
O clement, O loving, O sweet Virgin Mary.

Prayers from the Sacraments

Holy, Holy, Holy Lord

Holy, Holy, Holy Lord God of hosts.
Heaven and earth are full of your glory.
Hosanna in the highest.
Blessed is he who comes in the name of
    the Lord.
Hosanna in the highest.

Lamb of God

Lamb of God, you take away the
    sins of the world,
        have mercy on us.
Lamb of God, you take away the
    sins of the world,
        have mercy on us.
Lamb of God, you take away the
    sins of the world,
        grant us peace.

Gloria

Glory to God in the highest,
and on earth peace to people of good will.

We praise you,
we bless you,
we adore you,
we glorify you,
we give you thanks for your great glory,
Lord God, heavenly King,
O God, almighty Father.

Lord Jesus Christ, Only Begotten Son,
Lord God, Lamb of God, Son of the Father,
you take away the sins of the world,
    have mercy on us;
you take away the sins of the world,
    receive our prayer;
you are seated at the right hand of the
Father,
    have mercy on us.

Sanctus, Sanctus, Sanctus

Sanctus, Sanctus, Sanctus
Dominus Deus Sabaoth.
Pleni sunt coeli et terra gloria tua.
Hosanna in excelsis.
Benedictus qui venit in nomine Domini.
Hosanna in excelsis

Agnus Dei

Agnus Dei, qui tollis peccata mundi:
miserere nobis.
Agnus Dei, qui tollis peccata mundi:
miserere nobis.
Agnus Dei, qui tollis peccata mundi:
dona nobis pacem

For you alone are the Holy One,
you alone are the Lord,
you alone are the Most High,
Jesus Christ,
with the Holy Spirit,
in the glory of God the Father.
Amen.

Confiteor

I confess to almighty God
and to you, my brothers and sisters,
that I have greatly sinned,
in my thoughts and in my words,
in what I have done
and in what I have failed to do,
through my fault, through my fault,
through my most grievous fault;
therefore I ask blessed Mary ever-Virgin,
all the Angels and Saints,
and you my brothers and sisters,
to pray for me to the Lord our God.

Prayers from the Liturgy of the Hours

The Canticle of Zechariah

This hymn is sung during the Liturgy of the Hours, Morning Prayer.

Blessed be the Lord, the God of Israel;
he has come to his people and set them free.

He has raised up for us a mighty savior,
born of the house of his servant David.

Through his holy prophets he promised of old
that he would save us from our enemies,
from the hands of all who hate us.

He promised to show mercy to our fathers
and to remember his holy covenant.

This was the oath he swore to our father
    Abraham:
to set us free from the hands of our enemies,
free to worship him without fear,
holy and righteous in his sight
all the days of our life.
Based on Luke 1:68–75

The *Magnificat* (Mary's Canticle)

This hymn is sung during the Liturgy of the Hours, Evening Prayer.

My soul proclaims the greatness of the Lord,
my spirit rejoices in God my Savior;
for he has looked with favor on his lowly
servant.
From this day all generations will call me
blessed:
the Almighty has done great things for me,
and holy is his Name.

He has mercy on those who fear him
in every generation.
He has shown the strength of his arm,
he has scattered the proud in their conceit.
He has cast down the mighty from their
thrones,
and has lifted up the lowly.
He has filled the hungry with good things,
and the rich he has sent away empty.
He has come to the help of his servant Israel
for he has remembered his promise of mercy,
the promise he made to our fathers,
to Abraham and his children for ever.
Based on Luke 1:46–55

Personal and Family Prayers

Morning Prayer

God be in my head, and in my
understanding;
God be in my eyes, and in my looking;
God be in my mouth, and in my speaking;
God be in my heart, and in my thinking;
God be at my end, and at my departing.
Amen.

Evening Prayer

Lord, from the rising of the sun to its
setting, your name is worthy of all praise.
Let our prayer come like incense before
you. May the lifting up of our hands be
as an evening sacrifice acceptable to you,
Lord our God.
Amen.

Act of Faith

O God, we firmly believe that you are one God in three divine Persons, Father, Son, and Holy Spirit; we believe that your divine Son became man and died for our sins, and that he will come to judge the living and the dead. We believe these and all the truths that the holy Catholic Church teaches because you have revealed them, and you can neither deceive nor be deceived.

Act of Hope

O God, relying on your almighty power and your endless mercy and promises, we hope to gain pardon for our sins, the help of your grace, and life everlasting, through the saving actions of Jesus Christ, our Lord and Redeemer.

Act of Love

O God, we love you above all things, with our whole heart and soul, because you are all-good and worthy of all love. We love our neighbor as ourselves for the love of you. We forgive all who have injured us and ask pardon of all whom we have injured.

Act of Contrition

My God, I am sorry for my sins with all my heart.
In choosing to do wrong
and failing to do good,
I have sinned against you
whom I should love above all things.
I firmly intend, with your help,
to do penance,
to sin no more,
and to avoid whatever leads me to sin.
Our Savior Jesus Christ
suffered and died for us.
In his name, my God, have mercy.

The Jesus Prayer

Lord Jesus Christ, Son of God, have mercy on me, a sinner.

Eternal Rest

Eternal rest grant to them, O Lord,
and let perpetual light shine upon them.
May they rest in peace.
Amen.

Devotional Practices

When we pray with the Saints, we ask them to pray to God for us and to pray with us. The Saints are with Christ. They speak for us when we need help.

As the Mother of Jesus, the Son of God, Mary is called the Mother of God, the Queen of all Saints, and the Mother of the Church. There are many prayers and practices of devotion to Mary. One of the most revered is the Rosary. It focuses on the twenty mysteries that describe events in the lives of Jesus and Mary.

How to Pray the Rosary

1. Pray the Sign of the Cross and say the Apostles' Creed.
2. Pray the Lord's Prayer.
3. Pray three Hail Marys.
4. Pray the Glory Be.
5. Say the first mystery; then pray the Lord's Prayer.
6. Pray ten Hail Marys while meditating on the mystery.
7. Pray the Glory Be.
8. Say the second mystery; then pray the Lord's Prayer.

Repeat 6 and 7 and continue with the third, fourth, and fifth mysteries in the same manner.

9. Pray the Hail, Holy Queen (see page 384).

The Mysteries of the Rosary

The Joyful Mysteries
The Annunciation
The Visitation
The Nativity
The Presentation in the Temple
The Finding in the Temple

The Sorrowful Mysteries
The Agony in the Garden
The Scourging at the Pillar
The Crowning with Thorns
The Carrying of the Cross
The Crucifixion and Death

The Glorious Mysteries
The Resurrection
The Ascension
The Descent of the Holy Spirit
The Assumption of Mary
The Coronation of Mary in Heaven

The Luminous Mysteries
The Baptism of Jesus
The Wedding at Cana
The Proclamation of the Kingdom
The Transfiguration
The Institution of the Eucharist

The Chaplet of Divine Mercy

1. Begin with the Sign of the Cross

2. Pray the Our Father.

3. Pray the Hail Mary.

4. Say the Apostles' Creed.

5. Then pray, on the large bead before each decade on the Rosary:

Eternal Father,
I offer you the Body and Blood,
Soul and Divinity,
Of Your Dearly Beloved Son,
Our Lord, Jesus Christ,
in atonement for our sins
and those of the whole world.

6. One the small beads of each decade, say:

For the sake of his sorrowful Passion,
have mercy on us and on the whole world.

7. Then say three times:

Holy God,
Holy Mighty One,
Holy Immortal One,
have mercy on us,
and on the whole world.

Stations of the Cross

The devotional practice of the Stations of the Cross began in the early Church. Pilgrims would visit the various sites in Jerusalem that were associated with Christ's suffering and death. The Stations of the Cross focus on fourteen scenes of Christ's Passion.

First Station: Jesus is condemned to death on the Cross.

Second Station: Jesus accepts his Cross.

Third Station: Jesus falls the first time.

Fourth Station: Jesus meets his sorrowful mother.

Fifth Station: Simon of Cyrene helps Jesus carry his Cross.

Sixth Station: Veronica wipes the face of Jesus.

Seventh Station: Jesus falls the second time.

Eighth Station: Jesus meets and speaks to the women of Jerusalem.

Ninth Station: Jesus falls the third time.

Tenth Station: Jesus is stripped of his garments.

Eleventh Station: Jesus is nailed to the Cross.

Twelfth Station: Jesus dies on the Cross.

Thirteenth Station: Jesus is taken down from the Cross.

Fourteenth Station: Jesus is placed in the tomb.

Angelus

V. The angel spoke God's message to Mary,
R. and she conceived of the Holy Spirit.
Hail, Mary. . . .
V. "I am the lowly servant of the Lord:
R. let it be done to me according to
   your word."
Hail, Mary. . . .
V. And the Word became flesh,
R. and lived among us.
Hail, Mary. . . .
V. Pray for us, holy Mother of God,
R. that we may become worthy of the
   promises of Christ.
Let us pray.
Lord,
fill our hearts with your grace:
once, through the message of an angel
you revealed to us the incarnation of your Son;
now, through his suffering and death
lead us to the glory of his Resurrection.
We ask this through Christ our Lord.
R. Amen.

Litany of Saint Joseph

Lord, have mercy.	Lord, have mercy.
Christ, have mercy.	Christ, have
mercy.	
Lord, have mercy.	Lord, have mercy.
Good Saint Joseph,	pray for us.
Descendant of the House of David	pray for us.
Husband of Mary,	pray for us.
Foster father of Jesus,	pray for us.
Guardian of Christ,	pray for us.
Support of the holy family,	pray for us.
Model of workers,	pray for us.
Example to parents,	pray for us.
Comfort of the dying,	pray for us.
Provider of food to the hungry,	pray for us.
Companion of the poor,	pray for us.
Protector of the church,	pray for us.

Merciful God,
grant that we may learn from Saint Joseph
to care for the members of our families
and share what we have with the poor.
We ask this through Christ our Lord. Amen.

A

abba the Aramaic word with the English equivalent of "daddy" or "papa" (**81**)

abortion the deliberate termination of a pregnancy by killing an unborn child. It is a grave sin. (**229**)

absolution words spoken by the priest during the Sacrament of Penance and Reconciliation to grant forgiveness of sins in God's name (**280**)

Advocate literally means "he who is called to one's side." The Holy Spirit is our Advocate, guiding and comforting us, strengthening us to know and live by the truth. (**118**)

Anointing of the Sick one of the Sacraments of Healing for people who are seriously ill or in danger of dying. In the Sacrament, the person's forehead and hands are anointed with the blessed oil of the sick. (**283**)

Annunication the Angel Gabriel's announcement to Mary that she would be the Mother of God and give birth to the Savior (**109**)

Apostles the twelve men Jesus chose to be his closest followers and to share in his work and mission in a special way (**177**)

apostolic a Mark of the Church. The Church is apostolic because her teaching authority comes directly from Jesus and his chosen Apostles, handed down through the bishops of the Church, who are direct successors of the Apostles. (**177**)

B

Baptism the Sacrament of in which a person is immersed in water or has water poured on him or her. Baptism takes away Original Sin and all personal sin, and makes a person a child of God and member of the Church. (**199**)

Beatitudes Jesus' eight teachings about the meaning and path to true happiness; they depict the way to live in God's Kingdom now and always, working toward the eternal holiness or blessedness to which God calls all people (**150**)

C

canon of Scripture the Church's complete list of inspired books included in Sacred Scripture (**6, 66**)

Cardinal Virtues the four principal moral virtues—prudence, temperance, justice, and fortitude—that help us live as children of God and from which the other moral virtues flow. We strengthen these good habits through God's grace and our own efforts. (**240**)

catholic a Mark of the Church. The Church is catholic because she is universal, meant for all people in all times and in all places. (**200**)

Church the community of all baptized people who believe in the Holy Trinity and follow Jesus. The word is often used for the Catholic Church because we trace our origins back to the Apostles. (**177**)

Confirmation the Sacrament of Initiation through which the spiritual life received in Baptism is strengthened and the person is sealed with the Gifts of the Holy Spirit (**269**)

consecrated religious life a state of life lived by religious sisters, brothers, and priests in community and characterized by the vows of poverty, chastity, and obedience (**298**)

conscience the God-given ability that helps individuals judge whether actions are right or wrong (**214**)

contrition true sorrow for disobeying God and the commitment to try to avoid sin in the future (**279**)

covenant a sacred promise or agreement between humans or between God and humans (**79**)

D

discernment the process by which a person reflects, discusses, and prays about how God might be calling him or her to live out a particular vocation (**297**)

disciples people who learn from and follow the example of a teacher. The disciples of Jesus are those who believe in him, follow his teachings, and put them into practice. (**175**)

discipleship accepting Jesus' invitation to believe in and follow him by studying his ways and putting them into practice (**139**)

Divine Inspiration the gift of the Holy Spirit which assisted the human authors in writing the Bible to ensure it contained the truths God wanted us to know (**66**)

Divine Revelation the process by which God makes himself known. The chief sources of revelation are Sacred Scripture and Sacred Tradition. (**55**)

doctrine official Church teachings on matters of faith and morals. Catholics are obligated to believe these truths. (**177**)

domestic Church a name for the Catholic family, because it is the community of Christians in the home. God made the family to be the first place we learn about loving others and following Christ. (**295**)

E

Emmanuel the name given to the Messiah by the prophet Isaiah, meaning "God is with us" (**109**)

eternal the term that means "God is" and "has always been," even before the beginning of time, and will be forever (**58**)

eternal life life forever with God for all who die in his friendship (**200**)

Eucharist the Sacrament of Initiation during which the bread and wine become the Body and Blood of Christ and all who receive him in Holy Communion are brought closer to him and one another (**270**)

euthanasia the deliberate action or inaction which causes the death of someone who is sick, dying, or suffering because of disabilities or a debilitating condition. It is a grave sin. (**229**)

Evangelists the four inspired human authors of the Gospels: Matthew, Mark, Luke, and John (**69**)

F

faith the Theological Virtue that makes it possible for us to believe in God and the things that he has revealed to us. Faith leads us to obey God. It is both a gift from God and a free, human choice. (**95**)

free will the God-given freedom and ability to make choices. God created us with free will so we can have the freedom to choose good. (**199**)

G

Gifts of the Holy Spirit seven powerful gifts God gives us to follow guidance of the Holy Spirit and live the Christian life. We are sealed with the Gifts of the Holy Spirit at Confirmation. (**269**)

Gospel a word that means "Good News." The Gospel message is the Good News of God's Kingdom and his saving love. (**69**)

grace God's free, loving gift of his own life and help to do what he calls us to do. It is participation in the life of the Holy Trinity. (**98**)

H

Heaven the state, or experience, of the full joy of living eternally in God's presence (**321**)

Hell the state, or experience, of eternal separation from God because of a choice to turn away from him and not seek forgiveness (**321**)

hierarchy the organization of the Church into different levels of leadership and membership (**186**)

Holy Trinity the mystery of one God in three Divine Persons: Father, Son, and Holy Spirit (**8, 96**)

human dignity the worth each person has because he or she is made in the image of God (**227**)

I

image of God the Divine likeness in all human beings that comes from being made by God and includes the ability to think, choose, be free, love, and be in relationship with God and others (**57**)

Incarnation the truth that the Second Divine Person of the Holy Trinity, the Son of God, assumed human nature in order to save all people; Jesus Christ is both true God and true man (**106**)

intellect the God-given ability which makes it possible for humans to think, reason, and judge (**215**)

intercession a form of prayer that involves praying to God on behalf of another; also called intercessory prayer (**121**)

J – L

justice the constant and firm desire to give God and other people what is their due as children of God, made in his image and possessing equal human dignity (**306**)

Kingdom of God God's rule of peace, justice, and love that exists in Heaven, but has not yet come in its fullness on Earth (**147**)

laity all baptized members of the Church who share in Jesus' mission and witness to him and his message but are not priests or consecrated sisters or brothers; sometimes called lay people (**295**)

Last Judgment God's final triumph over evil that will occur at the end of time when Christ returns and judges all the living and the dead. Then, all will fully see and understand God's plan for creation. (**322**)

M

Mediator the title given to Jesus because, as true God and true man, he alone is able to reconcile all people to God the Father, bringing us closer to God the Father by his words and saving actions (**136**)

miracle an event for which there is no scientific explanation because it happened by the power of God. Jesus worked miracles to help us see the presence of the Kingdom of God. (**110**)

mortal sin a grave (very serious) sin by which someone turns completely away from God and breaks his or her relationship with God (**215**)

murder the deliberate killing of another person when the killing is not in self-defense. It is always gravely sinful. (**227**)

mystery a truth of faith that cannot be fully understood but that is believed because God has shown it in Scripture, in the life of Jesus, or in the teachings of the Church (**55**)

Mystical Body of Christ a name for the Church, whose baptized members are all united to Christ and one another through the Holy Spirit, forming one holy people with Christ as her head (**186**)

N

natural moral law precepts about goodness that are written by God in our hearts and accessible through our God-given reason (**83**)

New Commandment Jesus' command for his disciples to love one another as he has loved us (**83**)

O

one a Mark of the Church. The Church is one because the power of the Holy Spirit unites all the members through one faith and one Baptism (**188**)

Original Holiness the state of goodness that humanity enjoyed before our first parents, Adam and Eve, chose to sin against God (**159**)

Original Sin the sin of our first parents that wounded human nature and introduced sin, suffering, and death into the world; all humans are born with Original Sin and are thus tempted to sin (**159**)

parable a short story Jesus told using examples from everyday life or nature to illustrate moral or spiritual truths (147)

Particular Judgment the individual judgment by God at the time of a person's death; when God decides, after a person's death, where that person will spend eternity according to his or her faith and works (321)

Paschal Mystery Christ's work of redemption through his Passion, Death, Resurrection, and Ascension (162)

peace a state of calm and harmony when things are in their proper order and people settle problems with kindness and justice (309)

penance the name for the prayer, offering, or good work the priest gives you in the Sacrament of Reconciliation (280)

Penance and Reconciliation the Sacrament of Healing that celebrates God's mercy and forgiveness and a sinner's reconciliation with God and the Church through absolution from a priest (279)

personal sin a deliberate thought, word, deed, or omission that violates the law of God (159)

Purgatory a state of final cleansing after death and before entering into Heaven that removes any remaining personal obstacles to eternal union with God. Purgatory frees the person from temporal punishment (being deprived of the entrance into Heaven for a time) due to sin. (321)

Real Presence a phrase used to describe the Catholic teaching that Jesus is really and truly with us in the Eucharist—Body, Blood, Soul, and Divinity (258)

Sacraments at the Service of Communion Holy Orders and Matrimony. They celebrate people's commitment to serve God and the community and help build up the People of God. (257)

Sacraments of Healing Penance and Reconciliation and the Anointing of the Sick. In these Sacraments, God's forgiveness and healing are given to those suffering physical and spiritual sickness. (257)

Sacraments of Initiation the three Sacraments that celebrate membership into the Catholic Church: Baptism, Confirmation, and Eucharist (257)

Sacred Scripture the Word of God written by humans acting under the Holy Spirit's inspiration and guidance; another name for the Bible (5, 66)

Saints those whom the Church declares led holy lives and are enjoying eternal life with God in Heaven (121)

salvation the loving action of God's forgiveness of sins and the restoration of friendship with the Father brought by Jesus Christ (160)

scandal the destructive behavior by which a person deliberately leads, through his or her own action or inaction, another person to sin (230)

Seven Sacraments effective signs of God's grace instituted by Christ and given to his Church. In the celebration of each Sacrament, there are visible signs and Divine actions that give grace and allow us to share in God's work. (255)

Sermon on the Mount the summary of key teachings of Jesus found in the Gospel according to Matthew (149)

solidarity a Christian principle that motivates believers to share their spiritual gifts as well as their material ones (310)

soul the spiritual principle of a human person that is individual, created by God, and will exist forever (215)

T

Ten Commandments the ten fundamental moral laws given by God to Moses, and recorded in the Old Testament, to help his People live by the covenant (**82**)

Theological Virtues gifts from God that help us believe in him, trust in his plan for us, and love him as he loves us; they are faith, hope, and charity (**239**)

transubstantiation the process by which, through the power of the Holy Spirit and the words and actions of the priest, the bread and wine are transformed into the Body and Blood of Christ (**270**)

V

venial sin a sin that weakens, but does not destroy, a person's relationship with God (**215**)

virtue a good spiritual habit that strengthens you and enables you to do what is right and good (**239**)

Visitation the event of Mary, who was pregnant with Jesus, visiting her cousin Elizabeth, who was pregnant with Saint John the Baptist (**135**)

vocation the purpose for which God made us and the particular way to answer and live out his call, whether as a lay person (married or single), a member of a religious community, or a member of the ordained ministry (**297**)

W

wisdom the spiritual gift that helps us to see God's purpose and plan for our lives. Wisdom is also one of the seven Gifts of the Holy Spirit. (**147**)

Works of Mercy actions that show care for the physical and spiritual needs of others (**322**)

Boldfaced numbers refer to pages on which terms are defined.

"Jesus, Compassionate High Priest" 38
Jesus Prayer, The 387
John Bosco, Saint 192
John II, Pope 355
John Paul II, Pope Saint 204, 290, 311,
  355, 360
  Gospel of Life 130, 233
John the Baptist, Saint 23, 135, 174, 365
John XII, Pope 362
John, Saint 27, 349
"Joy and Peace" 238
Joyful Mysteries 135
Jude Thaddeus, Saint 365
"The Judgment of the Nations" 190
justice 98, 147, 158, **306**, 307, 308, 309,
  311, 312, 342, 344, 379, 393

K

Kingdom of God 6, 47, 110, 146, **147**,
  150, 151, 170, 176, 179, 290, 297, 306,
  307, 308, 311, 323, 368, 369, 393

L

laity 10, **295**, 300, 368, 380, 393
Lamb of God 385
Last Judgment **322**, 369, 393
Last Supper 79, 176, 188, 270, 365, 366
"Last Supper Discourses" 136
Law of Moses 7, 161, 256
Lazarus 318, 319
Lent 30, 34–37, 44, 284, 372
  practices 35
Leo I (the Great), Pope 130, 354
Leo III, Pope 359
Leo XIII, Pope 312
Life and Dignity of the Human
  Person 334–335
"The Light of the World" 178
Litany of Saint Joseph 390
Litany of the Holy Name of Jesus 113
Litany of the Saints 181
liturgical year 23, 43, 369, 372
liturgy 7, 50, 124, 356, 366
Lord's Prayer, the 80, 202, 366, 382, 383
Lorenzo Ruiz, Saint 204
Ludmilla, Saint 260

M

Madeleine Sophie Barat, Saint 164
Magdalene, Mary 162
Magnificat, the 386
Margaret Ward, Saint 244
Maria Goretti, Saint 84
Maria, Saint 112
Marks of the Church
  apostolic 177, 368
  catholic 200, 201, 368
  holy 368
  one 188, 368
Martha 318, 319
Martin de Tours, Saint 232
Mary 28, 31, 32, 111, 135, 140, 200, 366,
  369, 372
  and Joseph 294
  God's plan 109
  model of goodness 32
  Mother of God 354
  mother of Jesus 365
  titles 60
Mary Zhao, Saint 112

Mass 108, 295, 297, 366, 372, 373, 380,
  382
  Concluding Rites 271
  Introductory Rites 270
  Liturgy of the Eucharist 270
  Liturgy of the Word 70, 259, 270
  Order of 270, 371
  prayer 121, 366, 367
  readings 36
  Scriptures 71
  Sign of the Cross 96
  Word of God 70
Matrimony, Sacrament of 257, 370, 394
Matthew, Saint 72
Maximilian Kolbe, Saint 140
Mediator **136**, 137, 199, 254, 393
Memorare 384
"The Ministry of Reconciliation" 275
miracle 27, 107, **110**, 393
moral law 82, 83
morality 216, 217, 337
Morning Prayer 386
mortal sin **215**, 279, 376, 393
Moses 82, 83, 366
murder 217, **227**, 228, 393
mystery **55**, 393
Mystical Body of Christ 170, **186**, 191,
  393

N

natural moral law 82, **83**, 217, 373, 393
New Commandment **83**, 219, 242, 373,
  393
new covenant 31
New Testament 6, 7, 9, 66, 67, 270, 348,
  350, 353, 365
Nicene Creed 108, 162, 270, 322, 352,
  354, 367, 368, 369
Nicholas, Pope 360
"Nicodemus" 146
Old Testament 6, 7, 31, 57, 59, 66, 68, 69,
  78, 82, 270, 350, 353, 364
  covenant 79

O

one (Mark of the Church) **188**, 368, 393
"One Body, Many Parts" 183
Option for the Poor and Vulnerable
  340–341
Ordinary Time 18, 19, 31
Original Holiness **158**, 163, 393
Original Sin 82, 130, **158**, 159, 160, 198,
  199, 267, 376, 393

P

parable 67, 147, 308, 320, 394
"The Parable of the Mustard Seed" 308
Particular Judgment 320, **321**, 369, 394
Paschal Mystery 43, 130, **162**, 163, 256,
  267, 366, 372, 394
Passion (or Palm) Sunday 39
Passover 39, 259, 348
Patrick, Saint 354
Paul, Saint 67, 187, 190, 191, 198, 238,
  319
  conversion 170, 348
peace 28, 48, 98, 147, 271, 283, 306, 308,
  309, 311, 312, 321, 344, 366, 379, 381,
  394

penance 23, 35, 279, **280**, 281, 351, 373,
  394
Penance and Reconciliation, Sacrament
  of 36, 163, 250, 257, 270, **279**, 280,
  281, 283, 284, 372, 373, 378, 394
Pentecost 47, 250, 256, 348
personal sin 159
Peter, Saint 349, 368
"Peter's Speech" 42
Pius IX, Blessed Pope 324
"Plea for Unity and Humility" 103, 122,
  131
"Praise of God the Creator" 51
prayer 4, 5, 69, 70, 122, 123, 152, 178,
  179, 203, 210, 219, 220, 232, 281, 290,
  295, 296, 299, 311, 361, 381, 382
  adoration 29, 60
  Blessing and Adoration 382
  Church 90
  contemplative 180
  contrition 280
  for Life 233
  for Peace, A 49, 205
  for the Readers 251 forms 10, 203
  guidance 130
  intercession 121
  intercessory 382
  Jewish traditions 259
  Lord's, the 309
  of Adoration 85
  of Mercy, A 41
  of Petition 37, 73, 153, 313, 382
  of Praise 21, 45, 165
  of Thanksgiving 141
  of the Faithful 270
  Marian, A 33
  Praise 382
  Thanksgiving 382
  to Saint Joseph 261
  to the Holy Spirit 125, 384
  types 123
  Vocation 301
  Waiting, A 25
"Prayer and Conduct" 137
"The Prayer of Jesus" 91
Prayer of the Faithful 121
"The Preeminence of Christ" 155
Presentation of the Child Jesus at the
  Temple, the 135
Priest, Prophet, and King 296, 297
Psalm
  23, Praying 325
  of Lament 285
Purgatory 200, 320, **321**, 369, 394

R

Rafqa (Rebecca), Saint 124
"The Raising of Lazarus" 318
Real Presence **258**, 271, 394
Reconciliation, Sacrament of 278
Reflect on the Trinity 101
Renewal of Baptismal Promises 273
"Renunciation of Vice" 235
Rights and Responsibilities of the Human
  Person 338–339
Rights of Workers 343, 379
Rite of Christian Initiation of Adults 267
Rosa, Saint 112
Rosary, the 60, 367
  Mysteries 135, 388, 389
  pray 388
Rose of Lima, Saint 340

Endnotes

1. *Indulgentiarum doctrina*, 5.

© Our Sunday Visitor